THE ARDEN EDITION OF THE
WORKS OF WILLIAM SHAKESPEARE

THE THIRD PART OF
KING HENRY VI

Edited by
ANDREW S. CAIRNCROSS

METHUEN
LONDON AND NEW YORK

The general editors of the Arden Shakespeare have been
W. J. Craig (1899–1906), R. H. Case (1909–44) and
Una Ellis-Fermor (1946–58)

Present general editors: Harold F. Brooks, Harold Jenkins and
Brian Morris

This edition of *King Henry VI, Part III*, prepared by Andrew S. Cairncross,
first published 1964 by
Methuen & Co. Ltd
11 New Fetter Lane, London EC4P 4EE
First published as a University Paperback 1969
Reprinted 1982

Published in the USA by
Methuen & Co.
in association with Methuen, Inc.
733 Third Avenue, New York, NY 10017

Editorial matter © 1964 Methuen & Co. Ltd

ISBN 0 416 47220 6 (hardbound edition)
ISBN 0 416 27910 4 (paperback edition)

Printed and bound in Great Britain by
Richard Clay (The Chaucer Press) Ltd, Bungay, Suffolk

36174

CONTENTS

Frontispiece: The England of *Henry VI*

APPENDICES

ABBREVIATIONS

The abbreviations for Shakespeare's works, and customary terms, are from *A Shakespeare Glossary*, by C. T. Onions. References to the plays, other than *3 Henry VI*, are to *The Cambridge Shakespeare*, 1891–3.

Elizabethan authors are cited from the following editions:

Greene	Prose: A. B. Grosart, Huth Library, 1881–3.
Jonson	C. H. Herford, Percy and Evelyn Simpson, Oxford, 1925–50.
Kyd	F. S. Boas, Oxford, 1901.
Lyly	R. W. Bond, Oxford, 1902.
Marlowe	C. F. Tucker Brooke, Oxford, 1910.
Marston	H. Harvey Wood, Oliver and Boyd, 1934–9.
Nashe	R. B. McKerrow, Oxford, 1904–10.
Spenser	J. C. Smith and E. de Selincourt, Oxford, 1912.
Abbott	E. A. Abbott, *A Shakespearian Grammar*, 1869, edn of 1878.
Alexander	Peter Alexander, *Shakespeare's 'Henry VI and Richard III'*, Cambridge, 1929.
Baldwin	See *Sm. Lat.*
Boswell-Stone	W. G. Boswell-Stone, *Shakespere's Holinshed*, 1896.
Brooke	C. F. Tucker Brooke, in *Transactions of the Connecticut Academy of Arts and Sciences*, 1912.
Carter	Thomas Carter, *Shakespeare and Holy Scripture*, 1905.
Chambers, *ES.*	Sir Edmund K. Chambers, *The Elizabethan Stage*, 1923.
——, *WS.*	Sir Edmund K. Chambers, *William Shakespeare*, 1930.
Cooper	Thomas Cooper, *Thesaurus Linguae Romanae & Britannicae*, 1565, edn of 1578.
Fabyan	Robert Fabyan, *The New Chronicles of England and France*, 1516, repr. of 1811.
F.Q.	Edmund Spenser, *The Faerie Queene*.
Franz	W. Franz, *Shakespeare-Grammatik*, Heidelberg, 1909, repr. of 1924.
French	George R. French, *Shakespeareana Genealogica*, 1869.
Greg, *EDD.*	Sir Walter W. Greg, *Dramatic Documents from the Elizabethan Playhouses*, Oxford, 1931.
——, *Ed. Pr.*	Sir Walter W. Greg, *The Editorial Problem in Shakespeare*, 1942, edn of 1951.
——, *Pr. Em.*	Sir Walter W. Greg, *Principles of Emendation in Shakespeare* (Proceedings of the British Academy, xiv), 1928.

Greg, *ShFF.*	Sir Walter W. Greg, *The Shakespeare First Folio*, 1955.
H.F.B.	Harold F. Brooks.
Hall	Edward Halle, *The vnion of the two noble and illustre famelies of Lancastre and Yorke*, 1548, repr. 1809.
Hart	H. C. Hart, *The Third Part of Henry the Sixth*, Arden edn, 1910.
Hinman	Charlton Hinman, *The Printing and Proof-Reading of the First Folio of Shakespeare*, 1963.
——, *S.B.*	Charlton Hinman, 'The Prentice Hand in the Tragedies of the Shakespeare First Folio: Compositor E', in *Studies in Bibliography*, ix (1957).
Hol.	Raphael Holinshed, *Chronicles of England, Scotland, and Ireland*, 1577, repr. of 1807–8.
Jenkins	Harold Jenkins, *The Structural Problem in Shakespeare's 'Henry the Fourth'*, 1956.
Madden	D. H. Madden, *The Diary of Master William Silence*, 1897, edn of 1907.
Malone	Boswell's Variorum edition of *Malone's Shakespeare*, 1821.
Man. Voc.	*Manipulus Vocabulorum*, 1570, repr. EETS, 1867.
Metam.	Ovid, *Metamorphoses*.
Mirror	*The Mirror for Magistrates*, ed. Lily B. Campbell, Cambridge, 1938.
——, *Add.*	*Parts added to The Mirror for Magistrates*, ed. Lily B. Campbell, Cambridge, 1946.
MLR.	*The Modern Language Review.*
Noble	Richmond Noble, *Shakespeare's Biblical Knowledge*, 1935.
NQ.	*Notes and Queries.*
NSS.	*The New Shakespere Society.*
O.D.P.	*Oxford Dictionary of Proverbs.*
OED.	*A New English Dictionary*, Oxford, 1888–1928, *Supplement* 1933.
Onions	C. T. Onions, *A Shakespeare Glossary*, 1911, repr. of 1951.
PMLA.	*Publications of the Modern Language Association of America.*
Ps. (SH).	Sternhold and Hopkins, *The Whole Book of Psalms* (in metre), edn of 1628.
Pollard, *Sh. Fight*	A. W. Pollard, *Shakespeare's Fight with the Pirates*, 1917.
——, *ShFQ.*	A. W. Pollard, *Shakespeare Folios and Quartos*, 1909.
RES.	*The Review of English Studies.*
Rhodes	R. Crompton Rhodes, *Shakespeare's First Folio*, 1923.
Price	Hereward T. Price, *Construction in Shakespeare*, University of Michigan, 1951.
Rossiter	*Woodstock, A Moral History*, ed. A. P. Rossiter, 1946.
Rothery	Guy Cadogan Rothery, *The Heraldry of Shakespeare*, 1930.
Root	R. K. Root, *Classical Mythology in Shakespeare*, 1903.
Rowe 3	*The Works of Shakespeare*, ed. Nicholas Rowe, 8 vols., 1714.
Satchell	Thomas Satchell, 'The Spelling of the First Folio', *TLS.* (3 June 1920), 352.

Schmidt	Alexander Schmidt, *Shakespeare-Lexicon*, Berlin and London, 1874–5, 2nd edn, 1886.
Scott-Giles	C. W. Scott-Giles, *Shakespeare's Heraldry*, 1950.
SB.	*Studies in Bibliography* (University of Virginia).
SH.	Sternhold and Hopkins, *The whole Book of Psalms* (in metre), edn of 1628.
Sh. Bawdy	Eric Partridge, *Shakespeare's Bawdy*, 1947.
Sh. Lib.	*Shakespeare's Library*, ed. W. C. Hazlitt, 1875.
Sh. Qu.	*The Shakespeare Quarterly*, Washington.
Shroeder	John W. Shroeder, *The Great First Folio of 1623: Shakespeare's Plays in the Printing House*, The Shoe String Press, 1956.
Sm. Lat.	T. W. Baldwin, *William Shakspere's Small Latine & Lesse Greeke* (Urbana), 2 vols., 1944.
Smart	John Semple Smart, *Shakespeare: Truth and Tradition*, 1928.
Sp. Tr.	Thomas Kyd, *The Spanish Tragedy*.
S.P.	Thomas Kyd, *Soliman and Perseda*.
S. Ph.	*Studies in Philology*.
Sugden	Edward H. Sugden, *A Topographical Dictionary to the Works of Shakespeare and his Fellow Dramatists*, 1925.
Thomson	J. A. K. Thomson, *Shakespeare and the Classics*, 1952.
Tilley	M. P. Tilley, *A Dictionary of the Proverbs in England in the 16th and 17th Centuries*, 1950.
Tillyard, *EWP*.	E. M. W. Tillyard, *The Elizabethan World Picture*, 1943.
——, *SHP*.	E. M. W. Tillyard, *Shakespeare's History Plays*, 1948.
TLS.	*The Times Literary Supplement*.
TR.	*The Troublesome Raigne of King Iohn*, 1591, repr. in The Shakespeare Classics, ed. F. J. Furnivall and John Munro, 1913.
Vaughan	Henry H. Vaughan, *New Readings and Renderings of Shakespeare's Tragedies*, 1886.
Willoughby	Edwin Elliott Willoughby, *The Printing of the First Folio of Shakespeare*, Oxford, for the Bibliographical Society, 1932.
Wilson	John Dover Wilson, *1–3 Henry VI*, New Shakespeare, Cambridge, 1952.
——, *MSH*.	John Dover Wilson, *The Manuscript of Shakespeare's 'Hamlet'*, 2 vols., 1934.

INTRODUCTION

I. TEXTUAL

THE TEXTS

There are two basic texts of *3 Henry VI*—that of the Quarto (*The true Tragedie of Richard | Duke of Yorke, and the death of | good King Henrie the Sixt, | with the whole contention betweene | the two Houses Lancaster | and Yorke, as it was sundrie times | acted by the Right Honoura- | ble the Earle of Pem- | brooke his seruants. | Printed at London by P. S. for Thomas Milling- | ton . . . | 1595.*); and that of the First Folio (1623).[1]

The first edition of the Quarto (Q1)[2] appeared without previous entry in the Stationers' Register; possibly it was assumed to be covered by the same publisher's 1594 entry of *The First Part of the Contention of York and Lancaster* (*2 Henry VI*), of which, as the title implies, it was a continuation and completion. The second Quarto (Q2) was printed from Q1 in 1600, by 'W[illiam] W[hite] for Thomas Millington'. The third (Q3), which formed part of the notorious 'Pavier' collection of reprints,[3] was also printed from Q1, in 1619, by William Jaggard, who later printed the First Folio; and, together with *The Contention*, was given the inclusive title of *The | Whole Contention | betweene the two Famous | Houses, Lancaster and | Yorke*. It was unjustifiably claimed on the title-page to be 'newly corrected and enlarged'; and was the first edition of the play to bear Shakespeare's name.

The Folio text occupies pages 147 to 172 (signatures o4 to q4^v) of the histories. It is not divided into acts and scenes; except that it opens with the usual *Actus Primus. Scoena Prima.*

A change in the running-titles after signature o is evidence of a break in printing similar to, and connected with, those after b and c in *Richard II*.[4] These breaks are explained by trouble with Mat-

---

1. The symbol F will be used for the First Folio text, Q for that of the quartos. Differences among the quartos will be distinguished by the use of Q1, Q2, and Q3.

2. Strictly, an octavo; but the familiar Q is retained for simplicity.

3. See A. W. Pollard, *Shakespeare Folios and Quartos* (1909).

4. Willoughby, 33–4, 40 ff.; Shroeder, 50 ff., 73–7, 89.

thew Law, who held the copyright of *Richard II, 1* (and probably *2*) *Henry IV*, and *Richard III*, of which he had published the quartos. Work had been stopped on *Richard II* after the completion of quire b with the first two pages; a gap was left; and setting continued with *Henry V, 1* and *2 Henry VI*, to this point in *3 Henry VI*. At this stage an arrangement must have been reached with Law, and *Richard II* was completed, though with another break at the end of signature c, and then the two parts of *Henry IV*, before continuing with the rest of *3 Henry VI*, from signature p, and *Richard III*.

Spelling analysis suggests that the copy for F may have been distributed between compositors A and B as follows:

A	147–52	o4^r–o6^v	I. i. 1–II. i. 75
B	153–8	p1^r–p3^v	II. i. 76–III. ii. 1
A	159–61	p4^r–p5^r	III. ii. 2–III. iii. 151
B	162	p5^v	III. iii. 152–IV. i. 4
A	163–4	p6	IV. i. 5–IV. iii. 41
B	165^1	q1^r	IV. iii. 42–IV. vi. 15
A	166–70^1	q1^v–q3^v	IV. vi. 16–V. v. 43
B	171–2	q4^r	V. v. 43–end

There is considerable doubt, however, as to some pages here attributed to compositor B, including p2^v(b), p3^r(b), p4^r, and especially q1^r, which depart from B's spelling and other preferences. Professor Charlton Hinman notes q1^r for special attention. Although apparently by B, it was set, abnormally, from case x, which was A's.[2] 'Yet,' says Hinman, 'spelling evidence shows that it was set by compositor B. Which seems very odd, since there is abundant evidence that B always, normally, worked at case y.' This page is in many ways peculiar—so peculiar that it is difficult, if not impossible, to imagine B as the compositor. There do occur, indeed, many characteristic B spellings—do, go, heere, greefe; but also many not characteristic. The result is a curious mixture: we have thus: here/heere; heire/heyre; the non-B young; three out of four exits begin with lower-case letters (though this may have another explanation); mixed speech-prefixes like *King Edw.*/*King Ed.*/*K. Ed.*; a badly centred stage-direction (the first); the non-B Gloster; and two omissions of final s; and at least two omitted apostrophes. It seems, then, that, as Hinman suggests, B was called away, and that another compositor may have taken his place. Compositor D might have set it.[3] But D had already disappeared in the middle of the comedies. The possible alternative is E, who was to begin work

---

1. 165 is misnumbered 167; 166 is given as 168; in uncorrected copies there are also the errors 163 for 153, and 154 for 164.
2. Hinman, ii. 116.   3. *Ibid.*, i. 378.

in the tragedies not long after, and who may have been even here trying out his prentice hand. Certainly the result looks more typical of him than of any of the others. E's presence might also explain the peculiarities to be observed on some of the other pages and it would be consistent with the presence (as will be suggested later) of printed quarto copy among the material he worked on.

THE BAD QUARTO

It is now generally agreed that Q is a reported or bad version[1] of the text later printed in F, and not an early play or version of a play afterwards revised by Shakespeare. There was probably a slight element of revision between the two texts,[2] and of adaptation required by a reduction in the cast or by the censor. The main differences, however, are best explained by reporting.

Q is shorter than F by about a third. The main plot and substance are the same, and many of the speeches identical, or very close. But reporting is evident in the Q transpositions of words, phrases, and even scenes (e.g. IV. v, iv; vii, vi); use of paraphrases and synonyms; vulgarization, defective and inferior metre, printing of prose as verse and verse as prose, actors' connective phrases, and 'recollections' from other plays.[3]

Some of the abbreviation must, of course, be due to the reporters' lapses of memory; some, however, must be deliberate—the version reported must have been 'cut'. The main intention was, as Chambers thinks, to reduce the time required for performance rather than the number of the cast. One or two minor characters are indeed saved, such as the three watchmen in IV. iii, and possibly the two aldermen in IV. vii, and the (mute) Lieutenant of the Tower in V. vi. But the main cuts seem to have fallen on rhetorical, poetical, and allusive passages, which could easily be spared without affecting the progress of the action. Such are the classical allusion to the Thracian steeds (IV. ii. 19–25), the report of Edward's flight (IV. vi. 77–102), Henry's reflections (IV. viii. 92–100), the sorrows of Margaret (III. iii. 4–43), and much of Gloucester's soliloquy (III. ii) and Henry's (II. v. 22–54).

Other passages, again, were more probably omitted for reasons of censorship, as where Henry resigns the crown to Warwick and Clarence, Edward is pronounced a traitor, and Warwick and Clarence agree that 'succession be determined' (IV. vi. 1–37, 48–64); the character of Edward as a tyrant and usurper (III. iii. 67 ff.), of

1. Cf. _2 H 6_ (New Arden), Introduction; Alexander; Malone, xviii. 553; Wilson.

2. See below, xxii; and _MLR._, no. 4 (Oct. 1955), 492–4.

3. Chambers, _WS._, i. 281 ff., and Appendix IV.

Warwick as a traitor (iv. viii. 63–4), and in particular the single line (iv. iii. 38) referring to Edward's polygamous tendencies. Some of these, however, may be no more than reporter's omissions, since Q does preserve references to usurpation, deposition, and tyranny.

PEMBROKE'S MEN

We know from the title-page of the quarto that *3 Henry VI*, and, by implication, *2 Henry VI*, had been acted by Pembroke's. This company is first mentioned in 1592, and 'broke' in the summer of 1593. The breaking was probably the occasion for the compiling, by some of the actors, of the memorial or quarto versions of these two plays, and doubtless of others in their repertory.

A study of the external 'recollections'[1] in the quartos of *2* and *3 Henry VI, Richard III*, and *Romeo and Juliet* offers evidence that they were the work of such a group of Pembroke's men, or of groups that had at least one member in common. These recollections are drawn from a recognizable body of plays, mainly Shakespeare's, which included, besides the plays reported, *1 Henry VI, Titus Andronicus*, Marlowe's *Edward II*, Kyd's *Spanish Tragedy* and *Soliman and Perseda*, and the anonymous *Arden of Faversham*. *Titus*, like *3 Henry VI*, is associated through its title-page with Pembroke's; as may also be *Edward II* through Kyd's letter to Puckering, about 1591, referring to Marlowe's employment by a noble lord who may perhaps be identified as Pembroke.[2] The influence of the plays on each other confirms the ascription; attention need hardly be drawn to that of *The Spanish Tragedy* on Shakespeare, of *Henry VI* on *Edward II*, of to the similarities in *Arden of Faversham* to the rest. Two examples or what may be called cross-recollections may be sufficient to illustrate and establish the element of common reporting: they link the quarto of *3 Henry VI* with that of *2 Henry VI* on the one side and with that of *Richard III* on the other:

(a) *3 Henry VI* and *Richard III*

... steept in Rutlands blood,— A *handkercheefe*, ... And bid her *wipe* her *weeping eyes withall.* 　　　*Richard III*, iv. iv. 275–8	a *handkercher* steept in Rutlands blood, And bid her *dry* her *weeping eyes* therewith 　　　　　　*Richard III*, Q
. . . gaue him, to *dry* his Cheekes,	Gaue him a *handkercher* to *wipe* his *eies*

---

1. That is, words and phrases from other plays introduced into the quartos by the actors' faulty recollection. See Appendix IV.
2. Alexander, 203 ff.

A napkin, steeped in the harm-
   lesse blood
Of sweet young Rutland,
    3 Henry VI, ii. i. 61–3

Dipt in the bloud of sweet
   young Rutland
By rough Clifford slaine: who
   weeping tooke it vp
      True Tragedy, 590

(b) *2* and *3 Henry VI*

Away my Lord . . .
We shall to Lòndon get, . . .
But flye you must: . . .
    2 Henry VI, v. ii. 72, 81, 86

Away my Lord, and flie to London straight,
Make hast, for vengeance comes
   along with them,
Come *stand* not to expostulate,
      Contention, 568

Away: for vengeance comes
   along with them.
Nay, stay not to expostulate,
   make speed, . . .
    3 Henry VI, ii. v. 134–5

Awaie my Lord for vengeance
   comes along with him:
Nay *stand* not to expostulate
   make hast, . . .
      True Tragedy, 602[1]

In the first case, it will be noticed that the 'napkin' of *3 Henry VI* has become in report the 'handkercher' of *Richard III*; that 'dry' and 'wipe' have changed plays; and that 'weeping' and 'eyes' have been added to *The True Tragedy* from *Richard III*. In the second example, besides the appropriation by *The Contention* of the bulk of the *3 Henry VI* passage, 'my Lord' has been added to 'Away' from *2 Henry VI* to *The True Tragedy*, not to mention the common 'stand' for 'stay', and 'hast' for 'speed', from whatever source.[2]

The 'acting' origin of Q is confirmed by the incorporation of cues,[3] e.g.:

i. iii. 47   . . . no cause.
          Clif. No cause? Thy Father slew my father, therefore
              Die.
iii. ii. 111–12   . . . marrie her.
          Cla. Marrie her my Lord, to whom?
          (F *Clarence.* To who, my Lord?)
iv. iii. 30–1   . . . heere is the Duke.
          Edw. The Duke, why Warwike when we parted
              Last, thou caldst me king?
          War. I, but the case is altred now.
          (F omits 'Last' and 'now')

The first and third examples are uncorrected in F. The third, in a passage imperfectly corrected and still metrically unsatisfactory,

1. From *Sh. Qu.*, xi (1960), 3. 337, 340.   2. Cf. also Appendix IV (*b*).
3. Cf. e.g. *H 5*, v. i. 38–9, 'astonisht him. *Flew.* Astonisht him. . .' (Q).

might be debated. It is clear, however, that some cues appear in Q.

The stage-directions also suggest that Q is an actors' version, and probably made for actors to perform in the provinces. Many details of dress and business, not in F or deducible from the text, are given in Q. Thus the opposing factions appear at the opening with white and red 'Roses in their hats'; the forces which come on the Duke of York in i. iv are directed to 'Fight and take him'; Clifford enters wounded (ii. vi) 'with an arrow in his necke', an authentic detail from the chronicles[1] and *The Mirror for Magistrates*; and Clarence at Coventry (v. i) 'takes his red Rose out of his hat, and throwes it *Warwike*'.

Again, the F 'Gabriel' (i. ii. 48) was almost certainly Gabriel Spencer, whose name appears in a suit of 1597 as one of Pembroke's servants;[2] the company, after breaking, evidently had a continued provincial existence, probably in conjunction with some former Admiral's men. It was possibly for a provincial tour that Q was made.

The main reporters certainly include those identified by Professor Alexander for *2* and *3 Henry VI*—Warwick and Suffolk/Clifford.[3] To these may perhaps be added York;[4] and perhaps some 'bit-parts', such as John E. Jordan suggested for *2 Henry VI*.[5]

Imperfect as the quarto text may be, it has a special interest and value as a record of the play performed about 1592. It preserves some lines and characters later modified, and many words and forms 'sophisticated' in F. As will also appear, it has an even greater importance as the copy from which, after correction, a great deal of the F text was printed.

THE FOLIO TEXT

It will be suggested that

(*a*) F derives from the author's manuscript, as annotated by the prompter, and slightly modified by (i) revision, and (ii) re-casting;

(*b*) a transcript of this manuscript was sent to the printer;

(*c*) this transcript was often collated in the printing-house, where possible and profitable, with an exemplar of Q (Q3, and possibly also Q2), sometimes imperfectly; in one passage collation was neglected, and Q used as copy without alteration;

(*d*) the transcript was 'sophisticated', mainly by the printing-house collator.

F has a number of inconsistencies and irregularities that have been held to support a contrary theory implying multiple author-

1. Hall, 255; *Mirror*, 191, 195.
2. C. W. Wallace, *Englische Studien*, xviii, 357.   3. Alexander, 82 ff.
4. *2 H 6* (New Arden), xix–xx.   5. *PMLA.*, vol. 64 (1949), 45–6.

hip, or general revision, Shakespeare being one of the authors, or
he reviser of other men's work. These irregularities, however, can
be adequately explained as above, and in any case are themselves
nsufficient to support a theory of revision or of multiple author-
hip.[1]

It is obvious that F was *based* on the author's manuscript. The
tage-directions, as Sisson notes, are elaborate and literary,[2] and
hus presumably authorial, e.g. *Enter the King with a prayer booke*;
He giues his hand to Warw.; . . . *foure stand on one side, and foure on the
ther*; *Enter three Watchmen to guard the Kings Tent*; . . . *bringing the
King out in his Gowne, sitting in a Chaire*; *Layes his Hand on his Head.*
Some are missing when action is implicit in the text, and, to an
author or even an actor, unnecessary. Thus there is no '*Exit*' for
.hree characters at I. i. 190, 192, and 194, or for another four at
213 ff.; and an '*Exeunt*' at IV. viii. 32 leaves Henry and Exeter on
he stage.

Duplication and misplacement of stage-directions for music suggest the prompter's notes on the autograph. At IV. vii. 71 we have
Flourish. Sound.', which Wilson notes as 'perhaps marginal duplication'[3] by the prompter. Similar marginal annotation probably
ed to the misplacement in the printed text of '*Flourish*.' at the end
of I. i, and '*Alarum*.' at the end of I. ii. Both of these belong to the
beginning of the following scenes.

A more controversial feature is the occurrence in F of three
actors' names. Stage-directions read *Enter Gabriel* at I. ii. 48, and
Enter Sinklo and Humfrey at III. i. 1. All three names are also used as
speech-prefixes throughout their parts. This resembles the direction *Enter Beuis, and Iohn Holland* in *2 Henry VI*, IV. ii, where the
names are likewise carried through the speech-prefixes. Are these
due to Shakespeare, writing with particular actors in mind; or to
the prompter's jottings?

Since Allison Gaw's articles,[4] opinion has generally been in
favour of the author. Gaw found it natural, indeed inevitable, that
Shakespeare should mentally cast his parts as he wrote, from a
company with whose abilities and qualities he must have been in-
timate; and 'natural that in a special case he should note the name
of a given subordinate actor in his copy'.[5] This would be the more
natural in the case of Sinklo who obviously took the part of the thin

1. See further below, xli ff.; *2 H 6* (New Arden). xiii ff.; and *1 H 6*, xiii–xxxvii.
2. William Shakespeare, *The Complete Works*, 651.
3. *3 H 6* (New Shakespeare), note *ad loc.*
4. 'Actors' names in basic Shakespearean texts', *PMLA.*, 40 (1925), 530–50;
'John Sinklo as one of Shakespeare's actors', *Anglia*, xxxvii (1926), 289–303.
5. *Anglia*, xxxvii. 294.

officer in *2 Henry VI*, v. iv,[1] and may have been cast for the famine-starved apothecary in *Romeo and Juliet*. Sinklo's physical characteristics do not seem to have any special relevance in *3 Henry VI*. But Gaw argues that the use of the actor-names throughout the scene is most significant. 'Granted that the prompter might have noted them once in his copy, it is very unlikely that he would have replaced *1 Keeper* and *2 Keeper*, or their equivalent, with actors' names eighteen times in one brief scene. One each would have been quite sufficient to indicate the actors' parts that were to be prepared.'[2] McKerrow brings a further argument to support this view. 'I believe,' he says, 'that there is no case in any play having the clear marks of being, or being printed from, a prompt-copy, of an actor's name being given *alone* without that of the character whom he was to represent.'[3] In short, there seems every likelihood that the actor-names are Shakespeare's, and not prompter's jottings in his manuscript; and little of their being derived through a prompt-book, if such a further copy of the author's manuscript was made. It is hard to see why Greg, who admitted that the author may have used actor-names 'for some particular trait', should have objected that 'it is not of the least consequence who took these minor parts, and their assignment cannot possibly be attributed to the author'. Wilson is strongly in favour of Gaw and McKerrow; and their views agree with the evidence already drawn from stage-directions.[5]

F has indeed none of McKerrow's marks of surviving manuscript prompt-books: (*a*) advance warnings for actors and properties (*b*) the mention in entries of properties a character will require later in the scene; (*c*) the mention of actors' names as a gloss; and (*d*) entry of characters before the proper time.[6] To these Wilson would probably add obvious inconsistencies that the prompter might be expected to clear up. On the other hand, it may be suggested that the absence of these marks does not necessarily invalidate prompt-book copy in texts from which they are absent. Any further directions might well be added, and inconsistencies ironed out in the players' parts and the tiring-house 'plot'.

It is thus possible that Shakespeare's own manuscript, as annotated by the prompter, became the actual prompt-book.[7] The existence of such an annotated authorial copy, bearing the licenser'

---

1. He is named in Q; as also in *The Taming of the Shrew*, Induction, and Marston's *Malcontent*, Induction.

2. *Anglia*, xxxvii, 297.

3. R. B. McKerrow, 'The Elizabethan Printer and Dramatic Manuscripts' *The Library* (4 series), xii. 272.

4. Greg, *ShFF*, 183; *Ed. Pr.*, 55.   5. J. Dover Wilson, *3 H 6*, 119–21.

6. McKerrow, *op. cit.*, 270 ff.   7. But see Greg, *Pr. Em.*, 55; *ShFF*, 182–3.

'allowance' and therefore of prime value to the company, would help to explain the use of a transcript from it[1] for the printers of the F in 1623.

In favour of the use of the autograph as prompt-book are a few authorial alterations in the cast and the text. Some were made before the Q report, and therefore appear in both Q and F; others must have been made after, and appear in F alone.

Common to Q and F is the extrusion of Falconbridge from I. i, and of old Salisbury from I. ii, both replaced by Montague. As Shakespeare very well knew (II. i; IV. i), Montague was York's nephew; yet in the first two scenes (but not later) he is described as 'brother'. And both Falconbridge and old Salisbury were York's brothers-in-law. The two alterations leave the inconsistency that Montague is represented as saying, on his departure at the end of I. i,

> And I vnto the sea from whence I came,

only to reappear, in I. ii, at York's castle in the north. Montague had no particular connection with the sea. Falconbridge had. Though Shakespeare confused two Falconbridges, father and son, both of whom, in Hall, are mentioned in connection with keeping the Straits of Dover, he was historically correct in referring to this post at I. i. 246:

> Sterne Falconbridge commands the Narrow Seas.

Montague's three speeches in I. i, with three references to York as brother, together with the references to the sea and to Falconbridge, seem to confirm the substitution of Montague, to whom none of these references apply, for an original Falconbridge.

We learn from 1 Henry VI that 'Lord Falconbridge' was one of the many titles of Talbot, who was also Lord Strange. Strange was the patron of Shakespeare's company from at least 1594, but perhaps earlier.[2] It is thus possible that the adaptation was due to his influence. If so, it must have taken effect at an earlier date, since the Q was almost certainly a report of performance before 1593. On the other hand, the substitution might be no more than an economy in casting.

The substitution of Montague for Salisbury is also probable. In I. ii, there are further references to York's 'brother'; at I. i. 245 Warwick is described as 'Chancelor', an office given in the chronicles to Salisbury; and at II. iii. 14 ff. Q (correctly) describes him as Warwick's father. In this case, the text seems to have been altered to conform with the change, to

1. See below, xxxiii.   2. See below, xlv ff.

Warwick is Chancellor and the Lord of Calais

from

Salisbury is Chancellor, Warwick Lord of Calais.

(I. i. 245)

Warwick was Lord of Calais, but never Chancellor.

There seems to be no special reason for the elimination of Salisbury beyond economy of casting. It does not seem to have any connection with the alteration of a whole passage describing Salisbury's death at II. iii. 14 ff., an alteration that would not, in any case, affect the cast. Here the change from 'father' to 'brother' involves the correction of an error, and may thus contain an element of revision. The chronicles refer, not to old Salisbury, but to the 'bastard of Salisbury'—a rather ambiguous phrase. A description of the 'bastard's' death has been substituted in F for the Q description of the death of old Salisbury who thus disappears entirely from the F text.

Another possible alteration affects the name 'Brooke'. As is well known, 'Brooke' was changed to 'Broome' in *The Merry Wives of Windsor*; and 'Oldcastle' in *Henry IV* and *The Merry Wives* to 'Falstaff'. Since 'Brooke' was the family name of Lord Cobham, and Sir John Oldcastle one of Cobham's ancestors, the changes have usually been ascribed to his influence as Lord Chamberlain. William Brooke, seventh Lord Cobham, succeeded as Chamberlain on the death of the Shakespearean company's patron, the first Lord Hunsdon, in July 1596. Brooke held the office till his death in March 1597. The Players were retained by the second Lord Hunsdon, who himself succeeded Brooke as Chamberlain in 1597. In the interval 1596–7, the company was known as Hunsdon's Men, but would come under the jurisdiction of Brooke. This is therefore a possible time and occasion for these changes, and, in *3 Henry VI*, for the elimination of the name in the F line I. ii. 40,

You *Edward* shall vnto my Lord *Cobham*,

which appears in Q as

Edward, thou shalt to *Edmund Brooke* Lord *Cobham*.

1. See further the discussion of these phenomena in *MLR.*, 4 (Oct. 1955) 492–4. The following table may be useful:

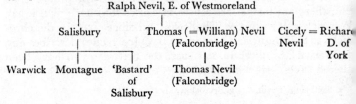

Ralph Nevil, E. of Westmoreland

Salisbury	Thomas (=William) Nevil (Falconbridge)	Cicely = Richard Nevil D. of York
Warwick Montague 'Bastard' of Salisbury	Thomas Nevil (Falconbridge)	

Some of the 'inconsistencies' in *3 Henry VI*, those, for example, affecting Montague, have thus been induced by minor alterations in the cast. Others are to be expected in authorial copy, from slips or errors on the author's part, or from his adoption of an error in his sources. Thus Clifford's death by 'the Swords of common Souldiers' (I. i. 9) is inconsistent with his death in single combat with York (*2 H 6*, v. ii. 28; *3 H 6*, I. iii. 5, etc.). But the inconsistency is Hall's (223, 255), whose conflicting accounts Shakespeare follows exactly. The marriages arranged for Warwick's daughters, Isabel and Anne, to Prince Edward and Clarence respectively, are the opposite of the correct arrangement given in Hall and *Richard III*. In this case, however, the inconsistency may be due either to (*a*) an error on Shakespeare's part—the particular order is of no consequence for the course of events—or (*b*) an error by the Q reporters, carried through the Q copy without correction into F.[1] Similar mistakes in the Christian names of Grey (III. ii) and Montgomery (IV. vii. 40) may likewise be due to either of the same causes.[2]

It is therefore probable that F was based (through a transcript) on Shakespeare's manuscript, as annotated by the prompter, and slightly altered for various reasons of casting, censorship, and historical accuracy. There is no need to call in theories of revision or of multiple-authorship to account for any of the phenomena.

Q COPY FOR F

It has hitherto been assumed that F gives a text bibliographically independent of Q. The original Pollard–Wilson theory[3] of 'good' and 'bad' quartos differentiated them partly by this criterion—that no use was made of the 'bad' (by correction or annotation or even consultation) in the preparation of the F text. It is now becoming clear that the criterion is unsound and that most, if not all, of the quarto versions were in fact used as far as practicable, the difference among them being only a matter of degree.[4] *The True Tragedy*, at least, seems to have been used extensively.

An exception was usually made for one short passage (IV. ii. 1–18) which is identical in Q and F. Here McKerrow is representative in suggesting that this was due to a defect in the manuscript, to supply which resort was had to an edition of Q—he thought Q1. In a further note he added a second passage—v. vii.[5] Such iden-

---

1. See below, xxiv ff.   2. Cf. 'Nell' for 'Meg' in *2 H 6*.
3. Greg, *Ed. Pr.*, 9; Pollard, *Sh. Fight*, 46 ff.
4. See e.g. my notes on *2 H 6* (New Arden), xxxii ff.; on *H 5*, in *SB.*, VIII (1956), 67–93.
5. *RES.*, xiii (1937), 64–72.

tity, of course, can be as well, if not better, explained by the use of Q as copy for F, and as illustrating a lapse on the 'corrector's' part.

That Q was in fact used in this way in *3 Henry VI* can be shown from the number of common errors and variants (especially Q2,F and Q3,F agreements against Q1) in readings, punctuation, italics, speech-prefixes, lineation, and spelling, as well as by patent signs of marginal or interlinear correction. As a body, these are obviously beyond the reach of coincidence, common variation, manuscript origin, or scribal misreading.

The following list (not intended to be exhaustive) illustrates the extent of such variants, in most of which F agrees with Q3:

			Q1	Q2	Q3	F
I.	i.	24	heauens	heauens	heauen	Heauen
II.	i.	123	He	Who	He	Who
	ii.	46	euill	euill	ill	ill
		104	flee	flee	fly	fly
		106	that droue	that droue	droue	droue
	vi.	24	our	our	out	out
III.	ii.	183	that that	that that	that which	that which
IV.	i.	28	my	my	mine	mine
		134	neerest	neerest	neere	neere
v.	vii.	38	Ranard	Ranard	Reynard	Reynard

This takes no account of (*a*) probable common corrections for sense or metre, e.g. *deafe* for Q1 *death*; *lesson* for Q1,2 *lesson, boy* (II. ii. 61); *stand* for *fie, stand* (IV. vii. 58); (*b*) probable common sophistications like that of Q1,2 *and* to *if* (III. ii. 30; v. i. 75; v. vii. 21), *whilst* to *while* (I. i. 177), and *thine* to *thy* (I. i. 202) in Q3 and F; and (*c*) instances where alternative sources of variation or lack of textual evidence make the true reading uncertain, e.g. v. vi. 80; v. vi. 90. Only one Q2,F variant is given; there may well be others not so obvious, but bibliographically important. The significance of this will be discussed below.

The listed variants, in which F derives from Q2 or Q3, have no probable authority. They are palpable Q misprints, like *out* for *our*; omissions—*droue* for *that droue*; modernizations—*Reynard* for *Ranard* (*Renard*); or they run counter to the trend of sophistication, as *mine* for *my*. These are therefore unlikely to be due to any common factor or agreement in variation.

The element of latent error in F arising from failure to correct the Q copy is of course seen at its clearest in the identical Q,F patch at IV. ii. 1–18. Here 'Towne' (15) is certainly an error for 'Townes', as at IV. iii. 15; and probably 'Somerset and Clarence *comes*' (3) for *'come'*. There may be other latent errors in this short passage. The second line

> The common people by numbers swarme to vs

seems more likely to have read

> The common people swarme to vs by numbers.

Line 12 seems also to contain a recollection from line 6, and its correction would improve both metre and general sense:

> Then gentle *Clarence*, welcome vnto *Warwicke*,   6
> And welcome *Somerset*: . . .
> But welcome sweet *Clarence*, my Daughter shall be thine.   12

The 'welcome' of line 12, almost certainly a recollection of those above, is superfluous, and would read naturally and metrically 'come'.

Elsewhere common errors are evident from excess or defect in the metre. While defects of omission can seldom be supplied with certainty, excess can often be dealt with by simple omission of intrusive elements. At I. iv. 120, for example,

> Were shame enough to shame thee, / Wert *thou* not shamelesse

'thou' is superfluous to the metre, and just the sort of particle commonly supplied by reporters to fill a Shakespearean ellipsis.

A special case is that, already noticed, of Q cues incorporated in the text.[1]

Other retained errors may have originated with the Q printer rather than with a reporter, as in

> My Father was as thou art, Duke of Yorke,
> Thy Grandfather *Roger Mortimer*, Earle of March.
>   (I. i. 105–6)

where 'Grandfather' is a palpable error for 'Grandsire', as at line 129, and was probably caught by the Q printer from 'Father' in the line above.

In many cases, naturally, it is clear that both Q and F are corrupt, but impossible to restore the original reading. For example, at I. i. 55–6:

> And thine, *Lord Clifford*, & you both haue vow'd reuenge
> On him, his sonnes, his fauorites, and his friends.

any one of several words and phrases may be intrusive—it is uncertain which.[2]

1. See xvii above.   2. Cf. e.g. I. iii. 23; IV. i. 29–31.

The use of corrected Q copy may also appear in F mislineation, corresponding to that of Q or to what correction of Q would produce. For example:

iv. i. 17 ff.

Q   *Glo.* And shall, because our King, but yet such
              Sudden marriages sildome proueth well.
       Edw. Yea brother *Richard*, are you against vs too?
       Glo. Not I my Lord, no, God forfend, that I
              Should once gainsay your highnesse pleasure,
              I, and twere pitty to sunder them that yoke so well
                 together.

F   *Rich.* And shall haue your will, because our King:
              Yet hastie Marriage seldome proueth well.
       King. Yea, Brother *Richard*, are you offended too?
       Rich. Not I: no:
              God forbid, that I should wish them seuer'd,
              Whom God hath join'd together:
              I, and 'twere pittie, to sunder them,
              That yoake so well together.

Symptoms of the derivative, corrected, nature of the copy seem to appear in: (a) the metrical defect in the first F line, probably to be emended by Rowe's insertion of 'you' after 'And', to supply the Q,F omission; (b) the mislineation affecting the whole of Richard's second speech; the superfluous 'together', caught up with the marginal insertion;[1] the retention of the erroneous line-opening 'I, and 'twere pitty'; and possible sophistication in the change from 'forfend' to 'forbid'; and (c) the retention of the common memorial phrase 'Not I'.[2]

The passage might thus read, with the fifth line still imperfect:

       Rich. And you shall have your will, because our King:
              Yet hasty marriage seldom proveth well.
       Edw. Yea, brother Richard, are you offended too?
       Rich. No: God forfend that I should wish them sever'd
              Whom God hath join'd: ay, and 'twere pity
              To sunder them that yoke so well together.

Imperfect correction may also be seen in the following:

Q   This shoulder was ordain'd so thicke to heaue,
              And heaue it shall some weight, or breake my backe,
              Worke thou the way, and *thou shalt* execute.

                                              (v. vii. 23–5)

1. Cf. the similar repetition of 'cudgel'd' in *H 5*, v. i. 90, 93.
2. Cf. other memorial examples in the Qq of *Wiv.*, 425; *H 5*, 469, 499, 504; *Ham.*, 747; and the use of the phrase at iv. i. 123.

F is identical, except that the last line reads 'that shalt'. The corrector would seem to have altered 'thou' to 'that', but omitted to complete the correction by changing 'shalt' to 'shall'. 'Shalt' is therefore evidence of the Q copy, 'that' of the correction.[1]

Insertions have been sometimes treated as alternatives (scored on the left), as at:

1. i. 120 ff.

Q   *Yorke.* Peace sonnes.
        North. Peace thou, and giue King *Henry* leaue to speake.
        King. Ah *Plantagenet*, why seek'st thou to depose me?
           Are we not both *Plantagenets* by birth?
           And from two brothers lineally descent?
           Suppose by right and equity thou be King:
           Thinkst thou, that I will leaue my Kingly seate, ...

F   *Plant.* Sonnes peace.
        Henry. Peace thou, and giue King *Henry* leaue to speake.
        Warw. *Plantagenet* shal speake first: Heare him Lords,
           And be you silent and attentiue too,
           For he that interrupts him, shall not liue.
        Hen. Think'st thou, that I will leaue my Kingly Throne, ...

Both Q and F alternatives seem authentic. It seems likely that Warwick's three lines, omitted in Q, were added opposite Henry's at the foot of Q3 page I2ᵛ and the top of I3, and treated as alternatives, the prefix for Henry being carried forward. As Vaughan remarks, the Q lines are exactly those which would account for his followers feeling faint (129).

1. i. 173 ff.

Q   *Yorke.* Confirme the crowne to me, and to mine heires,
           And thou shalt reigne in quiet whilst thou liu'st.
        King. Conuey the souldiers hence, and then I will.
        War. Captaine conduct them into *Tuthill* fields.
        Clif. What wrong is this. ...

F   *Plant.* Confirme the Crowne to me and to mine Heires,
           And thou shalt reigne in quiet while thou liu'st.
        Henry. I am content: *Richard Plantagenet*
           Enioy the Kingdome after my decease.
        Clifford. What wrong is this. ...

v. vii. 58, where both lines are required, Q after F:

Q   Resolue your selfe, and let vs claime the crowne
F   Why Brother, wherefore stand you on nice points?

1. Cf. v. vi. 84, Q keptst; F keept'st (=keep'st).

v. i. 76 ff.:

Q   *Enter Clarence with Drum and Soldiors.*
        War. And loe where *George* of *Clarence* sweepes along,
             Of power enough to bid his brother battaile.
        Cla. *Clarence, Clarence,* for *Lancaster.*
        Edw. *Et tu Brute,* wilt thou stab *Caesar* too?
             A parlie sirra, to *George of Clarence.*
Sound a parlie, and Richard and Clarence whispers together, and then
Clarence takes his red Rose out of his Hat, & throwes it at Warwick
        War. Come *Clarence*, come, thou wilt if *Warwicke* call.

F   *Enter Clarence, with Drumme and Colours.*
        War. And loe, where *George* of Clarence sweepes along,
             Of force enough to bid his Brother Battaile:
             With whom, *an* vpright zeale to right, preuailes (F *in*)
             More then the nature of a Brothers Loue.
        Come Clarence, come: thou wilt, if *Warwicke* call.

With the deletion of the mostly superfluous Q stage-direction, an explanation in terms of alternative passages will account for the variation, and restore the original.[1]

The close similarity of some stage-directions, though not nearly so striking as in *2 Henry VI*, also points to F dependence on Q copy. Stage-directions are not memorial matter to anything like the same degree as text, and parts likely to carry them are scarce or absent in Q. There has been some editing, and occasionally adjustment to lose or save space. An interesting example, where the names omitted in Q have been merely tacked on to the Q direction, is (ii. vi. 29):

Q   Enter Edward, Richard, Warwicke, and Souldiors.
F   Enter Edward, Warwicke, Richard, and Soldiers,
                Montague, and Clarence.

or again, where specific information has been added:

Q   Enter Warwicke and Oxford with Soldiors.
F   Enter Warwicke and Oxford *in England,* with *French*
                Souldiors.

A line has been gained in each of the following, in the same F column, by padding the Q direction:

Q   Enter Gloster, Hastings, and Sir William Stanley.
F   Enter Richard, *Lord* Hastings, and Sir William
                Stanley.

Q   Enter Edward and a Huntsman.
F   Enter *King* Edward and a Huntsman
                 with him.

1. As in Alexander, *Tudor Shakespeare.*

Space has been saved where it was clearly needed, in II. iv, by similar adaptation:

Q   Alarmes, and then enter Richard at one doore,
                And Clifford at the other.
F   Excursions. Enter Richard and Clifford.

Q   Alarmes. They fight, and then enters Warwike and
             rescues Richard, and then exeunt omnes.
F   They Fight, Warwicke comes, Clifford flies.

It is especially interesting to note the following, which suggests Q copy, at the end of v. vii:

Q1	Q2	Q3	F
Exeunt Omnes	Exeunt Omnes	Exeunt omnes	Exeunt omnes

The F agreement with Q1,2 *Exeunt Omnes*, against Q3 *Exeunt omnes* at the end of II. i might be, of course, due to normalization rather than to use of Q2 copy.

In Q, IV. vi was preceded by IV. vii and followed by IV. viii. The Q stage-direction for IV. vi was able to serve for the very similar direction at IV. viii (omitting the short intervening text of IV. vi).

> Enter *Warwike* and *Clarence*, with the Crowne, and
> then king *Henry*, and *Oxford*, and *Summerset*,
> and the yong Earle of *Richmond*.

This was easily modified, chiefly by deletion, into the F:

> *Flourish. Enter the King, Warwicke, Mountague,*
> *Clarence, Oxford, and Somerset.*

Somerset has no part in IV. viii, though he had in IV. vi, but Exeter speaks and is addressed by name in the text; he should obviously have replaced Somerset in the stage-direction. The oversight has been attributed[1] to a process of revision carried out on the Q copy to transform it into F. The use of Q copy, however, gives an explanation just as adequate, and more in accord with the other evidence.

The speech-prefixes show a similar influence from Q. Even the conservative compositor A departs from his usual *Warw.* to adopt the Q form *War.* on p5^r (1), q2^r (3), and q2^v (14). More striking still, he abandons his normal *Plant.* to follow the Q *Yorke.* in the three examples occurring on *one page* of Q3 (I2),[2] and in these only. Com-

1. See note *ad loc.*
2. These are likewise the only examples on one page of Q1 (*York.*) and Q2 (*Yor.*).

positor B (?) is similarly affected. Thus we have *Mes.* at II. i. 206, but *Mess.* at II. ii. 67, both agreeing with Q3; and likewise *North.* at II. ii. 66, but *Nor.* at 108. The prefixes of B (normal *Ed.*) for Prince Edward are specially interesting:

	Q3	F		Q3	F
II. i. 89 ff.	Edw.	Ed.		Edw.	Edw.
	Edw.	Edw.		Edw.	Ed.
	Edw. (2)	Ed. (2)	II. iii	Edw. (4)	Ed. (4)
	—	Ed.		Edw.	Edw.
II. ii. 81 ff.	Edw.	Edw.	III. iii	P. Ed.	Prince Ed.
	Edw.	Ed. (2)		—	Prin. Ed.
	Prin.	Pr. Ed.	v. v	Ed.	Edw.
	Edw.	Ed.		Edw. (3)	Ed. (3)

The only exception to the general preference for *Ed.* and the influence of Q in the spelling and form used is the first example in v. v, and here the obvious cause is justification of the line, assisted by wide spacing and the expansion of *she* to *shee*.

These phenomena in themselves all support F use of Q copy. Their distribution lends further support. For they occur in those passages where Q and F are closest. Since they are the relics of imperfect correction, they tend to produce an irregular, contaminated text. This is generally distinguishable from the cleanness and regularity of those other passages where Q and F diverge too widely for Q copy to have been possible or worth while. The distinction is in itself a corroboration of the intermittent use of Q.

That such use was eminently feasible may be demonstrated by making the attempt on a facsimile of Q. Much of it can be so corrected as to provide printer's copy as clear and legible as corrected first proofs. Apart from omissions to be supplied—and these are often substantial—there were about a dozen out of sixty-four Q pages that would have been quite impossible. Omissions could, however, have been inserted on separate leaves between passages of good corrected text. A little use of scissors and paste could have produced long stretches of mainly printed Q copy. Jaggard's preference for this is hardly in doubt.

Such copy would offer several advantages. Its preparation would take editorial, not compositorial, time. It could be more legible. It could be made so as to be physically divisible between the two compositors, as well as into separate stints equivalent to F pages, where this would be an advantage. For both reasons, it would be easier to cast off.

There is thus a considerable body of evidence that Q3 was used as part of the F copy. Some of that evidence may indeed be dis-

counted on the grounds that both Q3 and F issued from the same
printing-house and that some of the Q3,F agreements may be due
to common trends and practices, such as 'sophistication', of Jaggard and his compositors. Even when all such allowances are made,
however, sufficient remains to justify the claim of Q3.

That some use was also made of Q2, especially near the beginning, is suggested by the collation of e.g. I. i. 45–59 of A2ᵛ (of Q2):

	Q1,2,F	*Lancaster*	Q3	Lancaster
47		Dares		Dare
52		Backt		(Back'd)
59		lets		Let's

or again, in the passage included in leaf A3 (of Q2):

93	remember it	remember't
	griefe,	greefe:
97	bloud	blood
105	*Yorke*, (F Yorke,)	Yorke:
106	stoupe	stoope
113	You are	Y'are
	Father	Father,
122	to ... sorrow	(to ... sorrow)

There are occasional minor agreements with Q3, as in the roman
'Yorke', which may be set down to compositor A's normal habits;
and a common semi-colon at 'Lose/loose' (113), which could be
normal Q3,F treatment of the Q1,2 comma, and the reverse of
which would not apply to the punctuation at 105. This Q2 copy
from A3 and A3ᵛ falls entirely within the F page o4ᵛ (148) set by
compositor A, who set continuously from the beginning of the play
(o4) to the end of the F signature.

It seems possible to identify another stretch of Q2 copy between
I. iv. 38 and the end (or a few lines short of it) of II. i. The outstanding variants are 'can I' (Q1,2,F); 'I can' (Q3); and 'Who' (Q2,F);
'He' (Q1,3); at I. iv. 151 and II. i. 123 respectively. An agreement
in '*Exeunt Omnes*' (Q1,2,F) against '*Exeunt omnes*' (Q3) may be a
normalization in F. Besides agreeing with Q2, F shows no exclusive
agreements with Q3; and indeed avoids a number of Q3 errors and
minor variants.

The passage begins on the Q2 page B4ᵛ and ends at the foot of
C3 (and of L3 in Q3). Though it spans two F pages and the work
of both compositors, it could still be used as continuous copy, without physical division. For the first F page was o6ᵛ, the last in the
gathering; A, who set it, could simply work to a point indicated,
and leave the rest for B to use for p1. A five-line omission had to be

made good at the end of this page; and the few lines needed to finish the scene, whatever the copy, need have caused no difficulty. The setting of II. ii could proceed conveniently with the single side (L3ᵛ) of Q3.

There is not enough certain evidence of this kind in *3 Henry VI* to work out a complete scheme of quarto-copy. The incidence of correction from manuscript, sophistication, and scribal influence, together with our inadequate knowledge of compositors and their spelling habits, permit at present only a general view. It seems clear, however, that both Q2 and Q3 formed part of the copy. This use of multiple quarto-copy is paralleled in other Shakespearean texts, and its presence, as far as I can see, cannot be escaped.[1]

Meanwhile, also, it is possible to make only a general conjecture as to the method employed. Since the printing-house agent who constructed the copy would work straight forward, he would naturally do so by F pages or series of pages, and cast off as he went. He might have in mind the normal distribution of copy between compositors, and the direction—back or forward—in which they would set;[2] or he might adapt their distribution to the nature of the copy —printed, manuscript, heavily or lightly corrected—that emerged. At times, according to the correctness of the Q report, it might be feasible to construct a continuous galley from one-sided Q leaves (Q2 and Q3 alternately), divisible both for the insertion of Q omissions, and at the transitions from one F page to another. Within the F page, or in the case of a compositor who would set forward, it would be equally feasible to use both sides of the Q leaf, provided no insertions were required that could not be accommodated on the leaf itself.

It may therefore be assumed that Jaggard possessed an exemplar of his own Q3, printed for Pavier a year or two earlier, and one of Q2. It is reasonable to suppose that, for the printing of Q3, he would have received from Millington an exemplar of Q1—from which Q3 was printed—and one also of Millington's Q2. All these represent the file-copies normally kept by printers and publishers for reference and reprints.[3] With these, Jaggard could easily have produced the Q copy required. It could have been produced, more-

---

1. See e.g. 'The Quartos and the Folio text of *King Lear*', *RES.*, vi (July 1955), 252–8; 'Quarto Copy for Folio *Henry V*', *Studies in Bibliography*, viii (1956), 67–93; 'The Quartos and the Folio Text of '*Richard III*', *RES.*, viii (Aug. 1957), 225–33.

2. Cf. above, xiv.

3. They might, of course, have sometimes been in the form of unsold sheets; though the fact of reprinting of quartos would suggest that previous editions had been sold out.

over, in his own time, and thus without any loss of time in the printing-house.

THE SCRIBE

Where Q copy was used with inadequate or no correction, the trail of the basic manuscript is of course hard to recover. A Q,F variant may be an error and not a correction; a Q,F agreement may be a latent error. Here it is difficult and often impossible to be certain of identifying the marks of other agents of transmission.

To isolate such agents, we must generally turn to the passages where use of Q copy was impossible or unlikely. Here we may generally attribute to a scribe those types of error found in the stints of both the compositors. These seem to conform, though on a more limited scale, to the types of scribal error found in *1 Henry VI*,[1] where no Q was available and the whole play was printed from manuscript. As in *1 Henry VI*, the scribe seems to rationalize inversions and ellipses and add titles, and to show the effects of haste or carelessness in misreading words from their general appearance or under the influence of associations from the context. Thus with ellipses, though these might have been supplied editorially:[2]

I. i. 224	Thou would'st haue left ...	
	Rather then [haue] made that sauage Duke thine Heire,	
III. ii. 161	Like to a Chaos, or [an] vn-lick'd Beare-whelpe,	
V. vi. 51	To wit, an indigest [ed and] deformed lumpe,[3]	

and titles:

IV. v. 16	Now brother of Gloster, [Lord] Hastings, and the rest,[4]
IV. vii. 1	Now brother Richard, [Lord] Hastings, and the rest,

Words were misread from their general appearance:

I. iv. 50	buckler	*read*	buckle
III. i. 24	the sour Aduersaries		thee, sour Adversity
III. ii. 110	very sad		vex'd
III. ii. 132	place		plant (Q)

Some of these misreadings might be the compositor's, as 'externall' at III. iii. 124 for 'eternall'; or they may have arisen from the scribe's type of handwriting, as with 'very sad', III. ii. 110. Either through his writing, or his own errors, however, the scribe would seem to be responsible for most.

1. Cf. *1 H 6* (New Arden), Introduction, xviii ff.
2. Another possible example is IV. iii. 13 (cf. III. ii. 15) : 'in Townes about [him].'
3. Alternatively rationalized by the corrector/editor from Q: 'To wit: an vndigest created lumpe'.
4. Cf. *1 H 6*, xx.

Words are also misread or misinterpreted through the influence of the context, e.g.:

	F	Read
I. iv. 15–16	Richard cry'de, Charge, ...	
	And cry'de, A Crowne, ...	Edward
I. iv. 35	My *ashes, as* the Phoenix, may ...	like (Q)
III. iii. 10–11	Where I must take like Seat ...	
	And to my humble *Seat* conforme ...	state (cf. line 2)
IV. i. 32	Is now dis-honored by this *new* Marriage[1]	omit
	(Cf. line 2, 'Of this new Marriage ...)	

In compositor B's (or E's) stint this kind of error recurs at II. i. 130–1:

the Night-Owles lazie flight,
Or like a *lazie* Thresher with a Flaile.   Q idle

The examples, however, are mainly A's, and as he was 'in general, the more attentive and the more faithful to copy,'[2] the errors are unlikely to be his. One of them, in any case, goes rather far back (IV. i. 32), and is more likely to have come from a scribe who had some familiarity with the play than from a compositor who had not.

Omissions[3] are impossible to allot in detail. They are most frequent in B's work, and most may be his; but the scribe may have been responsible for some.

'SOPHISTICATION'

The F text also bears clear signs of what has been loosely, if conveniently, called 'sophistication'. This has always been characteristic of language; and the passage of some forty years between the printing of Q (1595) and the First Folio (1623) gave ample scope for its operation. Its influence was general, and its direction, in the main, consistent. It worked through various channels, from authors to scribes and editors. Among others, it appears in certain well-marked forms in the printing-house of William and Isaac Jaggard. Its general object was to present the reader with a more 'modern', agreeable, 'correct', and readable text.

The main trend was the modernization of obsolescent forms. Thus the tendency was to alter 'mine' before a vowel to 'my', 'in sunder' to 'asunder', 'sware' to 'swore', 'albeit' to 'although', 'and'

1. Other possible examples are: II. ii. 152–4: to ... *to* (Q till) ... to; III. i. 98: Our newes ... / Stab Poniards in *our* (your?) flesh; III. ii. 119: your Foe ... *your* (Q as) Prisoner ... your ... Gate; IV. i. 13: our Choyce ... *our* (your?) abuse.
2. Alice Walker, *Textual Problems of the First Folio*, 10–12.
3. Cf. e.g. II. i. 182; II. vi. 80; III. iii. 156; V. vi. 46.

to 'if'. This was accompanied by some rather pedantic regularization, which would change accusative 'who' to 'whom', adjectives used adverbially to adverbs, and the expansion of some euphonious verbal inflections, such as 'thou bids' to 'thou bid'st', and 'blind' (past participle) to 'blinded'. A similar tendency towards pedantry and politeness is evident in the substitution of 'he' for the colloquial 'a'.

Elizabethan printers generally, either by direct editing, or through standing instructions to their compositors, practised a degree of sophistication or improvement of their copy. How far Jaggard, the printer of the 'Pavier' quartos in 1619 and of the Folio in 1623, went in this direction, and his special preferences, may be seen in the 1619 reprints, which include Q3 of both *2* and *3 Henry VI*. Throughout these ten reprints, some frequent sophistications are:

afeard—afraid	. . . (e)s—'st
amongst—among	whilst—while
and—if	who—whom
mile/year—miles/years	yea—I (=ay)
mine—my	

The same changes, among others, are found also in Jaggard's otherwise unaltered reprints of quartos in the First Folio. They are found again in his plays printed from corrected quartos, like *3 Henry VI*, especially in those parts where Q copy is evident. In all such cases, they may therefore be attributed to Jaggard himself, or his agent. Although no doubt an occasional example may have come through a scribe or a compositor, in general they occur indifferently in the work of all the F compositors and of the (probably) various scribes. The older, unsophisticated forms are therefore likely to be Shakespeare's; the newer, to be Jaggard's.

The incidence of sophistication in Jaggard's editions, however, is erratic. In some straight reprints there is very little. Older forms are sometimes sophisticated, sometimes not. Occasionally sophistication is made in the reverse direction, as if the sophisticator were slightly confused. Confusion seems to be increased in quarto-copy plays, where correction may restore from manuscript an older form that sophistication has elsewhere modernized.

The general trend, however, is quite clear and consistent, when present. It is confirmed by its virtual absence in manuscript-copy plays, like *1 Henry VI*. In other words, Jaggard seems to have confined his sophisticating activities to printed copy, and to have concentrated on corrected print more than reprints. Correction of the Q copy, that is, drew his attention to the old forms, and gave him the opportunity of sophisticating without making of it a separate operation.

The trend may be illustrated by a comparison between *1 Henry VI* (printed from manuscript) and *Richard III* (printed from corrected Q).

1 Henry VI			Richard III
amongst	Q	amongst	F among
be (subjunctive)		be	is/are
I (=ay)		I	yes
mine/thine		mine/thine	my/thy
misconster		misconster	misconstrue
... (e)s (2 pers. sing.)		... (e)s	...'st[1]
lift (past tense)		spake	spoke
broke, tane (pa. pple)		spoke	spoken
whilst		whilst	while(s)
who (acc.)		who	whom (i. iii. 54)
wont		wont	used (iii. vii. 29)
year (pl.)		mile	miles
yea		yea	I (=ay)

The general trend, then, is clear enough, and there is no doubt that, as a whole, the unsophisticated forms are more likely to be Shakespearean than the sophisticated. This presumption is all the more probable since further sophistication was likely to have been effected during transcription, and even by the compositors. Until we know more of these agents, however, and more of sophistication in general, there will remain a doubt as to the possibility of emendation in some *particular cases*. Shakespeare may have used both forms; the reporters may have confused them; an old-fashioned compositor may have reverted in 1623 to the unsophisticated form; the corrector may have been inconsistent, or torn between correcting to an old form, and sophisticating to a new. For example, Jaggard progressively sophisticates 'yea' to 'I (ay)' to 'yes', normally one stage at a time, but occasionally direct from 'yea' to 'yes'. On rare occasions, in quarto-copy plays, we have the opposite order, e.g.:

yes—I	*Lear*, i. iii. 3; i. iv. 336
I—yea	*H 5*, i. ii. 284

Since these Q texts were corrected with some care for F copy at these points, it may be assumed that these represent restorations from the manuscript. But if 'yea' is changed to 'yes', are we to

---

1. Cf. *3 H 6*, ii. ii. 142, shames/sham'st; 172, deniest/denied'st; iv. viii. 16, commands/command'st; also *Lr.*, i. i. 183, thinks/think'st; *Troil.*, v. i. 24, meanes/mean'st; *Mer.*, iv. i. 22, exacts/exact'st.

emend to 'yea' or to 'I'? Or may not 'yes' be in fact correct, and 'yea' due to the reporter?

There are, indeed, readings where F is probably from manuscript and correct in the use of the older form, but where Q has sophisticated, e.g. III. ii. 112: F to who—Q To whom. Taking such cases as a whole, there can be little doubt that the majority are correct in Q, and that consistent adoption of Q would result in a net gain. Since, however, it does not seem possible meantime to be absolutely certain in individual cases, and since there are the few examples running counter, it is best to retain the F readings.

There are, however, a few types of sophistication, chiefly affecting syntax and verbal inflections, where Shakespeare's practice and the trend of sophistication seem clear and consistent enough to justify emendation.

(a) so/such ... as sophisticated to *that*[1]

This may be illustrated from two passages by different compositors, and by speakers unlikely to be present on the stage during each other's speeches—Northumberland and Gloucester:

> his passions moue(s) me so,
> That [Q As] hardly can I check my eyes from Teares.
>
> (I. iv. 150–1)
>
> For I will buzze abroad such Prophesies,
> That [Q As] Edward shall be fearefull of his life,
>
> (V. vi. 86–7)

(b) *sware/swore*

The original seems clear in:

II. i. 172   He *sware* consent to your succession, (F swore)[2]

Compare the passage appearing in F alone, at III. i. 72–82:

> *Hum.* And we his subjects, sworne in all Allegeance,
>   Will apprehend you, as his Enemie.
> *King.* But did you neuer sweare, and break an Oath ...
>   And you were sworne true Subjects vnto me:
>   And tell me then, haue you not broke your Oathes?
>   Ah simple men, you know not what you *sweare*, ...
>
> (=sware)

'Sweare', possibly affected by the present 'know' (which would prevent the normal sophistication 'swore'), may alternatively be a homonym; but the reference throughout is clearly to swearing in the past. The two forms are exactly in line with the practice of Shakespeare and the sophisticator.

1. Cf. also *Ham.*, II. i. 95; *1 H 4*, IV. ii. 31; *R 3*, III. iv. 40; III. iii. 227.
2. Cf. e.g. *Tit.*, I. i. 6, ware—wear; II. i. 87, bare—beare; *H 5*, V. i. 83, gat—got; etc.

(*c*) A standard Elizabethan usage and its F sophistication concerns the use of the subjunctive, still current in other European languages, in clauses of condition, concession, and purpose, e.g.:

I. iv. 160	Q	if thou *tell*	F	tell'st[1]
II. ii. 165		though the edge *have* . . . hit		hath
II. vi. 41		wheresoe'er he *be*		is
v. v. 84		if a thing *come* in his head		comes

This F usage, in manuscript-copy plays, is virtually absent, and in this Q offers the exact parallel. The very rare exceptions may be attributed to scribe, or compositor, operating thirty years after Shakespeare. What may reasonably be taken as Shakespeare's normal usage at this period may be illustrated from *The Two Gentlemen of Verona* and *1 Henry VI*, plays of approximately the same period as *3 Henry VI*. *The Two Gentlemen* shows at least forty examples of the subjunctive—where it is different from the indicative—in conditional or concessional clauses. The only exception is at III. i. 257, 'if thou seest'. In *1 Henry VI* there are at least fifty-five examples, with a similar 'If thou canst', and a clear sophistication in 'If Salisbury *wants* . . .'. In *3 Henry VI* itself, passages not affected by Q copy show the same consistency. Apart again from 'If thou canst',[2] at I. iv. 46, there are three examples close together in II. iii–iv, namely, II. iii. 31, 'till . . . dea*th* ha*th*', where the scribe or compositor may have been influenced by the ending of 'death'; 38, 'if . . . it stands'; and II. iv. 2, 'Suppose this arm *is*'; and also 'say there *is*', at III. ii. 146. Five 'thou' forms with the indicative endings occur together in v. i and ii; two of them occur also in Q (v. i. 107, 114). There may thus have been a tendency already by 1593–5 to assimilate the second person singular of the subjunctive to the indicative. Allowing for this possibility, however, it seems still possible to regard the other F examples as sophisticated, and emend accordingly. This would involve the examples occurring in Q and sophisticated in F; and the four non-quarto examples given above.

(*d*) A similar Elizabethan usage under modification was that of 'stand' (Italian *stare*, Spanish *estar*) to 'is/are', e.g.:

II. ii. 55	Q	that thy head *stands* here	F	is[3]
v. iv. 80		yonder *stands* the wolf		is

---

1. Cf. *R 3*, I. iv. 225, If you be hir'd (F are); *Oth.*, IV. i. 193; *Troil.*, III. iii. 116; *Lr.*, III. i. 20; *Ham.*, III. iv. 38; *R 2*, v. v. 38; etc.

2. These may be covered by Abbott, 363, as cases 'where there is no reference to futurity and no doubt is expressed', and equivalent to 'When thou seest', and 'When thou canst speak'.

3. Cf. *R 2*, III. iii. 191; *R 3*, III. i. 196.

Another well-recognized F tendency was the simplification or vulgarization of unusual or of difficult words or constructions. The F improvement of *The Merchant of Venice*, I. i. 93, to

I am sir [an] Oracle

illustrates one type; another is apparent in the F 'bitter' for Q 'acerbe' in *Othello*, I. iii. 347; and *Lear*, III. vii. 57, 62:

		F
In his annoynted flesh *rash* borish phangs, ...		sticke
If wolues had at thy gate howl'd that *dearne* time		sterne

In the first case, the F *Merchant* is a straight reprint of Q, and the vulgarization may therefore be attributed to the printing-house. In the others, the variants might equally have originated with a scribe, and been incorporated from the transcript by the Q collator. In either case, there is little doubt that these variants arose during transmission, and have no authority.

The strongest example of this kind[1] in *3 Henry VI* occurs in York's description of Margaret, at I. iv. 142, as '*obdurate*, flintie, rough, remorselesse'. In Q the first adjective is given as 'indurate'. It seems most unlikely that any known agent of Q transmission would alter 'obdurate' to the more abstruse and obsolescent 'indurate'. On the other hand, any of the agents in the F transmission might easily and naturally have sophisticated in the other direction. That 'indurate' is no accident is shown by its occurrence more than once in Hall (1548); and by its use in a 'heart' context, in the Vulgate version of Pharaoh's attitude to the Israelites: 'induratum est cor Pharaonis', at Exodus, vii. 13, 22.

Similar grounds might justify the adoption of Q as against F in the following, though the first could be an actor's vulgarization:

I. iv. 129	Q	God he *wots*	F	... knowes
III. ii. 23		clap		blow
25		Godsforbot		God forbid
IV. i. 20		God *forfend*		... forbid[2]

The probable history of the text, then, is that it was printed by compositors A and (?) B from mixed copy. This was made up partly of leaves or pages from Q editions—mainly Q3, but with some probable use of Q2—corrected, not always perfectly, from a manu-

---

1. Other possibilities in a well-reported passage are:

II. i. 132	Q	smote	F	strucke	Cf. *Lr.*, III. ii. 7
144		his power		the soldiers	*H 5*, I. ii. 149
161		clad		wrap	clad/decke III. ii. 149
166		seeke		finde	*R 3*, I. iv. 39

2. Cf. *R 2*, IV. i. 129; *Troil.*, I. iii. 302; *R 3*, III. vii. 81.

script; and partly direct from the manuscript itself. The manuscript was a scribal copy of Shakespeare's autograph as annotated by the prompter. In the course of correction of Q from the manuscript, some sophistication was introduced.

The original had been modified, before the transcription and before the performances reflected in Q, by the substitution of Montague for Falconbridge; and later—after these performances—by the correction or revision of one passage concerning Salisbury. The censor or Lord Strange may also have been responsible for the excision of some lines and references.

EMENDATION AND EDITORIAL POLICY

Editorially, therefore, Q now assumes an importance it lacked so long as it was taken to be an independent text related to F only as a possible basic version (or even just a very imperfect report of a version) that Shakespeare revised and improved to form *3 Henry VI*. The F text has correspondingly much less authority. Readings common to Q and F, in particular, now no longer confirm each other, since F may derive from Q, and Q is memorial in origin. F, moreover, has probably passed through the hands of a scribe, a collator whose work is often imperfect, and a sophisticator (the collator?). Where the F text is from manuscript, it is also liable, like all texts, to compositors' misreadings, and omissions. Q may therefore enable us to restore some omissions, some forms of words sophisticated in F, some F misreadings, and some details of stage dress and business. F may also be restored where an imperfect correction of Q betrays the sort of error that has occurred. Where F follows Q2 or Q3 against Q1, it is also permissible to restore the Q1 reading, even though the Q3 and F common departure from Q1 may be not derivative but common variation. Q, finally, preserves, even though in a mutilated form, the original substance of a passage later revised.

The critical apparatus follows normal Arden practice. In this text, the bad quarto differs so widely from F that adequate recording of variants is impossible, short of a complete reprint of the quarto. All substantive departures from F, however, by the present text, are fully recorded. Q variants are given only where they are adopted, conjectured, seem possible, or help to throw light on a difficult passage, or on the history of the text, or on the performance of the reporter. Spelling, punctuation, and other accidentals are given only where they may seriously affect interpretation.

In the text, some older forms have been silently modernized. Speech-headings are standardized. In the stage-directions, words without equivalent in Q or F are enclosed in square brackets.

2. AUTHENTICITY, DATE, COMPANY, SOURCES

AUTHENTICITY

The authenticity of *3 Henry VI* has been under fire since Malone made the case for Robert Greene's hand in it. In his death-bed pamphlet, *A Groats-worth of Wit* (1592), Greene parodied a line from *3 Henry VI* (i. iv. 137), and attacked Shakespeare as an 'vpstart Crow, beautified with our feathers, that with his *Tygers hart wrapt in a Players hide*, supposes he is as well able to bombast out a blanke verse as the best of you: and beeing an absolute *Iohannes fac totum*, is in his owne conceit the onely Shake-scene in a countrey'.[1] Taken together with the idea that Q was an early form of a play later revised as *3 Henry VI*, a form in which Greene had a hand, this allusion was read as a charge against Shakespeare of plagiarizing Greene's work, including the line parodied.

The opposite theory—that Q is a report of *3 Henry VI*—is now generally accepted, and the introductory 'his' taken as attributing the line to Shakespeare, and with it the play.[2] What Greene is attacking is Shakespeare's 'bombast' as illustrated in *3 Henry VI*; and the fact that an actor should take on himself to rival, and probably displace, the dramatists to whom the actors had been indebted and without whom they could say nothing.[3]

A further argument in favour of Shakespearean plagiarism, however, survived, and was emphasized by Professor Dover Wilson.[4] A contemporary passage, from Sonnet ix of *Greene's Funeralls*,[5] by R. B. Gent., 1594, seems to allude to and corroborate Greene's own reference to the upstart crow 'beautified with our feathers'. The passage runs:

> Greene, is the pleasing Obiect of an eie:
> Greene, pleasde the eies of all that lookt vppon him.
> Greene, is the ground of euerie Painters die:
> Greene, gaue the ground, to all that wrote vpon him.
> Nay more the men, that so Eclipst his fame:
> Purloynde his Plumes, can they deny the same?

These lines, says Wilson, 'make it certain that there is substance of some kind in the traditional notion of Shakespeare as, at least in his early days, the reviser of other men's dramas'; they show 'how contemporaries understood that attack'.[6]

---

1. Bodley Head Quartos, ed. G. B. Harrison, 45–6.
2. Smart, 195–6.   3. See further *2 H 6* (New Arden), xiv ff.
4. 'Malone and the Upstart Crow', *Sh. Survey*, 4 (1951), 63 (cf. 59 and 64); and *2 H 6* (New Arden), xvii, xix.
5. McKerrow (*Greene's Newes*, 1593, and *Greene's Funeralls*, 1594), 81.
6. Cf. *The Essential Shakespeare* (1932), 45–6.

In an important recent article,[1] however, Warren B. Austin has argued convincingly that the passage has in fact a quite other reference. The fourteen poems in *Greenes Funeralls*, possibly by Richard Barnfield, were written in defence of Greene. They contain a series of 'bitter references to Gabriel Harvey and the pamphlets in which he had maligned Greene within days of the playwright's death'. Austin points to the opportunity offered, and taken, by Greene's notoriety and death for pamphlets such as Harvey's. Greene's friend Thomas Nashe reported that he had himself written an epistle 'to the Ghost of Robert Greene, telling him what a coyle there is with pamphleting on him after his death'.[2] R. B.'s lines, therefore, it is suggested, used the words 'wrote upon him' in the same sense as Nashe's 'pamphleting on', that is, 'about him', and not, as in Wilson's interpretation, using Greene's works as a base to build their own works on.[3] Greene's popularity 'gives the ground' or 'background colour' (*OED.*, sb. II. 6b) that the pamphleteers used in their sketches and 'wrote upon'. Similarly 'eclipsed his fame' may well mean, not 'surpassing' (as Shakespeare is alleged to have surpassed Greene), but 'casting a shadow over', Greene's reputation. The general sense, then, is 'that even those who had written on Greene in indignant terms, those who had sought to blacken his reputation, had themselves taken advantage of, or borrowed from, his writings'. Hence 'the real object of R. B.'s allusion in the final couplet is not Shakespeare, but Gabriel Harvey'. Austin's case is amply supported from the context of R. B.'s other 'sonnets'.

Finally, R. B.'s 'purloynde his Plumes', so naturally associated with Greene's 'beautified with our feathers', was almost certainly written before its publication. It refers rather to Harvey's own attack on Greene, where he says, 'Thanke other for thy borrowed and filched plumes of some little Italianated bravery'.[4] R. B.'s use of the word 'purloynde', the closest of synonyms for Harvey's 'borrowed and filched', and, of course, the word 'plumes', where the *Groats-worth* passage speaks of 'feathers', shows unmistakably that it was Harvey's employment of this figure that he was recalling to make his point.[5] And Harvey had himself borrowed and purloined this from Greene's 'pranct with the glorie of others feathers'.[6] Here is 'Harvey accusing Greene of borrowing *his* tricks of style,

1. 'A Supposed Contemporary Allusion to Shakespeare as a Plagiarist', in *Sh. Qu.*, VI (1955), no. 4, 373–80.

2. McKerrow, i. 153.

3. Cf. Malone, xviii. 571, 'plays, formed upon old dramas'.

4. *Foure Letters* (ed. Harrison), 37–8.   5. Austin, 380.

6. *Francesco's Fortunes* (1590), Grosart, viii. 132.

yet himself filching from Greene the very figure in which he makes the infamous charge!' There is thus no longer any evidence for plagiarism in the sense that *3 Henry VI* owed anything to Greene at any stage.

Nor is there any valid evidence for supposing that any dramatist shared with Shakespeare in the writing of the play. Such theories were originally based, starting with Malone, on the theory that *2* and *3 Henry VI* were revisions of *The Contention* and *The True Tragedy*. Now that the true relation has been established, with *The Contention* and *The True Tragedy* as bad quartos or memorial versions of Shakespeare's plays, the argument for other hands has fallen back on parallels of vocabulary with Greene, Peele, Nashe, or Marlowe; on inconsistencies in Shakespearean texts; and on the general idea of Shakespeare as an unlearned natural genius.

But textual parallels are weak evidence for an age when there was a common stock vocabulary in drama and when borrowing was universal. Inconsistencies may arise from the chronicle sources, errors in the course of transmission, modification of a text by censorship or reductions in the acting cast, or even from the author's pure absence of mind. To imagine Shakespeare quite incapable of classical allusions is to make a quite unjustified assumption as to his education and reading.[1]

The main positive general argument for Shakespeare's complete authorship remains—that of unity of conception and execution. As will appear, the planning of *3 Henry VI*, and its thorough integration with *1* and *2 Henry VI* and with *Richard III*, are the surest guarantees of Shakespearean authorship. The organization of the chronicle material, the running themes and general ideas, and the assimilation to them of the imagery and style, are all of a piece. Variations conform to the acknowledged ideal of decorum. None of Shakespeare's contemporaries or proposed collaborators could have approached the result in *Henry VI*. Marlowe's *Edward II* is a pale shadow in characterization and structure, and basically different in style. Neither Lodge, Nashe, nor Greene has anything of the organizing genius that Shakespeare imprinted on his material, conception, and plan. The very wealth of significance that emerges from consideration of the play as Shakespeare's alone is almost enough in itself to guarantee his sole authorship.

DATE

Greene's parody of i. iv. 137 fixes an extreme later limit for *3 Henry VI* at 3 September 1592, the date of Greene's death. Since

1. See further *1 H 6* (New Arden), xxxii ff.; *2 H 6*, xxxix ff.

the theatres in London had been closed that year from 23 June,[1] and since time must be allowed for writing, rehearsing, and acting, the limit must be taken back to the early part of 1592.

The extreme earlier limit is fixed by Holinshed's *Chronicle*, the second edition of which—that used by Shakespeare—appeared in 1587. All other probable sources, however, agree in suggesting a date towards the end of 1590 or the beginning of 1591; in particular, the influence of Spenser's *Faerie Queene*, I–III,[2] entered on the Stationers' Register on 1 December 1589, and with a preface dated 23 January '1589' (i.e. 1590). It was possible, of course, for Shakespeare to have become familiar with *The Faerie Queene* in manuscript before publication; its influence, however, not only in *3 Henry VI*, but also in *1* and *2 Henry VI* and *Richard III*,[3] is so widespread and so general that it seems much more likely to derive from frequent reading and assimilation, that is, from the printed book. In *3 Henry VI*, it is specially marked at II. i. 10 ff., where the imagery of *The Faerie Queene* has been completely fused with the cognate imagery of the metrical Psalm xix and with the subject.

Again, it is reasonable to assume that *3 Henry VI* was written to succeed *2 Henry VI*; and that play is strongly indebted to Marlowe's *Tamburlaine*, entered on the Stationers' Register on 14 August 1590. As with *The Faerie Queene*, Shakespeare may have been familiar with *Tamburlaine* before publication, that is, on the stage; but again, the influence is so widespread and so spontaneous as to suggest a complete absorption more likely to be due to frequent reading. *Tamburlaine*, besides, was printed as an Admiral's play; and this in itself casts doubt on the chances of Shakespeare's becoming to this degree familiar with it on the stage, either as spectator or as actor. Allowing, therefore, some time for the previous writing of *2* (and probably *1*[4]) *Henry VI*, it seems likely that *3 Henry VI* was written in 1591.

Whatever its relation to Shakespeare's *King John*, the anonymous *Troublesome Raigne of King Iohn*, published in 1591, borrows freely from many other plays. For example, it takes phrases from Peele's *Arraignment of Paris* (1584) and from *The Battle of Alcazar*;[5] and has numerous parallels, which may likewise be taken as derivative with *2* and *3 Henry VI* and *Richard III*. In at least one of these parallels—'a diuine instinct' (*R 3*, II. iii. 42; *2 TR.*, iii. 173)—Shakespeare follows his source for *Richard III* in Holinshed, while the

---

1. Chambers, *WS.*, i. 287.   2. See Appendix V (*b*).

3. For *1 H 6*, see notes at I. i. 124, I. vi. 6; *2 H 6*, at I. i. 33, IV. i. 5, V. ii. 4; *R 3*, cf. I. iv. 26–33 with *F.Q.*, I. iv. 36, II. vii. 5, 30.

4. See my Introduction, xxxv ff.

5. Dugdale Sykes, *Sidelights on Shakespeare*, 115–16.

phrase does not appear in any of the sources for the plays on John. It may therefore be reasonably assumed that other similar parallel phrases are borrowed in *The Troublesome Raigne* from *Henry VI* and *Richard III*. One long passage in particular suggests that the author of *The Troublesome Raigne* had been specially impressed by Warwick's account of his defeat at St Albans, II. i.[1] And there are a number of scattered phrases throughout *The Troublesome Raigne* that support this assumption; e.g.:

3 H 6, II. ii. 142		Sham'st thou not, knowing whence thou art extraught,
1 TR., i. 351		. . . whence I am extraught.
	404	And when thou know'st from whence thou art extraught,
	ii. 147	Sham'st thou not . . .

Compare:

R 3, I. ii. 1	Set downe, set downe your honourable load,
2 TR., vi. 1	Set down, set down the load not worth your pain!

All the available evidence thus converges on a date in 1591, and probably the first half rather than the second.

This agrees with the evidence for *1* and *2 Henry VI*, and sets the trilogy within the period 1590 to mid-1591.

COMPANY

This dating permits a return to the problem of Shakespeare's first company. Early theories placed him with the Strange-Chamberlain organization throughout his career. It would now be generally agreed, however, that Shakespeare 'is to be looked for during these years in Pembroke's company until its collapse and then in Sussex's, and that it was from this rather than directly from Strange's that he went to the Chamberlain's'.[2] So generally agreed, in fact, that Pembroke's can now be thought of as Shakespeare's first company,[3] to the exclusion of Strange's.[4] The case for Pembroke's in 1592–3 seems well established; but that for Pembroke's as his first company, i.e. in the period before 1592, open to doubt. The evidence is fragmentary and its interpretation often uncertain; but, especially as regards *2* and *3 Henry VI*, in favour of Strange's as Shakespeare's company before Pembroke's (as

---

1. See Appendix V (*c*).

2. Halliwell-Phillips, *Outlines*, i. 122, ii. 329; Chambers, *ES.*, ii. 130; Rhodes, 90.

3. Rhodes, *loc. cit.*; P. Alexander, *Shakespeare's Henry VI and Richard III*, 204.

4. A. W. Pollard suggested the Queen's (in Alexander, 13 ff.); as did Wentersdorf, *Jahrbuch*, lxxxiv–lxxxvi (1950), 114 ff.

well as after), and possibly in an earlier form[1] as his first company.

It is reasonably certain that some of Shakespeare's early comedies, as well as *1–3 Henry VI*, were in existence by the end of 1591. If they were written for an earlier and independent Pembroke's, it is more than surprising that such a company should not be mentioned anywhere in London or provincial records before 1592. It is further surprising that it should suddenly attain, in 1592–3, the eminence of appearing, like Strange's, twice at Court that winter.

A more serious difficulty for the theory of an independent earlier Pembroke's is the presence of the actor-names Holland and Sinklo (among others)[2] in *2* and *3 Henry VI* respectively. For these actors are also found in a surviving cast of the second part of *The Seven Deadly Sins*—which belongs to about 1590, and certainly before the Alleyn-Burbage quarrel of May 1591[3]—found among Alleyn's papers at Dulwich, and presumably part of the repertory of the Strange-Admiral's company under him. The actor-names are so written into the speech-prefixes as to suggest that they are authorial,[4] and that the plays were therefore written for the combined company while Holland and Sinklo, as well as Shakespeare, were members. In which case they can hardly have belonged to an alternative or earlier Pembroke's company.

This argument for Strange's would be consistent with reading the companies on the title-page of *Titus Andronicus* (Q1, 1594) as acted by the servants of Derby (i.e. Strange's men), Pembroke, and Sussex. The last two are in chronological order, and it would thus be natural to assume that Strange's acted it before Pembroke's.[5] There are recollections of *Titus* in the bad quartos of *2* and *3 Henry VI*, and it is otherwise probable that it antedates 1590. It is most likely, then, to have been written for Strange's, or the Strange-Admiral's combination, and passed with Shakespeare to Pembroke's, then Sussex's, and back to the Chamberlain's.

A play also familiar to the reporters of *2* and *3 Henry VI*, but apparently always the property of the Admiral's, is *The Spanish Tragedy*. The only possible period at which the reporters are likely to have become so familiar with it as to confuse it with other plays in their repertory is this of combined operations with the Admiral's.[6] Shakespeare's own familiarity with it, and his adoption of so many of its phrases into the fabric of his plays (see e.g. Appendix V (*a*)) would also be best explained on the same lines.

1. As Leicester's.   2. See above, xix.   3. *WS.*, i. 41 ff.
4. And not, as Chambers thought, 'written into the books either before or after the transfer to Pembroke's'.
5. *ES.*, ii. 129; *Edward II*, Arden edn (revised 1955), 24.
6. After 1594 it is found with the Admiral's only.

How Pembroke's originated, how the Shakespeare plays came to them, and how Shakespeare was related to them, are still most obscure. There was obviously much movement among the companies in this difficult period of plague and City opposition, but detailed conclusions as to their nature and direction can only be hypothetical. Pembroke's may have originated, as Dover Wilson thinks,[1] from the Alleyn–Burbage quarrel of 1591, as a company centred on Burbage and the Theatre; or, as Chambers suggested,[2] may have been an offshoot of the large Strange–Admiral's company under Alleyn in London. Chambers's idea seems to fit best with the sudden emergence of Pembroke's at an unpropitious time in 1592; but it does not seem to account for (a) the reference to the 'breaking' of Pembroke's[3] in August 1593 as if they were an independent company; (b) the passing of Pembroke plays, like *Titus Andronicus*, to Sussex's (December 1593–February 1594); or (c) the absence of Shakespearean titles from Henslowe's Strange–Admiral's lists for 1592 and 1593,[4] as contrasted with the frequency of such titles in the Queen's–Sussex's lists for 1593–4.[5] In any case, Pembroke's remain a sudden brief apparition, without apparent previous existence, and probably emerged from some *ad hoc* arrangement among fragments of other companies hit by prevailing theatrical conditions; and Shakespeare's work probably precedes their appearance, having been done for Strange's.

SOURCES

Apart from occasional influences already noticed like those of *The Faerie Queene*, i–iii, *The Mirror for Magistrates*, the metrical Psalms, Brooke's *Romeus and Iuliet*,[6] the Bible, and the classics, Shakespeare's main source in *3 Henry VI*, as in *1* and *2 Henry VI* and *Richard III*, was Hall's chronicle. Shakespeare was also familiar with the second edition of Holinshed's chronicle (1587), and adopted from it what phrases and material he thought fit.[7] But it was to Hall, rather than Holinshed, that he was chiefly indebted;[8] though Holinshed often follows Hall so closely that it is sometimes difficult to tell which Shakespeare used. It was Hall's basic conception of events and characters, and their interdependence, that determined Shakespeare's treatment and his conception of the march of events in their relation to the characters. In addition, Shakespeare was so intimately familiar with Hall that in any one of these four plays he

1. *2 H 6* (New Shakespeare), xii ff.   2. *WS.*, i. 41 ff.
3. *WS.*, ii. 314.   4. *Op. cit.*, 307–12.   5. *Op. cit.*, 317–18.
6. See Introduction, lxvi; and Appendices I (b) and V (b).
7. Fully dealt with in Boswell-Stone.
8. See Appendix I; and *RES.*, xiv (1953), 157–60.

ranged widely over the whole of Hall's history, picking up phrases and incidents freely, and weaving them into his more limited structure. There seems little doubt that he had long been acquainted with Hall, and that his knowledge of Holinshed, much more recently acquired (naturally), served him rather to supplement Hall than as a main foundation for these plays.

3. CRITICAL

POPULARITY

Modern neglect of the *Henry VI–Richard III* tetralogy contrasts curiously with its Elizabethan popularity. Thomas Nashe the dramatist bore witness to the 'ten thousand spectators, at the least' who, 'at several times', saw brave Talbot (in *1 Henry VI*) bleeding on the boards of the Theatre. When the dying Robert Greene looked round for a shaft to throw at his too successful rival, he found the line (not yet in print) of *3 Henry VI*, which he knew well enough to parody—'his tiger's heart wrapped in a player's [woman's] hide'. The first of Shakespeare's plays to be printed, after *Titus Andronicus*, were *2* and *3 Henry VI*, in pirated versions (1594, 1595), and *Richard III* followed not long after (1597). These versions of *2* and *3 Henry VI* were each twice reprinted before the Folio of 1623, that of *Richard III* five times. The quality of the reports, moreover, especially those of *3 Henry VI* and *Richard III*, was high. All these facts confirm the popularity of the series.

To the Elizabethans, the involved genealogy of York and Lancaster, so unfamiliar and difficult to us, was no obstacle to popularity, and no more difficult than the ramifications of the present royal family are to millions of the modern public. Familiar from the chronicles—essential in the very limited Elizabethan library—it was all part and parcel of their own recent history. The people and the places were those of their own London and their own countryside. The story was interesting as an old story, provided it was told with speed and action, and to the life. They saw it, moreover, on the stage for which it was written.

Not so, however, the intervening critics. To the eighteenth century it was a drum-and-trumpet affair; even now, *2* and *3 Henry VI* can be described[1] as a 'sprawling ten-act composition, which lacks a central figure, begins with Henry's marriage, and ends only because he is dead and a new play, *Richard III*, is already on the stocks'. To Middleton Murry,[2] *3 Henry VI* was a 'mere record', with

1. T. M. Parrott, in *Sh. Qu.*, v (1954), 183.
2. Middleton Murry, *Shakespeare*, 144.

'no trace of speculation on the causes of things'. Or again, Shakespeare 'has to wind his way through a kaleidoscopic series of Yorkist and Lancastrian victories and defeats, in order to come to Richard III, and we see him struggling, with a sort of dreary disgust, through unmanageable and embarrassing matter, . . . with his eyes fixed on the valiant crook-backed prodigy'.[1] Even Tillyard, who has shown a fine appreciation of the historical plays, thinks that Shakespeare here 'failed to control . . . the mass of chronicle material' and in the intermediate passages 'is either tired or bored: or perhaps both'.[2]

The Elizabethan popularity of the *Henry VI–Richard III* series has been fully justified, however, by modern performances. When, after three centuries, they were again put on the stage in San Francisco in 1903 (and 1935), and by the Birmingham Repertory Company (*2* and *3 Henry VI*), first at Birmingham in 1952, and later (*1–3 Henry VI*) at the Old Vic;[3] on the screen (*Richard III*) by Laurence Olivier in 1952; broadcast, and later televised as 'An Age of Kings' (*1 Henry VI* without Talbot) by the BBC in 1960; there could remain little doubt of their dramatic quality and appeal. They have yet to be performed *in full* as a series; the effect would be interesting, and probably surprising.

It is only now, with a change in the attitude of criticism and the theatre, that we have been able to recapture something of the original popular effect. Only now are we ridding ourselves of some of the misconceptions that stood between us and a reasonable literary appreciation. Much of the trouble has been in the critical attitude to authorship and to Shakespeare's genius in construction. So long as it was believed that the plays were mainly the work of one or more other dramatists, and that Shakespeare did little more than write or revise them to a limited extent, they received less than justice. Shakespeare was given credit for only a few touches that differentiate F from Q, but the credit for the original handling and shaping of the chronicle material went to others. And even where Shakespeare was acknowledged as author, though with reservations, the structural achievement and the dramatic purpose have seldom been adequately seen and appreciated. Now a revaluation is therefore necessary, and it cannot but add to the standing of these plays, and of Shakespeare's achievement in construction and imagination.

---

1. Roman Dyboski, *Rise and Fall of Shakespeare's Dramatic Art* (Shakespeare Association Papers, 1923), 9.

2. *Shakespeare's History Plays*, 90.

3. See Sir Barry Jackson, 'On Producing *Henry VI*', in *Sh. Survey*, 1953.

GENERAL PLAN

For each play in the *Henry VI–Richard III* tetralogy is more than a mere 'temporal sequence' of events, shown for their own interest; it is also (*a*) a structure (*b*) within the structure of the series (*c*) within a universal political and 'moral pattern'. Each single event thus gathers to it all the significance projected from its double framework, which in turn carries all the implications of a universal scheme. Rossiter was amply justified in claiming that 'the rôle of Shakespeare as inventor of the well-built History is due for reconsideration';[1] and Price in describing the conception of the histories as one never seen before except under the 'controlling moral idea' of Aeschylus.[2]

Shakespeare's general purpose in these plays was, through the medium of drama, to glorify England and assert eternal providence and a scheme of salvation for England.[3] The original crime—the deposition and murder of Richard II by Henry IV—was still unexpiated. God proceeded, in Hall's Biblical phrase, to 'punish the grandfather in the sonnes sonne'.[4] England had suffered the humiliation of the loss of France, a French queen, and the throes of civil war. Murder had begot murder, and vengeance vengeance. Now, in *3 Henry VI*, chaos has come again; the jungle is loose; and the innocent are involved with the guilty in the general ruin. Here is an up-and-down struggle, in which Rutland, York, Clifford, Prince Edward, and Henry are the main victims; Edward of York is crowned and Margaret banished; Richard is within sight of the crown, and England of her final expiation and the peace of the Tudors.

UNITY (*a*) *External*

It was this theme, in this context, and this material that set Shakespeare his main dramatic problem—that of unity. It was a double problem—external and internal; the play was independent, but also one item in a series.[5] This made for intrinsic weakness. Since each play must have an end and its successor a beginning, there would always be some awkward divisions between them, and some overlapping by way of anticipation and recapitulation. The endings of *2 Henry VI* with the battle of St Albans and of *3 Henry VI* with the birth of the prince are dramatically inconclusive, and probably chosen because, as A. W. Schlegel said, 'the uninterrupted series of events offered no more convenient resting-

---

1. Rossiter, 21.   2. Price, 26.   3. Ribner, 101-2.
4. Cf. Hall, 246-7, 286; *Mirror*, 120 ff.
5. Cf. the discussion in Price and Jenkins.

place'.[1] Similarly, the first scene of *3 Henry VI*, while packing a good deal of exposition into the opening lines, hardly suffices to present more than a very dim outline of the situation, and is relatively inadequate without some previous knowledge of *2 Henry VI*; as Gloucester's behaviour at the beginning of *2 Henry VI* is inadequate without the background of the last act of *1 Henry VI*. The soliloquies of Richard, again, at III. ii. 124 ff. and v. vi. 68 ff. of *3 Henry VI*, are partly repeated and recapitulated in the opening speech of *Richard III*, where the material is required as part of the exposition. The effective career of Margaret, begun in *2 Henry VI* with her arrival in England to marry Henry, ends appropriately in *3 Henry VI* with her return to France, ransomed with the sale of her father's petty territories; but the series is strengthened by her 'courtship' extension back to *1 Henry VI*, as by her appearance as the mouthpiece of retribution in *Richard III*.

Edward has had his age increased: he is to marry Lady Grey, and appear as king here and in *Richard III*. It is to be noted, however, that Rutland, who was senior to both Edward and Richard, remains the 'child' he was, so that the tragedy of his murder—which is his total rôle in the play—may complete the part of Clifford, and of itself add to the emotional impact.

b) Internal

The chronical material for *3 Henry VI* presented Shakespeare with a mass of material, so to speak, in the void. There was only a linear unity in the events—the unity of a chronicle or diary—a long series of victories and defeats, with significant dramatic developments only in the breach of faith of Edward's marriage, and the perfidy of Clarence. The rest was the completion of the Clifford–York duel of *2 Henry VI*; the preparation, in the murder of Prince Edward and the king, for *Richard III*; and a series of battle-scenes. The nearest approach to unity that could be claimed in the temporal sequence was provided by the attitudes of Henry and Margaret to the succession, and the coronation of Edward IV and the birth of the young prince: but no dramatic 'moral pattern'. Within the limits imposed by the chronicles, Shakespeare could have done little more. The wars he compressed quite ruthlessly, solving the problem of dramatic time by skilful identification of similar incidents, by omission, by occasional reporting, by references back and forward.

He begins, for example (as he did in *2 Henry VI* by telescoping the two battles of St Albans), by a jump of five years between the

1. *Lectures on Dramatic Art* (trans. John Black, 1846), 422, 434.

parliaments of 1455 and 1460, in both of which York was declare
Protector and heir-apparent; and by identifying York's two separ
ate arrivals from Ireland,[1] in 1452 and 1459. In the same way, h
eliminates the interval between Edward's two flights from Englan
(1470 and 1471), Margaret's two flights to France (Hall, 257, 261)
and the two assemblies in France (1461 and 1470).[2] To quote Hart'
comment on a similar amalgamation, that of Warwick's two visit
to France, in 1470 and 1471, 'A happier or more skilful feat tha
the welding together of these two historic assemblies into one dra
matic whole, coupled with the annihilation of much dreary an
featureless historic time, could not possibly have been hit upon.'

So, in order to streamline the action, liberties are taken wit
particular events and people, Montgomery is transferred fror
Nottingham to York (IV. vii; Hall, 292), Montague to London (IV
viii. 14), for dramatic convenience. In IV. vii, of the three events
(a) Warwick's departure from London for Coventry, (b) Edward'
arrival in London and throwing Henry into prison, and (c) th
meeting at Coventry, the second and third are transposed, whil
Henry is conveniently, but unhistorically, left in London all th
time. Events at Wakefield, Mortimer's Cross and after, and S
Albans are similarly telescoped. Inconvenient battles, like Mor
timer's Cross and the second St Albans, are disposed of by shor
reports.[4] Margaret comes to her parliament (I. i. 35), though in th
chronicles she was sent for, but 'denied to come'.[5]

This reorganization of material was supplemented, as usual, b
invention. Subsidiary characters, like the watchmen in Edward'
camp, the bishop of York's huntsman, and various messengers, ad
only an occasional ironical comment; but the keepers who captur
Henry contribute their mite to the themes of allegiance and per
jury, and develop the character of Henry. The introduction of th
young Richmond is much more significant, as a pointer to the ap
proaching end of anarchy and the peace of the Tudors. The mai
thematic invention, however, is the father–son–Henry scene,[6] wit
its ritualistic soliloquies. It is a key scene at the very centre of th
action; an ironic commentary on the griefs of civil war, set agains
a vision of the peaceful pastoral life so apparently remote.

ORDER AND DISORDER

Shakespeare not only pruned and streamlined the historical ma
terial, however; he seized the irreducible residue of disorder an
chaos, the theme of disunity, and used it, with reinforcements c

1. Hall, 233, 249.   2. Hall, 265, 281; III. iii. 334.   3. Hart, 108.
4. 3 H 6, II. i. 104 ff.   5. Hall, 249.
6. Perhaps suggested by Hall, 256.

illustration and symbol, to create a unity of impression. He made the play, in effect, a study in anarchy—anarchy in the state, in the family, in the mind of the individual.

In the state, anarchy springs from the weakness of the king, who should control, and maintain the bonds of society, the 'due of birth, Prerogative of age',[1] the sanctity of oath and custom. Henry unnaturally yields the succession to York, weakly allows himself to be silenced whenever he tries to intervene, and abdicates in favour of Warwick and Clarence. His final murder is the supreme outrage against the political order, and the divine order on which it rested. From his weakness sprang in turn the freedom of the nobles to seek their personal interest and indulge in the 'retributive reaction'[2] of revenge. Richard, the unlicked 'brave bear' of 2 Henry VI, is now developed into the most characteristic expression and product of civil anarchy. His disregard of all political and family and personal obligations is expanded in detail in his two long soliloquies. It is he who kills the prince and the king; who is later to kill his brother Clarence; and who will finally surrender the rule of his mind to superstitions and nightmares.

The basic social bond of the family is similarly disrupted. Shakespeare is at some pains to select and emphasize and add to scenes of family 'contention'. He begins, naturally, with the king. Henry shows himself an 'unnatural father', whose political weakness in disinheriting his son immediately provokes an outburst by Margaret, who divorces him from bed and board. The prince leaves him, to go to the field. York's three sons, at first united behind his ambition, and then by a common thirst for revenge, could not in the end be farther divided. Edward alienates Clarence by his obsession with the new queen and her family; Richard's ambition lies in wait for both. Clarence deserts his father-in-law at a critical moment. Among the commons, the theme is repeated in the Morality tableau where the father unwittingly kills his son and the son his father (II. v).

Individual morality—custom, trust, duty, self-control—is also dissolving. Men and women are passion's slaves. Unreasoning fury, anger, rage, and hate abound; pride and ambition flourish; the lust for gold and power justifies murder. We begin to hear of Machiavellian 'policy'. 'It is war's prize to take all vantages', says Northumberland, speaking for most of the characters. Edward, in peace, tries to take vantages with Lady Grey; in war, he will enter York by fair means or foul. The climax is reached in Richard's complete disregard, after his father's death, of all obligations what-

1. *Troil.*, I. iii. 106–7.   2. Rossiter.

soever, the end (the crown) justifying the means. 'Why, I can smile, and murder whiles I smile', he says characteristically; he can deceive with Ulysses, change shapes with Proteus for advantages, 'set the murderous Machiavel to school'. His epitome is, 'I am myself alone'.

Perjury, in particular, is a string to be harped on. Edward introduces the theme when he persuades his father to go back on his agreement with Henry. For a kingdom any oath may be broken: and Richard is ready with some typical equivocation to justify the breach (I. ii). Edward is again prepared to perjure himself to retain the support of Montgomery, to claim the crown as well as his dukedom (IV. vii); and breaks faith with Warwick and Lewis in marrying Lady Grey (III. ii). Clarence, to complete the trio, uses similar tactics to his father-in-law, Warwick:

> Perhaps thou wilt object my holy oath:
> To keep that oath were more impiety
> Than Jephthah's, when he sacrific'd his daughter.
>
> (v. i. 92–4)

But then Clarence 'uses to forswear' himself; 'perjur'd' is an epithet that comes to stick to him. Lewis, similarly, has no compunction in going back on his promise to Margaret (III. iii).

What these do out of self-interest, Henry does from weakness. He had formerly been persuaded to break faith with the Earl of Armagnac to whose daughter he was betrothed (*1 Henry VI*, v. i. 15 ff.) in order to marry Margaret (v. v). Now the Queen and the nobles

> Have wrought the easy-melting King like wax . . . .
> And now to London all the crew are gone,
> To frustrate both his oath and what beside
> May make against the house of Lancaster.
>
> (II. i. 171 ff.)

Clifford seems to be the only one to keep his oath; but it is an oath of blind allegiance to Henry and blind vengeance on the house of York.

The overwhelming prevalence of disorder and perjury, however, implies reference to order and faith. The contrast completes the picture, while providing a further unifying conception, as well as an element of dramatic conflict. Thus there is not only the major struggle between the rival houses; there is also the painful reassertion of the moral and political order against the prevailing anarchy. The signs are yet faint and few, but they are significant. The main forward-looking pointer is, of course, Henry's 'divining thoughts' hat young Richmond, who is dramatically superfluous here, will in time . . . bless a regal throne' (IV. vi. 69 ff.), and 'will prove our country's bliss'. The vehicle of expression for the concept of order s, of course, Henry himself. In spite of his own weakness, and the breaches of faith he has been led into, he is a standing protest against the horrors of the civil war. It is at least part of his motive in resigning the succession of his son that he can get York 'to cease his civil war' (I. i. 200). He registers an ineffectual protest against the barbarity of placing York's head on the gates; he sermonizes the keepers on the respect due to their oaths; for the sake of his people he will resign the government to Warwick and Clarence, embracing 'sour Adversity'; and above all, he calls down the pity of heaven on the victims of civil war, and soliloquizes on the sweet content of the shepherd's life, in a scene that epitomizes the entire situation (II. v).

Shakespeare further introduces certain running devices to strengthen the unity of impression. He adopts and invents many forms of looking before and after. The characters reflect on the past, drag it up, recapitulate; comment on past and present events; express future hopes and wishes, fears and intentions.

Whether or not Shakespeare was ever 'a schoolmaster in the country', he knew the value and effect of the schoolmaster's damnable iteration as a means of inculcating a fact or projecting a character. And iteration is in itself a unifying factor to bind the heterogeneous material of his history together. Further, it suits the subject, and many of the characters.

The contention of York and Lancaster provides a natural source of upbraiding, recrimination, and recollection, in which the past is continually raked over. The rights of the Yorkist case and the Lancastrian defence involve the history of Edward III's descendants from Richard II onwards. Especially in I. i, but also in III. iii. 81 ff.,[1] allusion and argument range over the deposition of Richard II, the greatness of John of Gaunt, the reign of Henry IV, the conquest of France under Henry V, the coronation of Henry VI at nine months old, the loss of France; the restoration of Richard Plantagenet 'to his blood' and title as Duke of York, and old Clifford's death at his hands.

As each successive injustice or crime calls out the need for its revenge or satisfaction, it has to be justified by an allusion to its origin. Clifford harps on the death of his father; Warwick, betrayed in his mission to Lewis and Bona, recalls his past injuries at the hands of Edward (III. iii. 101 ff., 186 ff.); York the death of Rut-

1. Cf. also II. ii. 149–50.

land; his sons the death of York; Clarence his brother's provision
of a wife for the Queen's kindred but not for him. Even where, as
in some of these, the reference is to new material, the effect is the
same—to thicken and unify the plot. Events recounted, as well as
shown, like the death of York, have the same effect and function
(i. iv; ii. ii). In the same way, Richard's reflections on his deformity
(iii. ii; v. vi), and York's vituperation of Margaret (i. iv; ii. ii; v.
vii) are a convenient channel for describing their origins.

All this is supplemented by a series of prophecies and curses that
we know to predict events to come. Threats, wishes, fears, and intentions constantly fulfil the same function. In the meantime, previous prophecies and curses are being fulfilled as we go; again with
a back reference to their fulfilment to underline the significance.

General prophecies of civil war and its consequences, begun in
the Temple Garden scene of *1 Henry VI* and continued in *2 Henry
VI*, still flow. Before Henry will leave his throne, for example, he
says:

> . . . first shall war unpeople this my realm;
> Ay, and their colours, often borne in France,
> And now in England to my heart's great sorrow,
> Shall be my winding sheet.   (i. i. 129–32)

When Henry has resigned the succession, Northumberland and
Clifford wish his future on him:

> *North.* Be thou a prey unto the house of York,
> And die in bands for this unmanly deed!
> *Clif.* In dreadful war may'st thou be overcome,
> Or live in peace abandon'd and despis'd!
>   (i. i. 188–91)

Most of these forecasts naturally concern revenge and retribution.
York (i. iv) for Clifford, Margaret, and the rest:

> My ashes, like the phoenix, may bring forth
> A bird that will revenge upon you all;   (35–6)

and specially for Margaret:

> And in thy need such comfort come to thee
> As now I reap at thy too cruel hand!   (165–6)

Richard will revenge his father's death (ii. i. 87); Warwick 'pluck
the diadem from faint Henry's head' (153). Henry wishes that his
death 'would stay these ruthful deeds' (ii. v. 95); in the event it
helps. Richard has forecast the death of Clifford 'ere sun set' (ii. i.
115), and 'mark'd him for the grave' (ii. vi. 40); his death follows
at once.

In his two long soliloquies (iii. ii; v. vi. 37 ff.), Richard refers to the omens that surrounded his birth, and looks forward to the achievement of the ambitions they justify; and finds that 'Gloucester's dukedom is too ominous' (ii. vi. 107), but, since the omens must be fulfilled, is persuaded to accept. Margaret, now assuming the rôle she is to play in *Richard III*, curses the murderers of her son:

> But if you ever chance to have a child,
> Look in his youth to have him so cut off
> As, deathsmen, you have rid this sweet young Prince!
> (v. v. 63–5)

Edward foretells Warwick's imminent death. Finally, Henry's 'divining thoughts' foresee the happy future of England's hope, the young Earl of Richmond (iv. vi. 68–76; 92–3), as he does the sorrows that Richard's ambitious course will entail for England. Only Rutland's wish for Clifford seems to go unfulfilled:

> Thou hast one son; for his sake pity me,
> Lest in revenge thereof, sith God is just,
> He be as miserably slain as I.   (i. iii. 40–2)

There is an element of dramatic irony in the disregard and ignorance of the characters as to the inevitability of these portents and prophecies. They share Warwick's attitude:

> Poor Clifford, how I scorn his worthless threats!
> (i. i. 101)

and recognize only too late the truth of what has been forecast.

The unifying effect of irony, however, goes far beyond this. There is, to begin with, the long series of instances in which the characters are ignorant of events that intimately concern them. They act and speak in ignorance of what we and the others already know. Or they speak more wisely than they know of the present or immediate future. The device is used consistently throughout as a typical reflection of the general theme. York, for example, is ignorant (i. iv) of Rutland's murder; his murderers use it to add to his final torments. His sons, unaware of York's death, stand ironically on the top of confidence, till the news, with that of Warwick's defeat (ii. i), comes to dash their mood. Warwick's remarks on Clifford as 'surely dead', and Edward's request that the groaning man they hear should 'be gently us'd', are made in ignorance of Clifford's death beside them (ii. vi). Margaret in France imagines Henry still in Scotland, unaware of his capture; like Warwick, she has not heard of Edward's marriage to Lady Grey, as Edward, later, is ignorant of their new alliance against him. Warwick does not know that Henry is already in the Tower (v. i; cf. iv. viii); or that Clarence is about to desert him (v. i. 76 ff.). The Watchmen do not realize the significance of their words as they talk of Edward's insecure position:

> *3.*   If Warwick knew in what estate he stands,
>   'Tis to be doubted he would waken him.
> *1.*   Unless our halberds did shut up his passage.
>
>   (IV. iii. 18–20)

Warwick arrives forthwith, and they flee. There is irony, too, in the arrival of Margaret's supporting forces from France at the very moment of Warwick's death, of which they do not know.

The characters also lend themselves to this ironic treatment and contribute to its unifying impression. They are simple, clearly presented, public figures. Each is marked by some distinctive feature, which is generally preserved and elaborated throughout the action and emphasized in the dialogue, and sometimes reflected in their own style. They are almost Morality types—the lustful Edward, perjured Clarence, the unscrupulously ambitious Richard, holy Henry, the revengeful Clifford, the she-wolf Margaret. Some have the simplicity of the obsessed, like Clifford with his 'Thy father killed my father'; Richard with his fixation on the crown; and Margaret in her attachment to her son. The very narrowness of their aims—revenge, ambition, pleasure—lends itself to the pervading irony. They are so many fragments in the chaos, ignorant and heedless of the general course of events as the wheel of Fortune turns and of the consequences of their own actions, the victims of the chain of revenge they have set in motion and which, though they cannot see it, will eventually overwhelm them. The play holds the pattern together, but they are unaware of anything but their own limited section of it.

Edward is the outstanding illustration of their self-centred fatuity. He has something of the 'dementia' of those whom Fortune has marked for perdition. It is ironical to note his confidence in the Warwick he has previously outraged and whom he is to betray on his mission to France:

> Lord Warwick, on thy shoulder will I lean;
> And when thou fall'st—as God forbid the hour!—
> Must Edward fall, which peril heaven forfend!
>
>   (II. i. 189–91)

and in the same vein:

> For in thy shoulder do I build my seat,
> And never will I undertake the thing
> Wherein thy counsel and consent is wanting.
>
>   (II. vi. 100–2)

His own fatuity appears at the suggestion that Warwick and Lewis will be offended by his breach of faith over the marriage proposal:

> ... I am Edward,
> Your King and Warwick's, and must have my will.
>> (IV. i. 15–16)

and his naivety in:

> What if both Lewis and Warwick be appeas'd
> By such invention as I can devise?   (33–4)

Similarly, on Clarence's discontent at marriages arranged by Edward for his wife's relations:

> ... It was my will and grant;
> And for this once my will shall stand for law.   (48–9)

He consoles the Queen with:

> What danger or what sorrow can befall thee
> So long as Edward is thy constant friend
> And their true sovereign whom they must obey?
> Nay, whom they shall obey, and love thee too,
> Unless they look for hatred at my hands;   (75–8)

The height of irony is reached when, faced with the forces of Clarence and Warwick, he holds himself superior to Fortune:

> My mind exceeds the compass of her wheel. (IV. iii. 47)

The whole ironic spirit of the play is supremely concentrated and symbolized in the scene (II. v) where the nameless father kills his son, and the son his father. Henry appropriately laments the pity of it; and the son makes the final all-embracing comment, 'I knew not what I did'.

Not only disorder itself, but its fluctuations, become a theme of unity. The very changes in the constantly changing situation are pressed into the service of unity. By selection and regrouping, Shakespeare has imposed a unifying pattern on the apparently formless course of events—a pattern of alternation. Analysis of the structure makes the point plain:

Act I

York+   (Temporary success of York carried over from *2 Henry VI*.) Henry agrees to York's succession; (Margaret's re-
York—   jection of this); Clifford's revenge on (*a*) Rutland, (*b*) York. Wakefield.

Act II

York+   Success of York—three suns; death of Clifford; coronation of Edward.

Act III
The capture of Henry.

York—   The turning-point—Edward's marriage with Lady Grey
        since it:
        (a) aroused the enmity of Warwick, on embassy;
        (b) caused Clarence's discontent (as to marriage);
        (c) presented Richard with further possible obstacles.

Act IV
Discontent and defection of Clarence; Warwick's vic
tory; capture of Edward.

York+   Edward's escape and return.

Act V
Success of York; Clarence returns to Edward; murder o
Prince Edward and Henry; defeat and death of War
wick; birth of son to Edward.

The scheme does not conform precisely with our act-divisions
It could not conform, in any case. The pattern cannot be alway
one of clean-cut separation between cause and effect, since cause
in history are complicated and take time to work, and chronicl
facts put some restraint on freedom of treatment. But on the whol
the scheme offers a similar five-fold division. And the marriage i
Act III, which recalls that other, Lancastrian, 'fatal marriage' i
2 Henry VI for its far-reaching consequences, is the natural clima
and turning-point in the Yorkist fortunes.[1]

York's 'Ay, but the case is alter'd' (IV. iii. 31) is a key phrase tha
might be applied almost anywhere in the action. It is, of course
the standard medieval theme of the mutability of human affair
Hall, Shakespeare's main source, never tires of moralizing on 'for
tune which gideth the destiny of man' and 'will turn her whele a
she listeth, whosoeuer saith nay'.[2] The fault is in our stars. 'It wa
taken for granted that the stars dictated the general mutability o
sublunary things, and that fortune was a part of this mutabilit
applying to mankind alone',[3] as opposed, that is, to the constan
heavens. Fortune and the stars are thus naturally recurring theme
in this play of varying fortunes and human mutability.

The wheel of Fortune is therefore an appropriate symbol in
Henry VI. Fortune's malicious and unpredictable reverses gover
the war. Margaret, for example, triumphs over those 'whom For
tune captivates' (I. iv); but the time comes when 'mischance an
misfortune' strike her (III. iii. 10–11) likewise, and she has to fin
refuge in France and 'take like seat unto my fortune'. The turn o
the wheel is well illustrated at the French court. Margaret is down
but hopeful of rising again. Warwick's arrival seems a final mis

1. Hall, 264–5.   2. Hall, 45.   3. *EWP.*, 48.

chance; but with the news of Edward's marriage she is up again and allied to the 'fortunate' Warwick. Warwick is one whose nativity, apparently, the heavens favoured, who 'rightly temper with their stars' (IV. vi. 29), fortunate in all his deeds, 'likely to be blest in peace and war'. But the wheel turns again, and his glory is nothing but 'earth and dust' (v. ii). Henry carries his ill-fortune with him; the Queen has best success when he is absent (II. ii). He would fain escape his 'thwarting stars' (IV. vi. 22) by embracing adversity, and resign his crown to live low 'Where Fortune cannot hurt me'. Edward's fortune, on the whole, 'keeps an upward course' (v. iii). In *1 Henry VI* he was restored to his blood as Duke of York. Captured, he 'needs must down' for a time; but he escapes and returns to reclaim his dukedom, and later the kingdom (II. i. 192–3). Ultimately, however, none of them except Richmond, 'fram'd to wear a crown and bless a regal throne' and destined to end the long struggle, is above the reach of Fortune.

Thus Fortune is linked with the passions and their control. According to the Renascence adaptation of the Boethius tradition, those who are ruled by the passions, and not by reason, are Fortune's slaves.[1] All the main chacters of *3 Henry VI* are so ruled—by lust, ambition, revenge, anger—and therefore cannot avoid the turn of the wheel. King Henry, indeed, aims at escape in a private life. As a king, however, he has betrayed his trust and authority, and succumbs like the rest. It is thus natural that Fortune should dominate the play; and ironical that few, if any, of the main characters should realize her domination.

Here and there a touch of irony is added to the fluctuations of Fortune by the fictitious co-ordination of events. Henry sits on York's molehill to reflect on the horrors of civil war. Clifford is taunted by York's sons as he had taunted York at the point of death; and his head is placed on the gates where he had placed York's.

IMAGERY

G. Wilson Knight devotes a volume to Shakespeare's pervading tempest–beast imagery of disorder.[2] This imagery is the background in sea, air, and sky, and in the animal kingdom, against which Shakespeare sets the human disorder of *3 Henry VI*. The unstable fortunes of the contending parties and the general chaos are there fitly reflected in the two main groups of imagery—the internal changes and contentions in nature, and the jungle and

1. See e.g. W. C. Curry, *Chaucer and the Mediaeval Sciences* (1926), chap. 10, 'Destiny in *Troilus and Criseyde*.'

2. *The Shakespearean Tempest*, especially ch. ii.

slaughterhouse. Change, strife, disorder, and bloodshed thus become a universal theme that unites with the mutability of the planets and of Fortune's wheel to illuminate and lend universal significance to local and particular events.

The main body of images, however, is grouped round the sea–wind–tide theme. This partly continues the idea of changing fortunes, but equally suggests the destruction of disorderly natural forces. The to-and-fro of war is reflected in the alternations of sun and cloud, summer and winter, calm and storm, ebb and flow,[1] noon and night.

> This battle fares like to the morning's war,
> When dying clouds contend with growing light...
>
> (II. v. 1–2)

For Clifford

> Dark cloudy death o'shades his beams of life.   (II. vi. 61)

For the fortunes of battle, it is

> as I have seen a swan
> With bootless labour swim against the tide,
> And spend her strength with over-matching waves.
>
> (I. iv. 19 ff.)

For the result

> Now sways it this way, like a mighty sea,
> Forc'd by the tide to combat with the wind:
> Now sways it that way, like the self-same sea,
> Forc'd to retire by fury of the wind.
> Sometime the flood prevails: and then the wind:
>
> (v. i. 5 ff.)

Individual changes of mind are also appropriately described in the same terms: Clarence is a 'quicksand of deceit'; Warwick is 'wind-changing'; the commons are feathers blown back and forth by the wind. This pattern, as Kernan pointed out,[2] suggests that an illusion of formlessness is 'the very effect the dramatist is striving for in order to illuminate the nature of civil war which has no more proportion or structure than a storm at sea.'

The tempest imagery, and its associations with storms, floods, tears, thunder, and the dangers of sands and rocks, is probably even more directed to the 'smashing and destructive power of the men engaged in a struggle for power, the elemental nature of their drives, their vigour and stamina'.[3] It is seen in its most concentrated

---

1. Cf. Hall, 256, 'ebbing and flowing'.   2. *S.Ph.*, 51 (1944), 441.
3. *Ibid.*

form in the simile of the storm-tossed ship (v. iv. 3 ff.), which describes the fortunes of Margaret and her party.[1] The play is so full of this type of imagery that it is sufficient to call attention to it.

With the tempest imagery goes that of the jungle and the slaughter-house, symbolic of the cruelty and wild justice of civil war. 'War makes beasts of men.'[2] As in *2 Henry VI*, the realm has become one great shambles, in which the devil-butcher cannibal Richard is the chief general executioner. Wild birds and beasts prey at liberty. They appear from the beginning with the falcon Warwick (I. i. 47), and Henry's premonition of the York

> Whose haughty spirit, winged with desire,
> Will cost my crown, and like an empty eagle,
> Tire on the flesh of me and of my son.   (I. i. 271–3)

Warwick and Montague, whose emblem is the bear, naturally suggest the bear baited with dogs, or the 'chafed bull'; while the lion-king symbol occurs more than once. Margaret is the tiger, the 'she-wolf of France', or the adder and serpent; and retorts on Richard in terms of 'venom toads, or lizards' dreadful stings'. Almost all the other references centre on the idea of harmless creatures trapped—the woodcock and the cony, the limed bird—or pursued and preyed on—the dove by the falcon, the hare by the greyhound, the lamb by the wolf.[3]

Of two minor groups of images, one springs from the plant–Plantagenet identification, and the root and branches of the genealogical tree; the other introduces the standard Shakespearean comment on treachery and ingratitude, of which Judas is the type and the Last Supper the background. The theme here may have been suggested by Hall's later description of Richard,[4] 'not lettynge to kisse whom he thought to kill', and by York's paper crown.[5] An echo of the same theme appears in the Son's 'I knew not what I did'.[6]

A similar function—though only occasionally in the form of imagery—is served by the accumulation of significant detail to create a pervading atmosphere of grief and tears, steel, blood, and death. Clifford 'mourns in steel', and Acts I, II, and V are full of the sword, rapier, falchion, poniard, and lance. The 'purple falchion' is 'painted to the hilt In blood'; Rutland's 'blood cleaving to my blade Shall rust my weapon, till thy blood, Congeal'd with his, do make me wipe off both', says Clifford. Richard's news of defeat is

---

1. See below, lxvi.   2. G. Wilson Knight, *The Sovereign Flower*, 15.
3. Cf. Furnivall, *NSS.* (1875–6), 280–3.
4. v. vii. 33–4; Hall, 343 (from Sir Thomas More).   5. I. iv; Hall, 251.
6. II. v. 69.

to 'stab poniards in our flesh'. Henry prophetically sees in the civil war his winding-sheet; the Father's heart will be his son's sepulchre, his breast the funeral bell. Clifford would dig up 'thy forefathers' graves, And hang their rotten coffins up in chains'. Hearts are as flinty as the weapons of steel, especially Margaret's 'iron of Naples'; or as hot with rage and fury as the blood shed; or steeped in tears from the prevailing grief.

STYLE

As befitted the current ideal of decorum, the style varies with the varying matter. Even the apparently similar battle-scenes, as Tillyard notes,[1] are varied among themselves; the rhetorical manner of the instigators of chaos at Wakefield, for example, being contrasted with the ritualistic approach of the victims at Towton. Though largely formal and rhetorical, the style ranges from the matter-of-fact, almost prosaic, speech of the watchmen, the keepers, and the mayor of York, and the straightforward battle reports, through the stichomythia of Edward's courtship and its running commentary by his brothers, to the Virgilian pastoral and elegy of Henry's lamentations, and the epic similes of the storm-tossed ship and the flight of Icarus, reaching its height perhaps in the concentrated outcry of Margaret on the murder of her son, 'O, kill me too!'[2]

On the whole, the style is more carefully elaborated, on the recognized classical models and medieval text-books, than is recognized. T. W. Baldwin has analysed in detail, for example, how York's great 'vituperatio' on Margaret as the she-wolf of France is carefully constructed according to the standard rhetorical pattern, denouncing successively her race, her country, and her ancestors, and passing to her personal qualities, or defects, of mind and body.[3] Construction may be studied with advantage in the simile of the ship (v. iv. 3–36), with its careful enumeration and application of mast, cable (or tackles), anchor, and helm; and of the dangers of the sea and its waves, the sands, and the rocks.[4]

The conclusion, apart from the absence of rhyme, might be a typical Shakespearean sonnet, thus:

> And what is Edward but a ruthless *sea*?
> What Clarence but a quick*sand* of deceit?
> And Richard but a ragged fatal *rock*?
> *All these* the enemies to our poor bark.

1. *SHP.*, 194.   2. v. v. 41.   3. *Small Lat.*, ii. 335.
4. On the *elocutio* here, especially amplification with variation, see Gladys O. Willcock, 'Language and Poetry in Shakespeare's Early Plays', *Proceedings of the British Academy*, XL (1954), 108–9.

> Say you can *swim*—alas, 'tis but a while!
> Tread on the *sand*—why, there you quickly sink:
> Bestride the *rock*—the tide will wash you off,
> Or else you famish; that's a *three-fold* death.
>
> *This* speak I, lords, to let you understand,
> If case some one of you would fly from us,
> That there's no hop'd-for mercy with the brothers
> More than with ruthless *waves*, with *sands*, and *rocks*.
>
> Why, courage, then! what cannot be avoided
> 'Twere childish weakness to lament or fear.
>   (v. iv. 25 ff.)

The first quatrain introduces the comparison of the three sons of York to the triple dangers of sea, sand, and rock, with summary; the second shows the futility of striving with these, and sums up; the third, with the summarizing 'This', returns to link the two sides of the comparison, emphasize their ruthlessness, and end with a repetition of the three dangers; the final couplet draws the conclusion.

A similar analysis would demonstrate the careful construction of other set speeches: Richard soliloquizes, for example, on the possible pleasures of the crown, and love; the obstacles to both, with appropriate similes; the decision to aim at the crown, with simile; and the Machiavellian course by which he hopes to attain it.[1] Or one may study the careful extension of the grief–sorrow–tears pattern, combined with that of eyes and heart, in the father–son episode;[2] or the sustained sun-imagery, derived from Spenser and the metrical Psalms, in the dialogue of Richard and Edward at Mortimer's Cross.[3]

Formalism of arrangement and style is also reflected in the wealth of classical allusion, particularly from Ovid. A line is quoted from the original in the *Heroides* (I. iii. 47), and there are several references to the *Metamorphoses*. Specially worth noting, perhaps, as suggesting the schoolmaster, is the familiarity with the marginal glosses in the contemporary editions as well as with the Latin text, shown in York's denunciation of Margaret at I. iv. 134–6. Other main classical sources already noted also in *1* and *2 Henry VI* are Aesop, Virgil, and Horace, and the stories of Troy, Julius Caesar, Nero, and Daedalus.

Among English sources making for an artificial rhetorical style are the Senecan *Spanish Tragedy* and *Soliman and Perseda*. Neither was yet published, and Shakespeare's familiarity with them may

1. III. ii. 128 ff.   2. II. v. 76 ff.   3. II. i. 10–40 and n.; Appendix V (*b*).

be due to their presence in his company's repertory. The episodes of Rutland's handkerchief[1] and the Watchmen owe something to *The Spanish Tragedy*; while I. iv has obviously been influenced by (or influenced?) III. iii–iv of *Soliman and Perseda*.[2] This possibility is strengthened by at least four passages in *The True Tragedy*[3] that look like 'recollections' of *Soliman and Perseda*, and others that seem to derive from *The Spanish Tragedy*, all of which seem to suggest that the reporting actors were familiar on the stage with the texts of these plays.

The constant debt to the English Bible goes without saying. The ship simile (v. iv) is borrowed from Brooke's *Romeus and Iuliet*. *The Faerie Queene*, whose influence appears in all parts of the tetralogy, is here blended with the metrical Psalms of Sternhold and Hopkins.

Apart from the action, which is considerable and maintains dramatic interest and movement throughout, *3 Henry VI* thus presents many of the features of the pageant and pageantry. The formal presentation and style, the formal opposition of the rival houses, the Senecan rhetoric, the symbolic red and white of Lancaster and York, the bright robes, the weapons and armour and banners and music all join to produce the effect of spectacle. J. P. Brockbank[4] elaborates the point from Nashe's comment on *1 Henry VI* and Talbot. It was as if these figures, who had lain in 'rustie brasse' in their tombs, had come to life in all the colour and glory suggested by their monuments and hatchments, and been brought 'fresh bleeding' to 'pleade their aged Honours in open presence'.[5] But *3 Henry VI* is much more than a pageant for the eye. It is part of a great all-embracing conception of a pageant in which England and man himself work out the expiation of an original crime towards the final reassertion of a divinely controlled universal order. And, although the conception was given in the Elizabethan world-picture, Shakespeare alone could so have shaped the chronicles to provide for it a dramatic habitation and a name.

1. Appendix V (a).

2. See notes at I. iv. 17, 84, 136, 152; II. i. 25, 177; II. iii. 40; II. iv. 21; II. v. 57; III. iii. 199.

3. Appendix III.

4. 'The Frame of Disorder—"Henry VI" ', in *Early Shakespeare*, ed. J. R. Brown and B. Harris, 1961.

5. McKerrow, I. 212.

THE THIRD PART OF
KING HENRY VI

DRAMATIS PERSONÆ[1]

KING HENRY THE SIXTH.
EDWARD, *Prince of Wales, his Son.*
LEWIS THE ELEVENTH, *King of France.*
DUKE OF SOMERSET.
DUKE OF EXETER.
EARL OF OXFORD. } *of King Henry's Party.*
EARL OF NORTHUMBERLAND.
EARL OF WESTMORELAND.
LORD CLIFFORD.
RICHARD PLANTAGENET, *Duke of York.*
EDWARD, *Earl of March, afterwards*
  King Edward the Fourth. } *his Sons.*
GEORGE, *afterwards Duke of Clarence.*
RICHARD, *afterwards Duke of Gloucester.*
EDMUND, *Earl of Rutland.*
DUKE OF NORFOLK.
MARQUESS OF MONTAGUE.
EARL OF WARWICK.
EARL OF PEMBROKE. } *of the Duke of York's Party.*
LORD FALCONBRIDGE.
LORD HASTINGS.
LORD STAFFORD.
SIR JOHN MORTIMER. } *uncles to the Duke of York.*
SIR HUGH MORTIMER.
HENRY, *Earl of Richmond, a Youth.*
EARL RIVERS, *brother to Lady Grey.*
SIR WILLIAM STANLEY.
SIR JOHN MONTGOMERY.
SIR JOHN SOMERVILLE.
Tutor to Rutland.
Mayor of York.
Lieutenant of the Tower.
A Nobleman.
Two Keepers.
A Huntsman.
A Son that has killed his father.
A Father that has killed his son.

QUEEN MARGARET.
LADY ELIZABETH GREY, *afterwards Queen to Edward the Fourth.*
BONA, *Sister to the French Queen.*

Soldiers, Attendants, Messengers, Watchmen, etc.

Scene: *England and France.*

1. First given imperfectly by Rowe; corrected by the Cambridge editors; and revised.

2

THE THIRD PART OF
KING HENRY THE SIXTH

ACT I

SCENE I —[*London. The Parliament House.*]

Alarum. Enter the DUKE OF YORK, EDWARD, RICHARD, NORFOLK, FALCONBRIDGE, WARWICK, *and Soldiers, with white roses in their hats.*

War. I wonder how the King escap'd our hands!

The . . . Sixth] *F* (The third Part of Henry the Sixt, / with the death of the Duke of / Yorke.); The true Tragedie of Richard Duke / of Yorke, and the good King / Henry the Sixt. *Q.*

ACT I
Scene I

ACT I SCENE I] *F* (*Actus Primus. Scœna Prima.*); *not in Q.*   London.] *Theobald; not in Q,F.*   The . . . House.] *Capell; not in Q,F.*   S.D. *Alarum.* . . . *Soldiers,] F* (*Alarum. Enter Plantagenet, Edward, Richard, Norfolke, Mountague, Warwicke, and Souldiers.*); Enter *Richard* Duke of Yorke, The Earle of *Warwicke,* The Duke of Norffolke, *Marquis* Montague, *Edward Earle of* March, Crookeback *Richard,* and the yong *Earle of* Rutland, with Drumme and Souldiers, Q*1.* Falconbridge] *This edn;* Mountague | *F;* Marquis Montague | *Q.*   with . . . hats.] *Q; not in F.*

The play opens with allusions to the battle of St Albans, 1455, with which the action of *2 Henry VI* ended. The similarity of events in 1455 to those of 1460 enabled Shakespeare to jump the comparatively insignificant years between, and proceed to York's acceptance as heir apparent in 1460. Both years included a battle (Northampton, 1460), the wounding or death of Buckingham, a return to London, and an appointment for York (in 1455 as Protector). See Hall, 233; Boswell-Stone, 290.

The play covers events to the battles of Barnet and Tewkesbury in 1471, but includes the capture of the Earl of Oxford in 1474, and the ransoming of Margaret in 1475.

Alarum.] trumpet-call to arms.

1. *I wonder*] Cf. II. i. 1. The phrase, still in colloquial use, is practically equivalent to a question, as the F punctuation shows. Cf. Marlowe, *Ed. 2*, 1119, 'I wonder how he scapt', and 1168, 'Yet . . . I haue scapt your handes'.

In fact, the King did not escape; he remained in St Albans, and there accepted the excuses of York, who, on the following day, escorted him to London (Boswell-Stone, 290).

York. While we pursu'd the horsemen of the north,
     He slily stole away and left his men:
     Whereat the great Lord of Northumberland,
     Whose war-like ears could never brook retreat,   5
     Cheer'd up the drooping army; and himself,
     Lord Clifford, and Lord Stafford, all abreast,
     Charg'd our main battle's front, and breaking in
     Were by the swords of common soldiers slain.

Edw. Lord Stafford's father, Duke of Buckingham,   10
     Is either slain or wounded dangerous;
     I cleft his beaver with a downright blow:
     That this is true, father, behold his blood.

Falc. And, brother, here's the Earl of Wiltshire's blood,
     Whom I encounter'd as the battles join'd.   15

2, 17. *York.*] *Q*; Pl., Plan. / *F*.   14. *Falc.*] *This edn; Mo(u)nt.* / Q,F.

2. York.] In I. i, with one exception, all Q pages had *Yorke.* altered in F to *Plant.* (*Plan., Pl.*).

5. *brook*] endure; put up with; cf. 60.

retreat] the bugle-call or sounding of retreat; cf. *2 H 6*, IV. viii. 4, 'Northumberland . . . was Henry Percy, son of that famous Hotspur . . . who met a similar fate at the battle of Shrewsbury. . . He was also father of that famous Earl of Northumberland who was slain in the same cause in the field of Towton' (Vaughan, ii. 425).

7–9. *Lord Clifford . . .*] This account of Clifford's death is, of course, inconsistent with the account of his death at the hands of York, in *2 H 6*, v. ii, and with the references below at 55 and 164, and at I. iii. 5 and 46. Both accounts, however, derive from Hall (233 and 251), the main version being that developed by Shakespeare from the hint at 251, 'Thy father slew myne'. This becomes a dominating theme, and is widened to embrace the unnatural chaos introduced by civil war into the natural order of the family, as in II. v.

8. *main battle*] main body of the army, as distinguished from the van

and rear, or from the wings; *OED*. 9.

10. *Buckingham*] grandson of Thomas of Woodstock, Edward III's sixth son.

11. *dangerous*] adj. for adv., as commonly in Shakespeare; Abbott, 1.

12. *beaver*] lower portion of the faceguard of a helmet (OF. *bavière*); the visor; cf. *Ham.*, I. ii. 230.

14. Falc. . . . *brother*] See my note in *MLR.*, iv (1955), 492–4. Falconbridge seems to have been removed from the cast, and replaced by Montague, before performance. Traces have been left in York's further reference to him as 'brother' (York was actually Montague's uncle) at 116, as well as at 212 and 245. Tucker Brooke (Yale edn, 1923) points out the inconsistency, and suggests the reason given. See also notes to 212 and 245, and I. ii. S.D.

Wiltshire] 'James Butler, Earl of Ormond and Wiltshire, after leaving his harness in a ditch at St Albans, lived to be again defeated, and again to save his life by flight, at . . . Mortimer's Cross in 1465. . . From . . . Towton he fled with less effect, was captured and executed' (Vaughan, ii. 426).

15. *battles*] battalions; *OED*. 8.

Rich. Speak thou for me, and tell them what I did.

                [*Throwing down the Duke of Somerset's head.*]

York. Richard hath best deserv'd of all my sons.

    But is your Grace dead, my Lord of Somerset?

Norf. Such hap have all the line of John of Gaunt!

Rich. Thus do I hope to shake King Henry's head.   20

War. And so do I. Victorious Prince of York,

    Before I see thee seated in that throne

    Which now the house of Lancaster usurps,

    I vow by heavens these eyes shall never close.

    This is the palace of the fearful King,   25

    And this the regal seat: possess it, York;

    For this is thine and not King Henry's heirs'.

York. Assist me then, sweet Warwick, and I will;

    For hither we have broken in by force.

Norf. We'll all assist you; he that flies shall die.   30

York. Thanks, gentle Norfolk. Stay by me, my lords;

    And, soldiers, stay and lodge by me this night.

              They go up.

War. And when the King comes, offer him no violence,

    Unless he seek to thrust you out perforce.

16. S.D. *Throwing . . . head.*] *Theobald; not in* Q,F.   18. But is] *Q,F;* Is *conj. this edn.*   19. hap] *Dyce;* hope *Q,F.*   21. I. Victorious] *Edd.;* I, victorious *F;* I victorious *Q.*   York,] *Edd.,* Q; *Yorke.* | *F.*   24. heavens] *Q1,2;* heaven *Q3,F.*   27. heirs'] *Q,F* (heires), *Warburton.*   28, 35, 43. *York.*] *Q; Plant.* | *F.*   29. we have] *F;* are we *Q.*   32. S.D. *They go up.*] *F; not in* Q.

17. *Richard*] As in *2 H 6*, the historical Richard was much too young to have taken part in these events; born in 1452, he was now three years old. The change is part of Shakespeare's telescoping technique with dramatic time.

18 ff. *Somerset . . . Gaunt . . . Lancaster*] See App. II.

19. *hap*] hap/hope is one of the commonest Elizabethan puns; cf. II. ii. 9.

23. *usurps*] The usurpation goes back to the deposition of Richard II by Henry IV in 1399.

25. *fearful*] in the original sense = full of fear; timorous.

26. *regal seat*] Holinshed. Hall has 'siege royall' (239), 'trone royall', 'seate', 'chaire' (245).

29. *broken in by force*] Hol., iii. 655/1/3; Boswell-Stone, 291, n. 4; not in Hall.

32. *lodge*] remain; pass the night; sleep; *OED.* 7.

S.D. They go up] scil. to the chair of state at the back of the stage. It is unlikely to have been on the upper stage; as Wilson points out (129), 'the dialogue . . . allows no time for "going up" by the stair in the tiring-house'.

33.] 'And' and 'him' are possibly intrusive in Q, and have thence been adopted into F.

York. The Queen this day here holds her Parliament,   35
　　　But little thinks we shall be of her Council:
　　　By words or blows here let us win our right.
Rich. Arm'd as we are, let's stay within this house.
War. The bloody parliament shall this be call'd,
　　　Unless Plantagenet, Duke of York, be king,   40
　　　And bashful Henry be depos'd, whose cowardice
　　　Hath made us by-words to our enemies.
York. Then leave me not, my lords; be resolute;
　　　I mean to take possession of my right.
War. Neither the King, nor he that loves him best,   45
　　　The proudest he that holds up Lancaster,
　　　Dares stir a wing if Warwick shake his bells.
　　　I'll plant Plantagenet, root him up who dares.
　　　Resolve thee, Richard; claim the English crown.

Flourish. Enter KING HENRY, CLIFFORD, NORTHUMBERLAND,
WESTMORELAND, EXETER, *and the rest, with red roses in their hats.*

36. Council] *F* (counsaile)*; not in Q.*   41. be] *Q; not in F.*   43. not, my
lords;] *Edd.;* not, my Lords *F;* not my Lords: *Q;* not; my Lords, *Wilson;* not,
my lords, *Rowe.*   47. Dares] *Q1,2,F;* Dare *Q3, Rowe.*   49. S.D.] *F;* Enter
King *Henrie* the sixt, with the Duke of *Excester,* The Earle of *Northumberland,* the
Earle of *Westmerland* and *Clifford,* the Earle of *Cumberland,* / *Q.*   with . . . hats. /
Q; not in F.

35. *holds her Parliament*] This was the
Parliament of 1460, which, with York's
'breaking in', is now telescoped with
the preceding events of 1455.

37. *win our right*] Cf. 26, 29, 35. York
'entred the palace' of Westminster
with his friends, went straight to the
house of peers, 'stept vp vnto the
throne roiall, and there, laieing his
hand vpon the cloth of estate, seemed
as if he meant to take possession of
that which was his right' (Hol., iii.
655/1/37).

41. *be*] a probable F omission, from
its similarity to '*depos*'d'.

42. *by-words*] Cf. Ps. xliv. 15, 'Thou
makest us to be a by-word among the
heathen' (Noble).

46. *holds up*] upholds; supports.

47. *shake his bells*] a metaphor from
falconry. The bell was attached above
the foot. See Madden, 202; and cf.

Lucr., 510–11, 'Harmeless Lucretia,
marking what he tells / With trembling
fear, as fowl hear falcons bells.'

48.] Note the pun; = establish;
cf. III. ii. 132.

49. *Resolve thee*] make up your mind;
determine.

S.D. Clifford] the 'young Clifford'
of *2 H 6*, whose father York had killed.

Westmoreland] 'No Earl of Westmoreland ever took either side person-
ally in the Wars of the Roses. One Earl
of Westmoreland lived before, lived
through, and lived after. . . But he had
a brother, Sir John Nevil, who . . . died
. . . at the Battle of Towton, on the side
of Henry VI. Unfortunately Fabyan
either mistook him for an Earl of Westmoreland, or by the omission of some
important words has handed him
down for such, or inadvertently wrote
Westm*erland* for Cumberland; and both

K. Hen. My lords, look where the sturdy rebel sits,   50
  Even in the chair of state! Belike he means,
  Back'd by the power of Warwick, that false peer,
  To aspire unto the crown and reign as king.
  Earl of Northumberland, he slew thy father,
  And thine, Lord Clifford; and you both have vow'd
   revenge   55
  On him, his sons, his favourites, and his friends.
North. If I be not, heavens be reveng'd on me!
Clif. The hope thereof makes Clifford mourn in steel.
West. What! shall we suffer this? Let's pluck him down:
  My heart for anger burns: I cannot brook it.   60
K. Hen. Be patient, gentle Earl of Westmoreland.
Clif. Patience is for poltroons, such as he:
  He durst not sit there had your father liv'd.
  My gracious lord, here in the parliament
  Let us assail the family of York.   65
North. Well hast thou spoken, cousin: be it so.
K. Hen. Ah, know you not the city favours them,
  And they have troops of soldiers at their beck?
Exe. But when the Duke is slain they'll quickly fly.
K. Hen. Far be the thought of this from Henry's heart,   70

---

50. *K. Hen.*] *Edd.; Henry. | F (and throughout the scene); King. | Q.* ⌐ 55. and you both] *Q,F; both conj. this edn.* 56. favourites] *Q,F; favourers Capell.* 69. *Exe.*] *Q, Theobald; Westm. | F.*

Hall and Holinshed have perpetuated the error' (Vaughan, ii. 430).

50. *sturdy*] with a suggestion of 'sturdy beggar'.

51. *chair of state*] throne.

Belike] as it seems; apparently.

54. *Northumberland . . . thy father*] Henry, second Earl of Northumberland, was killed by the Duke of York's forces at St Albans; cf. 4–9 above.

55. *Clifford*] See n. to 7–9.

55, 56.] Something is obviously wrong with the QF reading here, and various omissions have been proposed to restore the metre; none, however, can be adopted as certain.

56. *favourites*] normal Elizabethan for 'favourers'; *OED.* 4.

58. *steel*] armour.

59. *Let's*] F adopted 'lets' from Q2.

60. *for*] with; Franz, 479.

61. *gentle*] noble.

62. *poltroons*] lazy cowards.

65. *the family of York*] Hall, 245.

66, 72. *cousin*] loosely used of relatives (L. *consanguineus*).

67. *the city favours them*] This is contrary to 2 *H* 6, v. ii. 81, where London is expected to favour Henry; but is based on Hall, 236, where Margaret 'well perceyued the duke of Yorke to be had in more estimacion emonge the citezens & communaltie, then the kyng', and 253, where Edward is greeted with acclamation by the Londoners.

69. *Exe.*] The F error is proved by 72.

To make a shambles of the parliament-house!
Cousin of Exeter, frowns, words, and threats,
Shall be the war that Henry means to use.
Thou factious Duke of York, descend my throne,
And kneel for grace and mercy at my feet;   75
I am thy sovereign.

York.   I am thine. *Defies*

Exe. For shame, come down: he made thee Duke of York.

York. 'Twas mine inheritance, as the earldom was.

Exe. Thy father was a traitor to the crown.

War. Exeter, thou art a traitor to the crown   80
  In following this usurping Henry.

Clif. Whom should he follow but his natural king?

War. True, Clifford: that is Richard, Duke of York.

K. Hen. And shall I stand, and thou sit in my throne?

York. It must and shall be so: content thyself.   85

War. Be Duke of Lancaster: let him be King.

West. He is both King and Duke of Lancaster;
  And that the Lord of Westmoreland shall maintain.

War. And Warwick shall disprove it. You forget
  That we are those which chas'd you from the field   90
  And slew your fathers, and with colours spread

76, 78, 85. *York.*] Q,F (*Yorke.*).   76. *York.* I] F; Henry, I *Rowe;* Thou art deceiv'd: I Q.   78. 'Twas] Q; It was F.   mine] Q1,2; my Q3,F.   83. that is *Collier;* that's F; and that is Q1,2; and thats Q3; and that's F2+Edd.

71. *shambles*] Hart notes the continuation of butcher metaphors from *2 H 6.*

72.] Cf. the ineffectual Richard II on his return from Ireland.

74. *factious*] rebellious; originating party strife.

descend] scil. the dais steps leading from the throne.

76, 78, 85. York.] Here only in I. i does the Q form of the speech prefix survive in F. All three examples occur on page I2 of Q3, and also on a single page in Q1 and Q2; the simplest explanation being that the F collator overlooked the prefixes on this page. Cf. 2, 17, 28, 35, 43.

77.] See *1 H 6,* III. i. 149 ff.

78. *earldom*] scil. of March, by virtue

of which, through his mother Anne Mortimer, he claimed the crown; see App. II.

79. *father*] the Earl of Cambridge, who was executed in 1415 at Southampton for treason against Henry V; see *H 5,* II. ii.

82. *natural*] rightful; by right of birth.

83. *that is*] F deletes Q 'and', but fails to restore Q3 'thats' to Q1,2 'that is'.

91. *fathers*] There may be some latent errors in this and the following speeches (cf. n. to 55–6 above), which are almost identical in Q and F. Each of the three Lancastrians answers Warwick's 'fathers' with a singular. Two are mentioned at 54–5; and at

March'd through the city to the palace gates.

North. Yes, Warwick, I remember it to my grief;
And, by his soul, thou and thy house shall rue it.

West. Plantagenet, of thee and these thy sons,   95
Thy kinsmen and thy friends, I'll have more lives
Than drops of blood were in my father's veins.

Clif. Urge it no more; lest that, instead of words,
I send thee, Warwick, such a messenger
As shall revenge his death before I stir.   100

War. Poor Clifford, how I scorn his worthless threats!

York. Will you we show our title to the crown?
If not, our swords shall plead it in the field.

K. Hen. What title hast thou, traitor, to the crown?
Thy father was, as thou art, Duke of York.   105
Thy grandsire, Roger Mortimer, Earl of March.
I am the son of Henry the Fifth,
Who made the Dauphin and the French to stoop,
And seiz'd upon their towns and provinces.

War. Talk not of France, sith thou hast lost it all.   110

K. Hen. The Lord Protector lost it, and not I:
When I was crown'd I was but nine months old.

93. Yes] *F*; No *Q*.   102. *York.*] *Q*; *Plant.* / *F* (*and throughout*).   105. Thy] *Q*,
Rowe; My *F*.   106. grandsire] *This edn*; grandfather *Q,F*.

93 '*They* seek revenge'. Cf. also n. to
I. i. 3. Clifford's 'his' (100), however,
has no antecedent noun.

97. *my father's*] See notes to 49. S.D.
and 91. Westmoreland's father has no
more historical right here than himself. He replaces the historical Somerset: 'Somerset . . . Northumberland,
& Clifford, whose fathers were slayn
at saint Albons' (Hall, 237; cf. 254).
Vaughan suggests (ii. 430–1) that
'As the chronicles . . . wrote that there
was slain at Towton "the Earl of
Northumberland and the Earl of
Westmoreland", and as the Earl of
Northumberland's father certainly fell
at St. Albans, the poet . . . not im-
probably entertained the false belief
that his so declared companion in
death, the Earl of Westmoreland, also
had a father slain at St. Albans.'

101. *worthless threats*] ironical, in

view of Clifford's killing of Rutland
and York in revenge (I. iii and iv).

102. *title*] legal right.

105. *Thy father . . . York.*] York in
fact inherited from his uncle Edward
(killed at Agincourt), the elder brother
of the Earl of Cambridge (n. to 79);
App. II.

106. *grandsire*] Cf. 129. F probably
repeats a Q error, 'grandfather',
caught from 'father', 105, by Q reporter or printer.

108. *stoop*] yield.

110. *France . . . lost*] by giving Anjou
and Maine as a dowry to Reignier his
father-in-law, on his marriage with
Margaret; and allowing the rest to be
lost during his reign (see *2 H 6*).

sith] since.

111. *Protector*] Humphrey, Duke of
Gloucester.

112. *crown'd . . . nine months old*]

Rich. You are old enough now, and yet, methinks, you lose.
    Father, tear the crown from the usurper's head.

Edw. Sweet father, do so; set it on your head.   11 5

Falc. Good brother, as thou lov'st and honourest arms,
    Let's fight it out and not stand cavilling thus.

Rich. Sound drums and trumpets, and the King will fly.

York. Sons, peace!

North. Peace thou, and give King Henry leave to speak.   12c

War. Plantagenet shall speak first: hear him, lords;
    And be you silent and attentive too,
    For he that interrupts him shall not live.

K. Hen. Plantagenet, why seek'st thou to depose me?
    Are we not both Plantagenets by birth,   12 5
    And from two brothers lineally descent?
    Suppose by right and equity thou be king,
    Think'st thou that I will leave my kingly throne,
    Wherein my grandsire and my father sat?
    No: first shall war unpeople this my realm;   13c
    Ay, and their colours, often borne in France,
    And now in England to our heart's great sorrow,

---

116. *Falc.*] *This edn; Mo(u)nt.* | *Q,F.*   120. *North.*] *Q, conj. Lettsom; Henry.* | F
121–3.] *F; not in Q.*   124–7.] *Q; not in F.*

Henry was actually crowned in Paris in November 1431 (*2 H 6*, I. i. 91; cf. *1 H 6*, IV. i, and *R 3*, II. iii. 16–17). This refers rather to the proclamation of 1422 (Hall, 114), when Henry, 'beyng of the age of ix. monethes or there about with the sound of trumpettes' was caused 'openly to be proclaimed kyng of Englande and of Fraunce the xxx. daie of August'.

116. *brother*] See n. to 14.

117. *stand*] delay.

118. *Sound*] scil. for an onset.

120. North.] A good deal of correction or alteration of the Q copy must have taken place here. The substitution of *Henry.* for Q *Northum.* might easily have been caused by the appearance of *Henry.* in the margin to replace the Q *King.* in the next line. See n. to 121–7.

121–7.] Both Q and F versions seem authentic; F shows a gap in the sense and textual disturbance is already evident at 120 (see n. above). Three o the four Q lines occur at the foot o signature I2ᵛ in Q3, the copy at thi point. It is possible that Warwick' three lines were added at the foot o the page and the top of the next, bu were interpreted as alternative; or tha the compositor forgot to turn back fo the King's first four lines. The F scrib or compositor might have skippe from the first 'Plantagenet' to th second.

127. *by right and equity*] 'These are th words that made the lords feel faint (Vaughan, ii. 432); cf. 133.

130. *first shall war* . . .] Note the dra matic irony, and the contrast to 70–1 Was this meant to show the instabilit of Henry's character, and possibly t add to the accumulation of dramati fatalism?

Shall be my winding-sheet. Why faint you, lords?
My title's good, and better far than his.

War. Prove it, Henry, and thou shalt be king. 135

K. Hen. Henry the Fourth by conquest got the crown.

York. 'Twas by rebellion against his king.

K. Hen. [*Aside.*] I know not what to say: my title's weak.
Tell me, may not a king adopt an heir?

York. What then? 140

K. Hen. And if he may, then am I lawful king;
For Richard, in the view of many lords,
Resign'd the crown to Henry the Fourth,
Whose heir my father was, and I am his.

York. He rose against him, being his sovereign, 145
And made him to resign his crown perforce.

War. Suppose, my lords, he did it unconstrain'd,
Think you 'twere prejudicial to his crown?

Exe. No: for he could not so resign his crown
But that the next heir should succeed and reign. 150

K. Hen. Art thou against us, Duke of Exeter?

Exe. His is the right, and therefore pardon me.

York. Why whisper you, my lords, and answer not?

Exe. My conscience tells me he is lawful king.

K. Hen. [*Aside.*] All will revolt from me, and turn to him. 155

North. Plantagenet, for all the claim thou lay'st,
Think not that Henry shall be so depos'd.

War. Depos'd he shall be in despite of all.

North. Thou art deceiv'd: 'tis not thy southern power,
Of Essex, Norfolk, Suffolk, nor of Kent, 160

138, 155. *Aside.*] *Capell; not in Q,F.*　　138. title's] *Q2;* titles *Q1,3,F.*　　139. Tell
me, may] *Q,F;* May *conj. this edn.*　　148. his crown] *F;* the Crowne *Q, Capell;*
his claim *conj. Vaughan.*

133. *faint*] lose heart or courage;
show fear; *OED.* 1.

135.] metrically defective in Q and
F.

139.] QF 'Tell me' looks like an intrusive recollection found frequently
in the bad quartos, e.g. *Cont.,* 525, 560;
H 5, 504; *Wiv.,* 447; *Tr. Tr.,* 614, 617,
620, 631; and should almost certainly
be omitted.

142–7. *Richard . . . | Resign'd the*

crown . . . | . . . unconstrain'd] Hall, 12,
'The nobles and commons were well
pleased that kyng Richard shoulde
frankely and frely of his own *mere
mocion* (lest it shuld be . . . *reported*
that he therevnto were . . . *constrained*)
resigne his croune.'

159. *southern power*] 'Northumberland speaks as a Percy of the north'
(Brooke).

power] army; forces.

Which makes thee thus presumptuous and proud,
Can set the Duke up in despite of me.

Clif. King Henry, be thy title right or wrong,
Lord Clifford vows to fight in thy defence:
May that ground gape and swallow me alive,   165
Where I shall kneel to him that slew my father!

K. Hen. ¯O Clifford, how thy words revive my heart!

York. Henry of Lancaster, resign thy crown.
What mutter you, or what conspire you, lords?

War. Do right unto this princely Duke of York,   170
Or I will fill the house with armed men,
And o'er the chair of state, where now he sits,
Write up his title with usurping blood.

He stamps with his foot, and the Soldiers show themselves.

K. Hen. My Lord of Warwick, hear me but one word:
Let me for this my life-time reign as king.   175

York. Confirm the crown to me and to mine heirs,
And thou shalt reign in quiet whilst thou liv'st.

K. Hen. Convey the soldiers hence, and then I will.

War. Captain, conduct them into Tuthill Fields.

[Exeunt Soldiers.]

K. Hen. I am content: Richard Plantagenet,   180
Enjoy the kingdom after my decease.

Clif. What wrong is this unto the Prince your son!

War. What good is this to England and himself!

West. Base, fearful, and despairing Henry!

Clif. How hast thou injur'd both thyself and us!   185

---

172. o'er] *F2;* ouer *Q,F1.*   173. S.D.] *F;* Enter Souldiers. *Q (after 169).*   174.
me] *Q + Edd.; not in F.*   177. whilst] *Q1,2;* while *Q3,F.*   178-9.] *Q; not in F.*
179. S.D.] *This edn; not in Q,F.*   180-1.] *F; not in Q.*

---

165. *ground gape*] Cf. Numbers, xvi.
30-2; Ps. cvi. 17 (Noble, 127-8); *R 3,*
I. ii. 65.

166. *slew my father*] Cf. 54, 91; and
I. iii. 5, 46. Note the repetition of the
phrase; see n. at 7-9.

170. *right*] justice.

Duke of York] the title Henry had
given him in *1 H 6,* III. i. 173.

174.] 'hear' could be disyllabic.

177. *reign in quiet*] Hall, 432.

whilst] F follows Q3 copy.

178-9.] possibly lost to F through
the inserted lines 180-1 being taken as
alternative instead of complementary.

179. *Tuthill Fields*] open land in
Westminster, south of Tothill St, used
for duels, tournaments, archery, and
training of troops.

184. *fearful*] full of fear; timorous.

West. I cannot stay to hear these articles.

North. Nor I.

Clif. Come, cousin, let us tell the Queen these news.

West. Farewell, faint-hearted and degenerate king,
    In whose cold blood no spark of honour bides. *Exit.*   190

North. Be thou a prey unto the house of York,
    And die in bands for this unmanly deed!   *Exit.*

Clif. In dreadful war may'st thou be overcome,
    Or live in peace abandon'd and despis'd!   *Exit.*

War. Turn this way, Henry, and regard them not.   195

Exe. They seek revenge and therefore will not yield.

K. Hen. Ah! Exeter.

War.   Why should you sigh, my lord?

K. Hen. Not for myself, Lord Warwick, but my son,
    Whom I unnaturally shall disinherit.
    But be it as it may: [*To York*] I here entail   200
    The crown to thee and to thine heirs for ever;
    Conditionally that here thou take thine oath
    To cease this civil war and, whilst I live,
    To honour me as thy king and sovereign;
    And neither by treason nor hostility   205
    To seek to put me down and reign thyself.

York. This oath I willingly take and will perform.
                 [*Coming from the throne.*]

War. Long live King Henry! Plantagenet, embrace him.

K. Hen. And long live thou and these thy forward sons!

York. Now York and Lancaster are reconcil'd.   210

190. S.D. *Exit.*] *Q (after 187)*; *not in F*   192, 194. S.D. *Exit.*] *Q*; *not in F*;
Exeunt North., Clif., and West. | *Rowe (after 191).*   200. S.D. *To York.*] *Collier MS*
+*Edd.*; *not in F.*   202. thine] *Q1,2*; *an Q3,F.*   207. S.D.] *Capell*; *not in Q,F.*
208. King Henry] *Q,F*; *the king conj. this edn.*

186. *articles*] Hol., iii. 658/1/33;
Boswell-Stone, 293; not in Hall; =
terms of agreement.

188.] Q 'these newes' is probably a
recollection left undeleted by the F
collator.

191–4.] more characteristic prophecies.

192. *in bands*] in bonds or confine-
ment; cf. Marlowe, *Ed. 2*, 1289.

196. *They*] See n. to 91.

200. *entail*] bestow as an inalienable
inheritance.

202. *Conditionally*] on condition that;
Franz, 565.

oath] 'Item, the said Richard duke
of Yorke, shall promit and bind himself by his solemne *oth*, in maner and
forme as followeth:' Hol., iii. 658/1/33;
Boswell-Stone, 293.

203. *civil war*] Hall, 216.

209. *forward*] promising, hopeful.

Exe. Accurs'd be he that seeks to make them foes!

Sennet. Here they come down.

York. Farewell, my gracious lord; I'll take my leave,
     For I'll to Wakefield to my castle.   *Exit with his sons.*
War. And I'll keep London with my soldiers.   *Exeunt.*
Norf. And I to Norfolk with my followers.   *Exeunt.*
Falc. And I unto the sea from whence I came.   *Exit.*
K. Hen. And I with grief and sorrow to the court.   217

Enter QUEEN MARGARET *and the* PRINCE OF WALES.

Exe. Here comes the Queen, whose looks bewray her anger:
     I'll steal away.
K. Hen.   Exeter, so will I.   *scared of her*
Q. Mar. Nay, go not from me; I will follow thee.   220
K. Hen. Be patient, gentle Queen, and I will stay.
Q. Mar. Who can be patient in such extremes?
     Ah! wretched man, would I had died a maid,
     And never seen thee, never borne thee son,
     Seeing thou hast prov'd so unnatural a father.   225
     Hath he deserv'd to lose his birthright thus?

---

211. S.D.] *F;* Sound Trumpets. *Q.*   212–13.] *This edn;* Farewell my gracious
Lord, Ile to my Castle: *F;* My Lord Ile take my leaue, / For Ile to *Wakefield*
to my castell. *Q3* (. . . Wakefield / To . . . *Q1,2).*   213. S.D.] *Q3; Exit Yorke*
and his sonnes. *Q1,2; not in F.*   214–15. S.D.] *Q (Exit.); not in F.*   216. *Falc.*]
This edn; Mo(u)nt. / *Q,F.*   unto the sea] *F;* to the sea *Q1,3;* to sea *Q2.*   S.D.]
Q; not in F.   217. S.D.] *Rowe; Enter the Queene.* / *F; Enter the Queene and the*
Prince. / *Q.*

---

211. S.D. Sennet.] a special sounding of the trumpets for the arrival and
departure of processions.

212–13.] In Q3 (alone) the Q lines
are printed so that the eye could easily
pass from 'Ile' to 'to my Castle' in the
line below. 'Wakefield', which is not
mentioned elsewhere in this play,
comes from the chronicles, e.g. Hall,
250, 'The Duke by small iorneis, came
to his Castle of Sandall, beside Wakefelde'.

216. Falc. . . . *unto the sea*] See n. to
14.

217. S.D.] This dramatic entry and
interview is of Shakespeare's creation.

In fact, the Queen 'was sent for',
but 'denied to come', Hall, 249. Note
her increasing manliness and initia-
tive, contrasting with Henry's 'fearful-
ness'.

218. *bewray*] reveal, expose; *OED.*
6a. For Margaret's anger, cf. Hall,
241, 'the feare y^t thei had of the quene,
whose countenance was so fearfull,
and whose looke was so terrible, that
to al men . . . her frounyng was theyr
vndoyng, & her indignation, was their
death'.

222. *patient*] trisyllabic.

225. *unnatural a father*] another note
in the family chaos theme.

Hadst thou but lov'd him half so well as I,
Or felt that pain which I did for him once,
Or nourish'd him as I did with my blood,
Thou would'st have left thy dearest heart-blood there,
Rather than made that savage duke thine heir,   231
And disinherited thine only son.

Prince. Father, you cannot disinherit me:
If you be king, why should not I succeed?

K. Hen. Pardon me, Margaret; pardon me, sweet son: 235
The Earl of Warwick and the Duke enforc'd me.

Q. Mar. Enforc'd thee! Art thou King, and wilt be forc'd?
I shame to hear thee speak. Ah! timorous wretch,
Thou hast undone thyself, thy son, and me;
And given unto the house of York such head   240
As thou shalt reign but by their sufferance.
To entail him and his heirs unto the crown,
What is it but to make thy sepulchre,
And creep into it far before thy time?
Warwick is Chancellor, Salisbury Lord of Calais;   245
Stern Falconbridge commands the narrow seas;
The Duke is made Protector of the realm;
And yet shalt thou be safe? Such safety finds
The trembling lamb environed with wolves.
Had I been there, which am a silly woman,   250
The soldiers should have toss'd me on their pikes

---

231. made] *F2;* haue made *F1.*   245. Salisbury] *This edn; and the F; not in Q.*

231. *made*] F imported 'haue' either from the line above or by sophistication.

238. *shame*] am ashamed.

240. *given ... such head*] from horsemanship = not checked or held in with the bridle; given freedom; *OED*. 57.

241. *sufferance*] permission.

245. *Chancellor ... Lord ...*] Hall, 233, according to whom Salisbury was appointed Chancellor, and Warwick Lord of Calais. The text was probably altered here before performance to eliminate the part of Salisbury. See my note in *MLR.*, iv (1955), 492–4, and n. to I. ii. S.D.

246. *Stern*] fierce; cruel.

Falconbridge] Shakespeare seems here to have followed Hall, 301, identifying the elder Falconbridge with his bastard son who was appointed with Warwick to 'kepe the passage betwene Douer and Caleys'. The line is echoed in Marlowe's *Ed. 2*, 970, 'The hautie Dane commands the narrow seas'.

seas] plural to express the general idea; cf. *Ed. 2*, 970, 1029.

247. *Protector*] Hall, 249.

249. *lamb ... wolves*] a common touch from Aesop, as in *2 H 6*.

250. *silly*] the old sense of: simple; helpless; *OED*. 1b; cf. *Gent.*, IV. i. 72.

251. *toss'd*] carried aloft on the point of a pike; *OED*. 10.

Before I would have granted to that act;
But thou prefer'st thy life before thine honour:
And seeing thou dost, I here divorce myself
Both from thy table, Henry, and thy bed,   255
Until that act of parliament be repeal'd
Whereby my son is disinherited.
The northern lords, that have forsworn thy colours,
Will follow mine, if once they see them spread;
And spread they shall be, to thy foul disgrace,   260
And utter ruin of the house of York.
Thus do I leave thee. Come, son, let's away;
Our army is ready; come, we'll after them.

K. Hen. Stay, gentle Margaret, and hear me speak.

Q. Mar. Thou hast spoke too much already: get thee gone.

K. Hen. Gentle son Edward, thou wilt stay with me?   266

Q. Mar. Ay, to be murder'd by his enemies.

Prince. When I return with victory from the field
I'll see your Grace: till then I'll follow her.

Q. Mar. Come, son, away; we may not linger thus.   270
                    Exeunt Queen Margaret and the Prince.

K. Hen. Poor Queen! how love to me and to her son
Hath made her break out into terms of rage.
Reveng'd may she be on that hateful Duke,
Whose haughty spirit, winged with desire,
Will cost my crown, and like an empty eagle   275
Tire on the flesh of me and of my son!
The loss of those three lords torments my heart:

---

266. thou wilt] *F*; wilt thou *Q*.   with] *Q,F2+Edd.*; *not in F1*.   268. from]
Q,F2; to *F1*.   270. S.D.] *Rowe*; *not in F*; *Exit. (after 267) . . . Exit. (after 629) / Q*.
275. cost] *F*; coast *Warburton*.

252. *granted to*] assented to.

255. *table . . . bed*] an accurate legal phrase, still used of marital separation 'a mensa et thoro'.

258. *forsworn*] abjured.

271. *love to me*] Could dramatic irony go farther?

272. *break out into terms of rage*] Cf. *F.Q.*, III. i. 48, 'Eftsoones she grew to great impatience / And into termes of open outrage brust'.

275. *cost*] = coast, *OED.* 9—attack; assail; and 10—fly from the straight course so as to cut off the chased animal when it doubles (in hawking); or simply—cost me (Hart).

276. *Tire*] of a hawk or other bird of prey—to prey or feed ravenously on; see Madden, 203. Cf. *Ven.*, 55–6; *Selimus*, 1343, 'the vulture tireth on his heart'; *1 Tamb.*, 901, 'like a Harpye tires on my life'.

I'll write unto them and entreat them fair.
Come, cousin; you shall be the messenger.

Exe. And I, I hope, shall reconcile them all.   280

Flourish. Exeunt.

[SCENE II.—*Sandal Castle.*]

Enter EDWARD, RICHARD, *and* MONTAGUE

Rich. Brother, though I be youngest, give me leave.

Edw. No, I can better play the orator.

Mont. But I have reasons strong and forcible.

Enter the DUKE OF YORK.

York. Why, how now, sons and brother! at a strife?
   What is your quarrel? How began it first?   5

Edw. No quarrel, but a slight contention.

York. About what?

Rich. About that which concerns your Grace and us—
   The crown of England, father, which is yours.

York. Mine, boy? Not till King Henry be dead.   10

---

280. S.D. *Flourish.*] F (*at* I. ii. I); *not in* Q.

Scene II

[SCENE II] *Capell; not in* Q,F.   *Sandal Castle.*] *Edd., after Pope; not in* Q,F.
S.D. *Enter* . . . *Montague.*] *F2; Flourish. Enter* . . . | *F1; Enter Edward, and Richard,*
and Montague. | Q.   I. though . . . youngest] *F; and cosen Montague,* | Q.
3. S.D.] Q,F.

---

278. *entreat them fair*] be courteous to
them; treat them kindly; *OED*. 1.

280. *reconcile*] Apparently Exeter
succeeds; all appear together again
except for Westmoreland, who is
dropped from the play) at II. ii. I.

S.D. Flourish.] taken from the F
entry to I. ii, where it is out of place
(Wilson).

Scene II

Sandal Castle.] beside Wakefield.
See Hall, 250; and I. i. 213; and 63
below.

S.D. Montague] treated throughout
the scene as York's brother (4, 36, 55,
50), whereas he was in fact his nephew.

This also occurred in I. i, where Montague was substituted for Falconbridge
(see n. to I. i. 14). It is possible that
here he has replaced old Salisbury
(Hall, 250), to whom the relationship
would apply. In Q, he is called 'cosen
Mountague' throughout; and this, if
not a memorial error, may indicate a
later alteration in the actor's 'part'
(the 'book' being left uncorrected in
this respect).

6. *contention*] the contention, or dis-
pute, about the crown, from which the
Q version of *2 H 6* derived its title; a
title also applied as 'the whole contention' to the combined Q versions of
2 and *3 H 6* in Q3; see Intro., xiii.

Rich. Your right depends not on his life or death.
Edw. Now you are heir, therefore enjoy it now:
　　By giving the house of Lancaster leave to breathe,
　　It will outrun you, father, in the end.
York. I took an oath that he should quietly reign.　　15
Edw. But for a kingdom any oath may be broken:
　　I would break a thousand oaths to reign one year.
Rich. No; God forbid your Grace should be forsworn.
York. I shall be, if I claim by open war.
Rich. I'll prove the contrary, if you'll hear me speak.　20
York. Thou canst not, son; it is impossible.
Rich. An oath is of no moment, being not took
　　Before a true and lawful magistrate
　　That hath authority over him that swears.
　　Henry had none, but did usurp the place;　　　25
　　Then, seeing 'twas he that made you to depose,
　　Your oath, my lord, is vain and frivolous.
　　Therefore, to arms! And, father, do but think
　　How sweet a thing it is to wear a crown,
　　Within whose circuit is Elysium　　　　　30
　　And all that poets feign of bliss and joy.
　　Why do we linger thus? I cannot rest
　　Until the white rose that I wear be dy'd
　　Even in the lukewarm blood of Henry's heart.

---

13. By giving] *F; not in Q;* But give *conj. this edn.*　　17. I would] *Q,F;* I'd *Pope*

11. *right*] title; just claim.

13.] 'But' possibly misprinted 'By', and the verb adjusted to make sense. *breathe*] rest.

14. *outrun*] Cf. *2 H 6*, v. ii. 73, 'Can we outrun the heavens?', and the common Elizabethan phrase, 'to outrun the constable' (Tilley, C615)—'escape by running' (Schmidt).

16. *But . . . broken:*] typical Machiavellian doctrine. Hart refers to Cicero's 'Nam si violandum est ius, regnandi gratia violandum est' (*De Officiis*, III. c. 21). York actually obtained a dispensation from the Pope to release him from his oath; see n. to I. iv. 100.

18.] a characteristic piece of irony from Richard.

26. *depose*] take an oath.

27. *vain*] worthless; ineffectual.
frivolous] a legal term in pleading —'manifestly insufficient or futile' *OED.* 1b.

29–31. *to wear a crown . . . joy.*] Cf. *1 Tamb.*, 763–5: 'I thinke the pleasure they enioy in heauen / Can not compare with kingly ioyes in earth, / To weare a Crowne enchac'd with pearle and golde'; and 863, 878 ff.: 'The . . sweetnes of a crown, / . . . the ripest fruit of all, / That perfect blisse and sole felicitie, / The sweet fruition of an earthly crowne.'

30. *circuit*] circumference; cf. *2 H 6* III. i. 352.

34. *lukewarm*] a common Elizabethan expression, but here perhaps with a touch of irony.

York. Richard, enough; I will be king, or die.   35
　　Brother, thou shalt to London presently,
　　And whet on Warwick to this enterprise.
　　Thou, Richard, shalt to the Duke of Norfolk straight
　　And tell him privily of our intent.
　　You, Edward, shall to Edmund Brook Lord Cobham, 40
　　With whom the Kentishmen will willingly rise:
　　In them I trust, for they are soldiers,
　　Witty, courteous, liberal, full of spirit.
　　While you are thus employ'd, what resteth more
　　But that I seek occasion how to rise,   45
　　And yet the King not privy to my drift,
　　Nor any of the house of Lancaster?

Enter a Messenger.

　　But stay: what news? Why com'st thou in such post?
Mess. The Queen with all the northern earls and lords
　　Intend here to besiege you in your castle.   50
　　She is hard by with twenty thousand men;
　　And therefore fortify your hold, my lord.
York. Ay, with my sword. What! think'st thou that we fear
　　them?
　　Edward and Richard, you shall stay with me;

38. straight] *Q; not in F.*   40. to Edmund Brook] *Q;* vnto my *F.*   43. Witty]
F; Witty, and *Capell.*   47. S.D. *a messenger] Q, Theobald (after 47); Gabriel | F.*
49. Mess.] *Q; Gabriel. | F.*

36. *Brother*] See n. to 'Montague' at
the initial S.D.
　presently] the normal Elizabethan
sense of 'immediately'.
　40. *Cobham*] one of York's 'especiall
frendes' (Hall, 232). His own name,
'Edmund Brooke', was omitted in F,
either by inadvertence or through the
action of the censor, as in *Wiv.* it was
changed to 'Broome'.
　41–3. *Kentishmen . . . spirit.*] For
Shakespeare's praise of Kent, cf. *2 H 6,*
IV. vii. 56–9.
　41. *willingly*] Cf. I. i. 207. The QF
text, with its jingle 'will willingly', is
probably corrupt.
　43. *Witty*] intelligent; wise; *OED.* 2.
　liberal] gentleman-like.

44. *resteth*] in the Fr. sense—remains; *OED.* v². 3.
　46. *And*] expressing emphasis or ad-
ditional circumstance; Abbott, 95.
　drift] intention; purpose.
　47. S.D. a Messenger] The F
'Gabriel' probably stands for Gabriel
Spencer, later found with the Admiral's Men, and killed by Ben Jonson
in a duel on 22 September 1598. See
Intro., xix.
　48. *post*] haste, from 'post-haste'.
　51. *twenty*] a round number; Hall,
250, says twenty-two; but cf. *Mirror,*
188 (l. 130), 'With skant fiue thousand
souldiers, to assaye / Fower times so
many'; and 66, 71 below.
　52. *hold*] stronghold.

My brother Montague shall post to London.   55
Let noble Warwick, Cobham, and the rest,
Whom we have left protectors of the King,
With powerful policy strengthen themselves,
And trust not simple Henry nor his oaths.

Mont. Brother, I go; I'll win them, fear it not: 60
And thus most humbly I do take my leave.   *Exit*

Enter SIR JOHN *and* SIR HUGH MORTIMER.

York. Sir John and Sir Hugh Mortimer, mine uncles,
You are come to Sandal in a happy hour;
The army of the Queen mean to besiege us.

Sir John. She shall not need; we'll meet her in the field.   65

York. What, with five thousand men!

Rich. Ay, with five hundred, father, for a need.
A woman's general; what should we fear? *A march afar off*

Edw. I hear their drums: let's set our men in order,
And issue forth and bid them battle straight.   70

York. Five men to twenty! Though the odds be great,
I doubt not, uncles, of our victory.
Many a battle have I won in France,
When as the enemy hath been ten to one:
Why should I not now have the like success? *Exeunt.*   75

55. brother] *F;* Cosen *Q.*   61. S.D. *Exit.*] *F* (*Exit Mountague.*) *; not in Q.*   Ente
. . . Mortimer.] *Q; Enter Mortimer, and his Brother.* | *F.*   68. S.D.] *F; not in Q*
72. uncles] *Hudson;* uncle *F; not in Q.*   75. S.D. *Exeunt.*] *Q2; Exit.* | *Q1,3*
Alarum. Exit. | *F.*

58. *policy*] Cf. *2 H 6,* I. i. 79; political
cunning; *OED.* sb.[1] 3.
59. *simple*] foolish.
60. *fear*] doubt.
62. *uncles*] 'these were two bastard
uncles by the mother's side . . . but it

does not appear who was the father
(French, 194).
67. *for a need*] in case of necessity; a
a pinch.
70. *straight*] immediately.
74. *When as*] when.

[SCENE III.—*Field of battle between Sandal Castle and Wakefield.*]

Alarums. Enter RUTLAND *and his Tutor.*

Rut. Ah, whither shall I fly to scape their hands?
 Ah, tutor, look where bloody Clifford comes!

Enter CLIFFORD [*and Soldiers*].

Clif. Chaplain, away! thy priesthood saves thy life.
 As for the brat of this accursed duke,
 Whose father slew my father, he shall die.   5
Tut. And I, my lord, will bear him company.
Clif. Soldiers, away with him!
Tut. Ah, Clifford, murder not this innocent child,
 Lest thou be hated both of God and man.

       Exit[, *dragged off by soldiers*].

Clif. How now! is he dead already? Or is it fear 10
 That makes him close his eyes? I'll open them.
Rut. So looks the pent-up lion o'er the wretch

Scene III

SCENE III] *Capell; not in Q,F.   Field . . . Wakefield.*] *Theobald; not in Q,F.*
Alarums.] Q (*Alarmes, and then*); *not in F.   Enter Rutland*] F; *Enter the yong
Earle of Rutland* / Q.   2. S.D. *Enter Clifford*] Q,F.   *and Soldiers*] *Theobald; not
in Q,F.*   7. *Soldiers, away*] Q,F; *Away conj. this edn.*   *with him*] F; *not in Q;
and drag him hence perforce:* / *Awaie with the villaine. Q, Theobald, conj. this edn.*
9. S.D.] *Theobald; Exit.* / F; *Exit the Chaplein.* Q.

The scene is elaborated from Hall,
251.
 S.D. *Alarums.*] The fighting continues in the background.
 Rutland] 'scarce of the age of xii
yeares' (Hall); actually aged seven-
teen (French, 188).
 4. *brat*] child, 'sometimes used without contempt, though nearly always
implying insignificance', *OED*.
 5. *Whose father slew my father*] See n.
on I. i. 7–9, and *2 H 6*, v. ii. The first
two Acts are developing into a revenge
tragedy centring on Clifford's revenge
for his father, followed by the Yorkists'
revenge on him (II. vi). The whole is
part of the picture of civil war and its
results.

Whose] The antecedent is 'brat'.
 7.] The end of the line, given in Q,
seems to have been lost in the correction of the copy; and the Q 'Soldiers',
to remain uncorrected.
 9. *hated . . . man*] Cf. *F.Q.*, I. i. 13,
'whom God and man does hate', and
v. 48, 'scornd of God and man'.
 10. *dead already*] Cf. Kyd, *S.P.*, v. ii.
102, 'Ah, poore *Erastus*, art thou dead
already?'
 12–15.] Cf. Ps. xxii. 13–14 (*SH*),
'Much like a Lion roaring out, / and
ramping for his prey. / But I drop down
like water shed, / my ioynts in sunder
break'. The simile may have been
prompted by Hall's contrast (251) of
Clifford's conduct with the lion's true

That trembles under his devouring paws;
And so he walks, insulting o'er his prey,
And so he comes to rend his limbs in sunder.   15
Ah, gentle Clifford, kill me with thy sword,
And not with such a cruel threatening look.
Sweet Clifford, hear me speak before I die:
I am too mean a subject for thy wrath;
Be thou reveng'd on men, and let me live.   20

Clif. In vain thou speak'st, poor boy; my father's blood
Hath stopp'd the passage where thy words should enter.

Rut. Then let my father's blood open it again:
He is a man, and, Clifford, cope with him.

Clif. Had I thy brethren here, their lives and thine   25
Were not revenge sufficient for me;
No, if I digg'd up thy forefathers' graves
And hung their rotten coffins up in chains,
It could not slake mine ire nor ease my heart.
The sight of any of the house of York   30
Is as a Fury to torment my soul;
And till I root out their accursed line
And leave not one alive, I live in hell.
Therefore—   [*Lifting his hand.*]

Rut. O, let me pray before I take my death!   35
To thee I pray; sweet Clifford, pity me.

Clif. Such pity as my rapier's point affords.

14. o'er] *F* (o're); ouer *Q1,2*; ore *Q3*.   15. in sunder] *Q*; asunder *F*.   23.
father's blood] *Q,F*; father's *conj.* H. Brooks.   open it] *F*; ope it *Q*; open't *Pope*.
34. S.D.] *Johnson*; not in *Q,F*.

nature, to Clifford's disadvantage.
    12. *pent-up*] confined without food.
    14. *insulting o'er*] exulting proudly or
contemptuously over; cf. *R 3*, II. iv. 51,
'Insulting tyranny'. The sense of 'o'er'
(both here and in l. 12, where Q1
reads 'on') is that of an arrogant
mastering survey by someone who can
do it from a position of superior power;
cf. *R 3* (Q), IV. iii. 42, 'looks proudly
ore the crown' (H. F. B.).
    15. *in sunder*] F 'asunder' is probably
a sophistication; cf. *R 3*, IV. i. 34; and
see Ps. xxii in n. to 12–15.
    16. *Ah, gentle . . .*] Wilson compares

Lavinia's plea to Tamora, *Tit.*, II. iii.
168–9.
    23. *my father's blood*] The line re-
quires emendation, either by adoption
of Q 'ope' or by omission of 'blood' as
caught from 21. '*My* father's' is em-
phatic.
    25–6.] The principle is that of *Ham.*,
IV. vii. 128, 'Revenge should have no
bounds'.
    31. *a Fury . . . soul*] The Furies were
tormentors who possessed the souls of
the guilty with madness; cf. Ovid,
Metam., iv. 499, 'mens est quae diros
sentiat ictus'.

Rut. I never did thee harm; why wilt thou slay me?
Clif. Thy father hath.
Rut.   But 'twas ere I was born.
    Thou hast one son; for his sake pity me,   40
    Lest in revenge thereof, sith God is just,
    He be as miserably slain as I.
    Ah, let me live in prison all my days,
    And when I give occasion of offence
    Then let me die, for now thou hast no cause.   45
Clif. Thy father slew my father; therefore die.   [*Stabs him.*]
Rut. Di faciant laudis summa sit ista tuae!
Clif. Plantagenet, I come, Plantagenet!
    And this thy son's blood cleaving to my blade
    Shall rust upon my weapon, till thy blood,   50
    Congeal'd with this, do make me wipe off both.   *Exit.*

[SCENE IV.—*The same.*]

Alarum. Enter RICHARD, *Duke of York.*

York. The army of the Queen hath got the field:
    My uncles both are slain in rescuing me;

46. Thy] *This edn;* No cause? Thy *Q,F.*   46. S.D.] *Theobald; not in Q,F.*
47. Di] *Edd.; Dij / F.*   51. this] *F;* his *Hart, conj. anon.*   51. S.D.] *Q,F.*

Scene IV

SCENE IV] *Capell; not in Q,F.*   The same.] *This edn; Another . . . field. | Camb.+*
Edd.; Theobald continues the scene.   Enter . . . York.] *F;* Enter the Duke of Yorke
solus. | Q.

39. *ere I was born*] not historically true.

44, 45. *when . . . | Then . . .*] adversative use; Franz, 554, note.

46.] Q repeats Rutland's last words, probably as Clifford's cue, and F has failed to correct.

Thy father slew . . .] The phrase becomes a refrain, expressing Clifford's intense hate and desire for revenge.

47. *Di . . . tuae*] Ovid, *Heroides*, ii. 66 (Phyllis to Demophoon). It is interesting to note that Nashe used it later in *Haue with you to Saffron Walden* (Steev-

ens, i. 596), McKerrow, III. 71. 14. 'The gods grant that this may be the peak of thy glory!'

48. *Plantagenet, I come*] addressed to the Duke of York, Rutland's father. Note the forecast of York's capture and murder in the next scene.

Scene IV

The scene, with the death of York, carries the fortunes of the Lancastrians to a peak. The source is Hall, 250-1 (Hol., iii. 659); see n. to 67 below.

    1. *got*] won; gained.
    2. *uncles*] the two Mortimers of I. ii.

And all my followers to the eager foe
Turn back and fly, like ships before the wind,
Or lambs pursu'd by hunger-starved wolves.   5
My sons, God knows what hath bechanced them:
But this I know, they have demean'd themselves
Like men born to renown by life or death.
Three times did Richard make a lane to me,
And thrice cried 'Courage, father! fight it out!'   10
And full as oft came Edward to my side
With purple falchion, painted to the hilt
In blood of those that had encounter'd him:
And when the hardiest warriors did retire,
Richard cried, 'Charge! and give no foot of ground!'   15
Edward, 'A crown, or else a glorious tomb!
A sceptre, or an earthly sepulchre!'
With this we charg'd again: but out alas!
We budg'd again; as I have seen a swan
With bootless labour swim against the tide   20
And spend her strength with over-matching waves.

A short alarum within.

Ah, hark! the fatal followers do pursue,
And I am faint and cannot fly their fury;
And were I strong I would not shun their fury.

16. Edward] *This edn, conj. Lettsom;* And cri'de *F;* Ned cried *conj. Collier.*   19.
budg'd] *Johnson;* bodg'd *F.*   21. S.D.] *F; not in Q.*

3. *eager*] ardent; impetuous (L. *acer*).

4. *Turn back*] i.e. Turn their backs (Wilson); cf. Ps. xxxv. 4 (*SH*), 'turn back and flie'; and II. i. 185.

5. *lambs . . . wolves*] a continuation of the Aesopian animal imagery of *2 H 6.*

7. *demean'd*] conducted; behaved.

9. *lane*] scil. of slaughtered bodies.

12. *purple*] blood-red.

falchion] curved sword, with the edge on the convex.

14. *retire*] retreat; draw back.

16. *Edward*] F has a graphical error, probably complicated by 'cry'de' in the line above. Edward would natur-

ally cry for a crown, to which he was heir; cf. Kyd, *S.P.*, III. iii. 8, 'A glorious death or famous victorie.'

18. *out alas!*] a double or compound interjection expressing reproach or indignation; cf. *Mirror*, 276 (Hastings, 217).

19. *budg'd*] flinched; gave way; *OED.* 1 b.

20. *bootless*] useless; fruitless.

21. *with*] against; *OED.* 2.

over-matching] more than a match for; too powerful; cf. 64.

22. *fatal*] bringing with them fate or destiny. The word adds to the sense of inevitability in these events, and of the nemesis that runs through them.

> The sands are number'd that makes up my life; 25
> Here must I stay, and here my life must end.

Enter QUEEN MARGARET, CLIFFORD, NORTHUMBERLAND, *the*
young PRINCE, *and Soldiers.*

> Come, bloody Clifford, rough Northumberland,
> I dare your quenchless fury to more rage:
> I am your butt, and I abide your shot.

North. Yield to our mercy, proud Plantagenet.   30

Clif. Ay, to such mercy as his ruthless arm
> With downright payment show'd unto my father.
> Now Phaëthon hath tumbled from his car,
> And made an evening at the noontide prick.

York. My ashes, like the phoenix, may bring forth   35
> A bird that will revenge upon you all;
> And in that hope I throw mine eyes to heaven,
> Scorning whate'er you can afflict me with.
> Why come you not? What! multitudes, and fear?

Clif. So cowards fight when they can fly no further;   40
> So doves do peck the falcon's piercing talons;
> So desperate thieves, all hopeless of their lives,
> Breathe out invectives 'gainst the officers.

York. O Clifford, but bethink thee once again,

---

25. makes] *F;* make *Edd.*   26. S.D.] *F;* . . . *Northumberland, and* | *Q.*   33.
Phaëthon] *Q,F* (*Phaeton*).   35. like] *Q;* as *F.*   phoenix] *Q,F;* phoenix' *conj.*
Edd.

---

25. *makes*] See Abbott, 333.

27. *rough*] cruel; violent.

29. *butt . . . shot*] a metaphor from archery = a mark for shooting at.

32. *downright payment*] probably a quibble, as Wilson suggests.

33. *Phaëthon*] See Ovid, *Metam.*, ii. 1–237. The son of Phoebus Apollo, who attempted to drive his father's chariot (of the sun), and was killed in the process. The metaphor is particularly appropriate to York, since the sun was a Yorkist badge (Wilson).

34. *noontide prick*] the mark on the sundial face indicating noon; cf. *Lucr.*, 781.

35. *ashes . . . phoenix*] Cf. *1 H 6*, IV. vii. 93. 'The phoenix was a fabulous

Arabian bird which existed single and rose again from its own ashes' (Schmidt).

like] F *as* is probably a repetition of *a*shes.

36. *bird*] i.e. a young bird; here, Edward, who became Edward IV.

revenge] take vengeance.

38. *Scorning . . .*] the true heroic stoicism of the tragedian.

39. *multitudes, and fear?*] Cf. *Mac.*, v. i. 35, 'a soldier, and afeard?'

41. *doves . . . falcon*] another metaphor of prey; cf. *Ant.*, III. xiii. 197, 'in that mood | The dove will peck the estridge (goshawk)' (Hart).

42–3, 63–4. *thieves . . . robbers*] a new series of images.

And in thy thought o'errun my former time;   45
And, if thou canst for blushing, view this face,
And bite thy tongue that slanders him with cowardice
Whose frown hath made thee faint and fly ere this.

Clif. I will not bandy with thee word for word,
But buckle with thee blows twice two for one. [*Draws.*] 50

Q. Mar. Hold, valiant Clifford; for a thousand causes
I would prolong awhile the traitor's life.
Wrath makes him deaf: speak thou, Northumberland.

North. Hold, Clifford! do not honour him so much
To prick thy finger, though to wound his heart.   55
What valour were it, when a cur doth grin,
For one to thrust his hand between his teeth,
When he might spurn him with his foot away?
It is war's prize to take all vantages;
And ten to one is no impeach of valour.   60

[*They lay hands on York, who struggles.*]

Clif. Ay, ay, so strives the woodcock with the gin.

North. So doth the cony struggle in the net.

York. So triumph thieves upon their conquer'd booty;
So true men yield, with robbers so o'er-match'd.

North. What would your Grace have done unto him now? 65

---

50. buckle] *Q, Theobald;* buckler *F.*   50. S.D. *Draws.*] *Johnson; not in Q,F*
60. S.D.] *Johnson;* Fight and take him. *Q; not in F.*

45. *o'errun*] review.
46. *for*] on account of.
47. *bite thy tongue*] be silent; cf. *2 H 6,* I. i. 225.
48. *faint*] take fright; show fear; cf. I. i. 133.
49. *bandy*] a metaphor from tennis—to strike the ball (or words or blows) to and fro; cf. *Shr.,* v. ii. 172.
50. *buckle*] grapple or couple with in combat; *OED.* v. 3. The only example of F 'buckler' in this sense is this very one. Cf. *1 H 6,* I. ii. 95, 'In single combat shalt thou buckle with me'.
51, 54. *Hold*] hold your hand; refrain.
56. *grin*] show its teeth.
59. *prize*] privilege; advantage.

vantages] opportunities.
60. *impeach*] reproach of; detraction from.
valour] The normal standards of chivalry have been overthrown, like all civilized standards in this 'intestine discord'.
61. *woodcock . . . gin*] another image from the animal world, followed by one from robbers; cf. 62 and 63–4: both woodcock and rabbit were easily snared.
62. *cony*] rabbit; also commonly used for a dupe; a gull; the victim of the 'cony-catcher'; *OED.* 6.
63. *triumph*] exult.
64. *o'ermatch'd*] See n. to 21; and cf. 'being overmatcht by might', *Mirror* 187.

Q. Mar. Brave warriors, Clifford and Northumberland,
　　Come make him stand upon this molehill here,
　　That raught at mountains with outstretched arms,
　　Yet parted but the shadow with his hand.
　　What, was it you that would be England's king?   70
　　Was't you that revell'd in our parliament
　　And made a preachment of your high descent?
　　Where are your mess of sons to back you now—
　　The wanton Edward and the lusty George?
　　And where's that valiant crook-back prodigy,   75
　　Dicky your boy, that with his grumbling voice
　　Was wont to cheer his dad in mutinies?
　　Or, with the rest, where is your darling Rutland?
　　Look, York: I stain'd this napkin with the blood
　　That valiant Clifford with his rapier's point   80
　　Made issue from the bosom of the boy;
　　And if thine eyes can water for his death,
　　I give thee this to dry thy cheeks withal.
　　Alas, poor York! but that I hate thee deadly,
　　I should lament thy miserable state.   85
　　I prithee grieve, to make me merry, York.

---

67. *molehill*] not in Hall; Holinshed's version (iii. 659/2/37) runs: 'Some write that the duke of Yorke was taken aliue, and in derision caused to stand vpon a molehill; on whose head they put a garland in steed of a crowne, which they had fashioned and made of sedges and bulrushes; and, hauing so crowned him with that garland, they kneeled down afore him (as the Iewes did vnto Christ) in scorne, saieng to him: "Haile king without rule! haile king without heritage!" And at length, hauing thus scorned him with these and diuerse other despitefull words, they stroke off his head, which (as you haue heard) they presented to the queene.'

68. *raught*] reached.

69. *parted*] divided.

71. *revell'd*] led your party of riotous maskers (Wilson).

72. *preachment*] sermon. York's 'preachment' is not in I. i, where his high descent is mentioned only by Henry, but in his oration to the parliament, in Hall, 245–6. Cf. Marlowe, *Ed. 2*, 1328.

73. *mess*] set of four; cf. *LLL.*, IV. iii. 204; a group of persons, normally four, into a number of which the company at a banquet was divided.

74. *wanton*] the first indication of Edward's nature, to be developed by such remarks as Richard's at II. i. 41, and by his conduct in the scene with Lady Grey (III. ii).

75. *crook-back prodigy*] Hall, 342–5; cf. v. vi. 44 ff., and App. I (Hall, 342–3).
　　prodigy] monster; portent.

76. *grumbling*] querulous.

77. *mutinies*] quarrels; rebellions.

79. *napkin*] handkerchief.

84. *I hate thee deadly*] also in Kyd, *S.P.*, v. iv. 67.

86. *to make me merry*] Cf. 'to make me

What, hath thy fiery heart so parch'd thine entrails
That not a tear can fall for Rutland's death?
Why art thou patient, man? thou should'st be mad;
And I to make thee mad do mock thee thus.   90
Stamp, rave, and fret, that I may sing and dance.
Thou would'st be fee'd, I see, to make me sport;
York cannot speak unless he wear a crown.
A crown for York! and, lords, bow low to him:
Hold you his hands whilst I do set it on.   95
          [*Putting a paper crown on his head.*]
Ay, marry, sir, now looks he like a king!
Ay, this is he that took King Henry's chair,
And this is he was his adopted heir.
But how is it that great Plantagenet
Is crown'd so soon and broke his solemn oath?   100
As I bethink me, you should not be king
Till our King Henry had shook hands with Death.
And will you pale your head in Henry's glory,
And rob his temples of the diadem,
Now in his life, against your holy oath?   105
O, 'tis a fault too too unpardonable!
Off with the crown, and, with the crown, his head;
And, whilst we breathe, take time to do him dead.

Clif. That is my office, for my father's sake.

Q. Mar. Nay, stay; let's hear the orisons he makes.   110

91.] F; Q (*after 86*), Malone.   95. S.D.] *Rowe; not in* Q,F.

sport', 92. Shakespeare is thinking of
the death of Samson, particularly
Judges, xvi. 25, 'And it came to pass,
when their hearts were *merry*, that they
said, Call for Samson, that he may
make us sport. And they called for Samson out of the prison house; and he
made them sport'.

87. *entrails*] bowels, considered as the
seat of the sympathetic emotions;
OED. 4; cf. 'bowels', *OED*. 3.

91. *Stamp, rave*] Cf. *F.Q.*, III. x. 17,
'He rau'd, he wept, he stampt, he
lowd did cry'; *Mirror*, 224, 'to fret and
fume, / To stampe and stare' (Clarence).

94. *crown*] Hall, 251; not in Holin-

shed, who has 'a garland'. The scene
is recalled to Margaret in *R 3*, I. iii
174 ff., where the paper is also
mentioned. Note the irony latent in
I. ii. 29.

100. *broke . . . oath*] See I. i. 202, 207
and I. ii. 22 ff., and n. to I. ii. 16.
Holinshed describes this as 'a due
punishment for breaking his oth of
allegiance vnto his souereigne lord
king Henrie' (iii. 659/2/58).

103. *pale*] enclose in the pale or
circle of the crown; cf. 'impale', III. ii.
171; III. iii. 189.

106. *too too*] intensive repetition.

108. *time*] the opportunity.

110. *orisons*] prayers.

York. She-wolf of France, but worse than wolves of France,
Whose tongue more poisons than the adder's tooth!
How ill-beseeming is it in thy sex
To triumph like an Amazonian trull
Upon their woes whom Fortune captivates!   115
But that thy face is vizard-like, unchanging,
Made impudent with use of evil deeds,
I would assay, proud queen, to make thee blush.
To tell thee whence thou cam'st, of whom deriv'd,
Were shame enough to shame thee, wert not shameless.
Thy father bears the type of King of Naples,   121
Of both the Sicils, and Jerusalem,
Yet not so wealthy as an English yeoman.
Hath that poor monarch taught thee to insult?
It needs not, nor it boots thee not, proud queen;   125
Unless the adage must be verified,
That beggars mounted run their horse to death.
'Tis beauty that doth oft make women proud;
But God he knows thy share thereof is small.

---

116. is] *Q,F; is, Hart.*   117. deeds,] *Edd.;* deedes. *F;* deeds: *Q.*   120. wert]
This edn, conj. S. Walker; wert thou *Q,F.*   129. knows] *F;* wots *Q, conj. this
edn.*

---

111. ff.] a formal rhetorical invec-
tive on Margaret's parentage, personal
appearance, character, conduct, and
nationality, with appropriate com-
parisons, and general introduction.
See Baldwin, *Sm. Lat.,* ii. 335.
  She-wolf . . . adder] The metaphors
from natural history continue. There
may be an implication of the L. sense
of *lupa* = prostitute; cf. Plutarch,
Romulus, I. 35; and Cooper, *Thesaurus;*
and 'trull' below.
  113. *ill-beseeming*] unbecoming.
  114. *triumph*] exult.
  Amazonian trull] shameless female
warrior—alluding to her leadership of
the army. Possibly a reference to the
Scythian Tomyris (*I H 6,* II. iii. 6)
triumphing over Cyrus, the Amazons
being regarded as Scythians (Wilson).
  115. *captivates*] in the literal sense—
makes captive; subdues.
  116. *vizard-like*] as fixed in expres-

sion as a mask, such as seems to have
been worn on the Elizabethan stage;
e.g. 'the Visard of the ghost, which
cried so miserally (*sic*) at the Theator
. . . *Hamlet, reuenge*' (Lodge, *Wit's
Miserie*).
  117. *use*] custom; habitual practice.
  120. *wert not*] The intrusive F 'thou'
derives from Q.
  121. *Thy father*] 'King of Naples,
Sicilia and Jerusalem', *2 H 6,* I. i. 46.
  type] distinguishing mark; title;
OED. 3.
  122. *the Sicils*] Sicily and Naples.
  123. *yeoman*] freeholder; independent farmer.
  124. *insult*] exult contemptuously.
  125. *it boots thee not*] it is of no avail;
cf. 20.
  126. *verified*] proved true.
  128. ff.] Cf. *Mirror,* 420, 'seeing
women are by nature tender harted,
mylde, and pytefull'; and Hall, 159.

'Tis virtue that doth make them most admir'd;   130
The contrary doth make thee wonder'd at.
'Tis government that makes them seem divine;
The want thereof makes thee abominable.
Thou art as opposite to every good
As the Antipodes are unto us,   135
Or as the south to the Septentrion.
O tiger's heart wrapp'd in a woman's hide!
How could'st thou drain the life-blood of the child,
To bid the father wipe his eyes withal,
And yet be seen to bear a woman's face?   140
Women are soft, mild, pitiful, and flexible;
Thou stern, indurate, flinty, rough, remorseless.
Bid'st thou me rage? Why, now thou hast thy wish.
Would'st have me weep? Why, now thou hast thy will.
For raging wind blows up incessant showers,   145
And when the rage allays, the rain begins.
These tears are my sweet Rutland's obsequies,
And every drop cries vengeance for his death
'Gainst thee, fell Clifford, and thee, false French-woman.
North. Beshrew me, but his passion moves me so   150

---

137. tiger's] *F* (Tygres), *Rowe*, *Q* (Tygers); tygress' *Capell*.   142. indurate] *Q;*
obdurate *F*.   143. Bid'st] *F; Bids Q*.   150. passion] *Edd.;* passions *Q,F.*
moves] *F; moue Q*.

---

130. *admir'd*] wondered at.

132. *government*] becoming conduct; self-discipline; *OED*. 2b.

134–6. *opposite . . . / . . . south . . . Septentrion*] Ovid, *Metam.*, I. ii. 33, 34, 'septemq:triones . . . contraria tellus'. The marginal gloss, with which it seems likely from this passage that Shakespeare was familiar, runs 'Septentrioni *opposita*, quae est plaga *meridionalis*'.

Septentrion] north, from *septentriones*, the seven stars of the Great Bear, or Plough.

137. *O tiger's heart . . .*] Cf. *Rom.*, III. ii. 73, 'O serpent heart, hid with a flowering face!', and *Tit.*, II. iii. 136, 142, 'thou bear'st a woman's face, . . . / When did the tiger's young ones teach the dam?'

This is the famous line parodied by Robert Greene in his dying attack on Shakespeare. See *2 H 6*, Intro., xvi–xvii, and *3 H 6*, Intro., xli–xliii.

142. *indurate*] indúrate—induratus, *Manipulum*, 41; *OED*. 2: 'morally hardened, rendered callous. Often of the heart, referring to the phrase *induratum est cor Pharaonis* in the Vulgate (Exod., vii. 13, 22).' Cf. Hall, 238, 'indurate hartes'. F sophisticates.

rough] cruel; violent.

145–6. *raging wind . . . rain*] proverbial rain after storm; Tilley, R16; cf. *Lucr.*, 1788–90; *Mac.*, I. vii. 25.

146. *allays*] abates.

147. *obsequies*] rites for the dead.

150. *Beshrew me*] May evil befall me; a plague on me; *OED*. 3b.

As hardly can I check my eyes from tears.

York. That face of his the hungry cannibals
Would not have touch'd, would not have stain'd with
blood;
But you are more inhuman, more inexorable—
O, ten times more—than tigers of Hyrcania.   155
See, ruthless queen, a hapless father's tears.
This cloth thou dipp'd'st in blood of my sweet boy,
And I with tears do wash the blood away.
Keep thou the napkin, and go boast of this;
And if thou tell the heavy story right,   160
Upon my soul, the hearers will shed tears;
Yea, even my foes will shed fast-falling tears,
And say 'Alas! it was a piteous deed.'
There, take the crown, and with the crown my curse;
And in thy need such comfort come to thee   165
As now I reap at thy too cruel hand!
Hard-hearted Clifford, take me from the world;
My soul to heaven, my blood upon your heads!

North. Had he been slaughter-man to all my kin
I should not for my life but weep with him,   170
To see how inly sorrow gripes his soul.

Q. Mar. What, weeping-ripe, my lord Northumberland?
Think but upon the wrong he did us all,
And that will quickly dry thy melting tears.

---

151. As] *Q;* That *F.*   157. dipp'd'st] *F* (dipd'st); dipts *Q.*   160. tell] *Q;* tell'st *F.*

151. *As*] F sophisticates to 'That'; cf. Abbott, 109; Intro., xxxiv ff.

152.] Cf. Kyd, *S.P.*, III. i. 72, 'This face of thine shuld harbour no deceit'.

155. *Hyrcania*] the region of the Caspian (Hyrcanum) Sea. The association with tigers appears also in *Mac.*, III. iv. 101, and *Ham.*, II. ii. 444. The allusion is to *Aeneid*, IV. 367, 'Hyrcanaeque admorunt ubera tigres'.

157 ff.] Cf. the account of the same incident in *R 3*, I. ii. 155 ff., and IV. iv. 274 ff.

159. *napkin*] handkerchief.

160. *heavy*] in the L. figurative sense of *gravis* = serious, sad.

164. *my curse*] Hall, 251. One re-

venge breeds another, indefinitely. York's 'chyldren shortly reuenged their fathers querell, both to the Quenes extreme perdicion, and the vtter vndoynge of her husband and sonne'. Cf. Marlowe, *Ed. 2*, 2043, 'Here, take my crowne, the life of Edward too' (Brooke).

169. *slaughter-man*] slayer; killer.

171. *inly*] inward(ly).

gripes] grieves; afflicts.

172. *weeping-ripe*] ready to weep.

174. *thy melting tears*] the tears of thee melting: poss. pron. for gen. of pers. pron. (Abbott, 219).

melting] softened by my gentle or tender passion (Schmidt).

Clif. Here's for my oath, here's for my father's death.　　175
　　　　　　　　　　　　　　　　　　[*Stabbing him.*]
Q. Mar. And here's to right our gentle-hearted king.
　　　　　　　　　　　　　　　　　　[*Stabbing him.*]
York. Open thy gate of mercy, gracious God!
　　My soul flies through these wounds to seek out Thee.
　　　　　　　　　　　　　　　　　　　　　　[*Dies.*]
Q. Mar. Off with his head, and set it on York gates;
　　So York may overlook the town of York.　　　　180
　　　　　　　　　　　　　　　　　Flourish. Exeunt.

175. S.D.] *Pope; not in Q,F.*　　176. S.D.] *Rowe; not in Q,F.*　　178. S.D.] *Rowe; not in Q,F.*　　180. S.D.] *F (. . . Exit.); Exeunt omnes. | Q.*

176. *gentle*] noble—an interesting comment from Margaret, which should be compared with 1. i. 223 ff.

Margaret is not present, according to the chronicles, in this scene; her part in it, and particularly her share in the murder of York, accentuates her progress towards her character and attitude in *R 3*.

[ACT II

SCENE I.—*A Plain near Mortimer's Cross in Herefordshire.*]

A March. Enter EDWARD, RICHARD, *and their power.*

Edw. I wonder how our princely father scap'd,
Or whether he be scap'd away or no
From Clifford's and Northumberland's pursuit.

ACT II

Scene I

ACT II SCENE I] *Rowe; not in Q,F.*
in Q,F.   S.D. *A March] F; not in Q.*
and *Richard,* with drum and Souldiers. *Q.*

A Plain . . . Herefordshire.] *Malone; not*
Enter . . . power.] *F;* Enter *Edward*

This act sees the complete reversal, after the report of a further Yorkist defeat at the second battle of St Albans, of the fortunes of York and Lancaster. It ends with the triumph of York at Towton, and preparations for the succession and marriage of Edward IV.

An alternation of Yorkist and Lancastrian victories in the Chronicles is omitted or heavily telescoped; and all but Towton are reported. The main battles were:

Hall, 250 L+ Wakefield: 1460—reported II. i. 43 ff.
251 Y+ Mortimer's Cross: 2 February 1461—omitted, except for the three suns, II. i. 25.
252 L+ Second St Albans: 17 February 1461—reported, II. i. 95 ff.
255 Y+ Towton: 1461—dramatized, II. ii–vi.

The substantial omission of Mortimer's Cross, and the subsequent report of the *earlier* battle, Wakefield, gives the impression of a run of Lancastrian victories, followed by a permanent turn of the tide in favour of York.

The Act ends with Warwick's announcement of the coronation, and of the project for Edward's marriage, which is to form the theme of Act III.

S.D. *Richard*] actually abroad at this time; see n. to 143 below. In any case he was born in 1452, and therefore only eight years old. But, as in *2 H 6*, he is brought into the main action, no doubt in anticipation of his part in *R 3*.

Edward] was at Gloucester; see Hall, 251.

power] forces; army.

1. *I wonder*] Cf. I. i. 1, and n. The opening indicates the confusion and 'particularity' of the fighting, as in Tolstoi's *War and Peace* and Stendhal's description of Waterloo.

Note the dramatic irony of Edward's and Richard's ignorance of their father's fate.

3. *Clifford's and Northumberland's*] In the sources, these two are mentioned together only at the battle of Towton. Henry's Council 'committed the gouernaunce of the armye to the duke of Somerset, the erle of Northumberland, and yᵉ lord Clifford, as men desiring to reuenge yᵉ death of their

33

Had he been ta'en, we should have heard the news;
Had he been slain, we should have heard the news;   5
Or had he scap'd, methinks we should have heard
The happy tidings of his good escape.
How fares my brother? Why is he so sad?

Rich. I cannot joy until I be resolv'd
Where our right valiant father is become.   10
I saw him in the battle range about,
And watch'd him how he singled Clifford forth.
Methought he bore him in the thickest troop
As doth a lion in a herd of neat;
Or as a bear, encompass'd round with dogs,   15
Who having pinch'd a few and made them cry,
The rest stand all aloof and bark at him.
So far'd our father with his enemies;
So fled his enemies my warlike father:
Methinks 'tis prize enough to be his son.   20
See how the morning opes her golden gates,
And takes her farewell of the glorious sun;
How well resembles it the prime of youth,
Trimm'd like a younker prancing to his love!

Three suns appear in the air.

Edw. Dazzle mine eyes, or do I see three suns?   25

21. See] *F; Edw.* Loe *Q.*   24. S.D.] *Q (after 20); not in F.*

parentes slayn at the first battayle of
sainct Albons' (Hall, 254). Cf. n. to
I. i. 91.

9. *resolv'd*] freed from doubt as to.

10. *Where . . . is become*] Fr. usage,
common in Elizabethan works, *F.Q.*,
I. x. 16; = has betaken himself.

10–40.] For the imagery, see following notes, Intro., lxii, and App. V.

12. *singled*] a hunting term = to
select from the herd an animal to be
hunted; cf. II. iv. 1.

13. *Methought*] It seemed to me.

14 ff. *lion . . . neat . . . bear . . . dogs*]
a continuation of the animal metaphors from *2 H 6.*

14. *neat*] horned cattle.

16. *pinch'd*] bitten; nipped with the
teeth.

20. *prize*] privilege; cf. I. iv. 59.

21 ff. *morning . . . gates . . . sun . . . love*]
Cf. Ps. xix. 4; and *F.Q.*, I. v. 2, 'golden
orientall gate. . . / And Phoebus, fresh
as bridegroome to his mate, / Came
dauncing forth.'

22. *takes her farewell*] 'Aurora takes
for a time her farewell of the sun, when
she dismisses him to his diurnal course'
(Johnson).

23. *the prime of youth*] Cf. 'In prime
of youthly yeares', *F.Q.*, I. ii. 35.

24. *younker*] young man.

25. *Dazzle mine eyes*] Are my eyes
dazed, or dimmed? Hart notes Kyd,
S.P., II. i. 44, 'Dasell mine eyes, or ist
Lucinas chaine?'

three suns] Hall, 251. No doubt they
appeared in 'the heavens'; cf. Cham-

Rich. Three glorious suns, each one a perfect sun;
    Not separated with the racking clouds,
    But sever'd in a pale clear-shining sky.
    See, see! they join, embrace, and seem to kiss,
    As if they vow'd some league inviolable: 30
    Now are they but one lamp, one light, one sun.
    In this the heaven figures some event.
Edw. 'Tis wondrous strange, the like yet never heard of.
    I think it cites us, brother, to the field,
    That we, the sons of brave Plantagenet,   35
    Each one already blazing by our meeds,
    Should notwithstanding join our lights together,
    And over-shine the earth, as this the world.
    Whate'er it bodes, henceforward will I bear
    Upon my target three fair-shining suns.   40
Rich. Nay, bear three daughters: by your leave I speak it,
    You love the breeder better than the male.

Enter a Messenger, blowing.

    But what art thou, whose heavy looks foretell
    Some dreadful story hanging on thy tongue?
Mess. Ah, one that was a woeful looker-on   45
    When as the noble Duke of York was slain,

30. inviolable] *F;* inuiolate *Q, conj. this edn.*   32. heaven figures] *F;* heavens
doth figure *Q.*   40. fair-shining] *Edd.;* faire shining *Q,F.*   42. S.D. *Enter a
Messenger] Q3; Rowe (after 44); not in Q1,2; Enter one | F.*   blowing] *F; not in Q.*

bers, *ES.,* iii. 76; 77 n. Or did they
appear at all? The sun was, of course,
York's emblem.
  27. *racking clouds*] clouds packing,
and scudding like smoke (cf. reek)
(Hart). Cf. *2 Tamb.,* iv. 3 (4000),
'draw *|* My chariot swifter than the
racking cloudes'.
  28. *clear-shining sky*] Cf. Ovid,
Metam., ii. i. 1–2, 'Regia Solis . . . /
clara micante auro', and *F.Q.,* i. v. 21,
'shining cleare'.
  30. *inviolable*] possibly a sophistication of Q 'inuiolate'; cf. *A Shrew (Sh.
Lib.,* ii. 525), 'league . . . inuiolate';
and The Countesse of Pembroke
(1586), Ps. lxxviii, 5, 'They did not
hold inuiolate / The league of God'.

32. *figures*] reveals; discloses; fore-
shows; cf. *R 3,* i. ii. 194; *OED.* 5.
  34. *cites*] calls; summons.
  36. *meeds*] merits; *OED.* 3.
  38. *over-shine*] illumine.
  40. *target*] light shield.
  40–1. *suns . . . daughters*] a common
Shakespearean pun; cf. *LLL.,* v. ii.
170–2. Note the characteristic cyni-
cism of Richard, and the anticipation
of Edward's subsequent conduct.
  42. *You love . . .*] Compare Edward's
courtship of Lady Grey in iii. ii. The
line was perhaps suggested by Hall,
265, 'Edward, which loued well both
to loke and to fele fayre dammosels'.
  breeder] female; child-bearer.
  43. *heavy*] sad; sorrowful.

Your princely father and my loving lord!

Edw. O, speak no more, for I have heard too much.

Rich. Say how he died, for I will hear it all.

Mess. Environed he was with many foes,   50
  And stood against them, as the hope of Troy
  Against the Greeks that would have enter'd Troy.
  But Hercules himself must yield to odds;
  And many strokes, though with a little axe,
  Hews down and fells the hardest-timber'd oak.   55
  By many hands your father was subdu'd;
  But only slaughter'd by the ireful arm
  Of unrelenting Clifford, and the Queen,
  Who crown'd the gracious Duke in high despite,
  Laugh'd in his face; and when with grief he wept, 60
  The ruthless Queen gave him to dry his cheeks
  A napkin steeped in the harmless blood
  Of sweet young Rutland by rough Clifford slain:
  And after many scorns, many foul taunts,
  They took his head, and on the gates of York   65
  They set the same; and there it doth remain,
  The saddest spectacle that e'er I view'd.

Edw. Sweet Duke of York, our prop to lean upon,
  Now thou art gone, we have no staff, no stay.

---

55. Hews ... fells] *F;* Hew ... fell *Pope+Edd.*

48–9.] Hazlitt, *Sh. Lib.*, vi. 30, quotes Johnson, 'the generous tenderness of Edward, and savage fortitude of Richard, are well distinguished by their different reception of their father's death. The one was the natural ebullition of filial affection—the other ... all feeling of affection lost in the reflection that he has risen one step nearer the throne'; cf. 93–4.

50–1. *Environed ... Troy ...*] Cf. IV. viii. 25, 'my Hector, and my Troy's true hope'. From Virgil, *Aeneid*, ii. 281, 'spes O fidissima Teucrum!' (Root).

53. *Hercules ... odds*] Hall, 68, 'Hercules alone was not equiuolent vnto ii men'. Hart quotes the L. proverb in Aulus Gellius, 'Ne Hercules quidem

contra duos'; it became an Elizabethan commonplace; see Tilley, H436.

54–5. *many strokes ... fells the ... oak*] an old proverb, found in Lyly, *Euphues*, i. 225; ii. 108; Whitney's *Emblems* (ed. Greene), 13; Kyd, *Sp. Tr.*, II. i. 5, 'In time small wedges cleaue the hardest Oake'; cf. III. ii. 50 below. Tilley, S941, quotes Erasmus, *Adagia*, 'Multis ictibus deiicitur quercus'.

62. *napkin*] handkerchief.

63. *rough*] cruel; violent; cf. I. iv. 27.

68 ff.] Cf. Marlowe, *Massacre at Paris*, 1122 ff., 'Sweet Duke of Guise, our prop to leane vpon, / Now thou art dead, heere is no stay for vs'; and 87 below, and n.

69. *stay*] support.

O Clifford, boisterous Clifford! thou hast slain   70
The flower of Europe for his chivalry;
And treacherously hast thou vanquish'd him,
For hand to hand he would have vanquish'd thee.
Now my soul's palace is become a prison:
Ah, would she break from hence, that this my body   75
Might in the ground be closed up in rest!
For never henceforth shall I joy again;
Never, O never, shall I see more joy.

Rich. I cannot weep, for all my body's moisture
Scarce serves to quench my furnace-burning heart;   80
Nor can my tongue unload my heart's great burden;
For self-same wind that I should speak withal
Is kindling coals that fires all my breast,
And burns me up with flames that tears would
          quench.
To weep is to make less the depth of grief: 85
Tears then for babes; blows and revenge for me!
Richard, I bear thy name; I'll venge thy death,
Or die renowned by attempting it.

Edw. His name that valiant duke hath left with thee;
His dukedom and his chair with me is left.   90

Rich. Nay, if thou be that princely eagle's bird,
Show thy descent by gazing 'gainst the sun:
For chair and dukedom, throne and kingdom say,
Either that is thine, or else thou wert not his.

---

70. *boisterous*] savage; cf. *F.Q.*, I. viii.
o, 'his boystrous club' (Hart).

71. *flower of . . . chivalry*] Hall, 253,
where it is, however, applied to
Edward. *chivalry*] = prowess in war.

74. *soul's palace . . . prison*] a commonplace; cf. Lyly, *Campaspe*, i. 2, 36, 'the
bodie is the prison of the soule' (Hart).

82. *wind*] breath.

86–7. *revenge . . . bear thy name; I'll
venge . . .*] Marlowe, *Massacre at Paris*,
1124, continues, from 1123, as this does
from 68 ff.: 'I am thy brother, and ile
reuenge thy death.'

90. *dukedom . . . chair*] Edward asserts
his priority—a pointer to the coming
coronation.

90, 93. *chair*] throne.

91. *princely eagle*] The eagle was the
king, or prince (L. *princeps*), of birds.
Possibly a reference to York's badge of
the falcon (Scott-Giles).

bird] the young of any fowl; cf. I. iv.
36 above.

92. *gazing 'gainst the sun*] a very old
fancy, arising no doubt from the eagle's
powerful sight; cf. Pliny (tr. Holland),
xxix. 6, 'that Aegle (which I said here-
tofore, to prove and trie her yong birds,
useth to force them for to look directly
upon the sunne) . . .' (Hart); cf. Kyd,
S.P., III. i. 85–9, 'gase against the glorious Sunne'; and Spenser, *Hymn of
Heavenly Beauty*, stanza 20.

March. Enter WARWICK, MARQUESS MONTAGUE, *and their army.*

War. How now, fair lords! What fare? What news abroad?

Rich. Great Lord of Warwick, if we should recount   96
    Our baleful news, and at each word's deliverance
    Stab poniards in our flesh till all were told,
    The words would add more anguish than the wounds.
    O valiant lord, the Duke of York is slain!   100

Edw. O Warwick, Warwick! that Plantagenet
    Which held thee dearly as his soul's redemption
    Is by the stern Lord Clifford done to death.

War. Ten days ago I drown'd these news in tears,
    And now, to add more measure to your woes,   105
    I come to tell you things sith then befall'n.
    After the bloody fray at Wakefield fought,
    Where your brave father breath'd his latest gasp,
    Tidings, as swiftly as the posts could run,
    Were brought me of your loss and his depart.   110
    I, then in London, keeper of the King,
    Muster'd my soldiers, gather'd flocks of friends,
    And very well appointed, as I thought,
    March'd toward St Albans to intercept the Queen,
    Bearing the King in my behalf along;   115
    For by my scouts I was advertised
    That she was coming with a full intent
    To dash our late decree in Parliament,
    Touching King Henry's oath and your succession.

---

94. S.D. *March*] F; *not in* Q.   S.D.] F (... *Montacute* ...); Enter the Earle o
Warwike, Montague, with drum, ancient, and souldiers. Q.   96. recount] *F*
(recompt).   113.] Q, Steevens; *not in* F.

94. S.D. *Marquess Montague*] This
anticipates the first year of Edward's
reign, when 'lord Ihon Neuell, brother
to Richard Erle of Warwicke, he first
made Lorde Mountacute, and after-
wardes created hym Marques Mountacute' (Hall, 258).

95. *What fare?*] What state of things?
What cheer?

   abroad] about in the world.

97. *deliverance*] delivery; utterance.

97–8. *word's* . . . / *Stab poniards*] Cf.
Ado, II. i. 220, 'she speaks poniards and

every word stabs'. and *Ham.*, III. ii. 414
'I will speak daggers to her'.

104 ff.] This speech seems to be imi
tated in *2 T R.*, vi. 23–53; see App. V

109. *posts*] express messengers.

110. *depart*] verb used as noun; cf
IV. i. 91.

111 ff.] See Hall, 252.

113. *appointed*] equipped.

115. *behalf*] interest; advantage.

116. *advertised*] informed; notified.

118. *dash*] frustrate.

   our late decree] See above, I. i. 200 ff

Short tale to make, we at St Albans met,   120
Our battles join'd, and both sides fiercely fought:
But whether 'twas the coldness of the King,
Who look'd full gently on his warlike Queen,
That robb'd my soldiers of their heated spleen;
Or whether 'twas report of her success;   125
Or more than common fear of Clifford's rigour,
Who thunders to his captives blood and death,
I cannot judge: but, to conclude with truth,
Their weapons like to lightning came and went;
Our soldiers', like the night-owl's lazy flight,   130
Or like an idle thresher with a flail,
Fell gently down, as if they struck their friends.
I cheer'd them up with justice of our cause,
With promise of high pay and great rewards:
But all in vain; they had no heart to fight,   135
And we in them no hope to win the day;
So that we fled: the King unto the Queen;
Lord George your brother, Norfolk and myself,
In haste, post-haste, are come to join with you;
For in the Marches here we heard you were,   140
Making another head to fight again.

Edw. Where is the Duke of Norfolk, gentle Warwick?
And when came George from Burgundy to England?

War. Some six miles off the Duke is with the soldiers;
And for your brother, he was lately sent   145
From your kind aunt, Duchess of Burgundy,

---

131. idle] *Q, Capell + Edd.;* lazie *F.*

121. *battles*] main forces; cf. I. i. 8.
124. *spleen*] fiery temper; impetu-
osity; *OED.* 5.
126. *rigour*] cruelty; relentless sever-
ty (Schmidt).
140. *the Marches*] near Mortimer's
Cross, on the Welsh Marches or bor-
ders, near Shrewsbury, where the
people were favourable (Hall, 251).
141. *Making another head*] gathering
another force.
143. *George from Burgundy*] Hall, 253.
George and Richard were both sent to
Utrecht 'where they were of Philippe
Duke of Bourgoyne, well receyued and

fested, and so there thei remayned,
till their brother Edwarde had obteyned the Realme, and gotten the
regiment'. Shakespeare, as already
noted, brought Richard as an adult
into the action; it is now clear that he
modified the chronicles so as to give
him added prominence. This was no
doubt due to his desire for a foil to
Edward, as well as to preparation for
Richard III.]

146. *aunt*] Isabel, daughter of John I,
King of Portugal, by Philippe of Lan-
caster, eldest daughter of John of
Gaunt. She was therefore third cousin

With aid of soldiers to this needful war.

Rich. 'Twas odds, belike, when valiant Warwick fled:
Oft have I heard his praises in pursuit,
But ne'er till now his scandal of retire.   150

War. Nor now my scandal, Richard, dost thou hear;
For thou shalt know this strong right hand of mine
Can pluck the diadem from faint Henry's head,
And wring the awful sceptre from his fist,
Were he as famous and as bold in war   155
As he is fam'd for mildness, peace, and prayer.

Rich. I know it well, Lord Warwick; blame me not:
'Tis love I bear thy glories makes me speak.
But in this troublous time what's to be done?
Shall we go throw away our coats of steel,   160
And wrap our bodies in black mourning gowns,
Numbering our Ave-Maries with our beads?
Or shall we on the helmets of our foes
Tell our devotion with revengeful arms?
If for the last, say ay, and to it, lords.   165

War. Why, therefore Warwick came to seek you out,
And therefore comes my brother Montague.
Attend me, lords. The proud insulting Queen,
With Clifford and the haught Northumberland,
And of their feather many moe proud birds,   170

---

158. makes] *Edd.*; make *F.*

---

to Edward, not aunt. 'The dramatist
may have been thinking of Edward
IV's sister, Margaret Duchess of Burgundy, who assisted the adventurer
known as Perkin Warbeck, for the real
or ostensible reason that he was her
nephew, Richard Duke of York' (Boswell-Stone, 303). See also Hall, 473–4.

148. *odds*] inequality.

150. *scandal*] disgraceful imputation.
retire] retreat.

153. *can pluck the diadem*] Warwick is
the 'King-maker'.
faint] faint-hearted.

153–6, 162.] For Henry's character,
see Hall, 249, and *2 H 6*, I. iii. 53 ff.,
'But all his mind is bent to holiness, /
To number Ave-Maries on his beads'.

154. *awful*] awe-inspiring.

158. *makes*] may well have been
attracted into the plural by 'glories'.

159. *troublous time*] Hall describes
this reign as 'The troublous season of
Kyng Henry the VI'.

161. *mourning gowns*] Cf. the 'mourning cloaks' of *2 H 6*, II. iv. 1. S.D.

162. *Ave-Maries*] prayers, beginning
'Ave Maria' (Hail, Mary).

164. *Tell*] count, but with sword
strokes instead of beads.

166. *therefore*] for that reason.

168. *Attend*] listen to; *OED.* 1.
insulting] exulting proudly or contemptuously; *OED.* 1.

170. *moe*] old form of 'more'.

170–1. *proud birds . . . wax*] Cf. v. vi

Have wrought the easy-melting King like wax.
He sware consent to your succession,
His oath enrolled in the Parliament;
And now to London all the crew are gone,
To frustrate both his oath and what beside   175
May make against the house of Lancaster.
Their power, I think, is thirty thousand strong:
Now, if the help of Norfolk and myself,
With all the friends that thou, brave Earl of March,
Amongst the loving Welshmen canst procure,   180
Will but amount to five-and-twenty thousand,
Why, Via! to London will we march amain,
And once again bestride our foaming steeds,
And once again cry 'Charge upon our foes!'
But never once again turn back and fly.   185

Rich. Ay, now methinks I hear great Warwick speak.
Ne'er may he live to see a sunshine day,
That cries 'Retire', if Warwick bid him stay.

Edw. Lord Warwick, on thy shoulder will I lean;
And when thou fall'st—as God forbid the hour!—   190

172. sware] *Q;* swore *F.*   182. amain] *Q, Theobald + Edd.; not in F.*   190.
fall'st] *Steevens;* fail'st *F;* faints *Q.*

; 'in the background of the poet's
thought is Icarus who attached wings
to his back with wax and for whom
pride came before a fall' (Armstrong,
7).

172. *sware*] F 'swore' is most probably a sophistication, as at III. i. 82;
cf. *H 5*, v. i. 83, and *Troil.*, II. iii. 235
(gat/got); *R 3*, II. i. 108 (spake/spoke);
it., I. i. 6 (ware/wore); etc.

173. *enrolled*] written, or recorded,
in a roll of parchment, i.e. as official
and binding.

175. *frustrate*] annul.
what beside] Cf. 'what else', III. i. 51
= anything else.

177. *power*] regular Elizabethan
term for 'army'.

177, 181. *thirty . . . five-and-twenty*]
The Q figures are closer to Hall's
30,000 and 48,650. The F figure of
20,000, however, is repeated at II. ii.

68. Q ('Their power I gesse them fifty
thousand strong') may have been influenced by Kyd, *S.P.*, III. i. 48, 'Their
horse, I deeme them fiftie thousand
strong.'

179. *Earl of March*] Edward, 'the
erle of Marche, so commonly called,
but after the death of his father, in dede
and in right very duke of Yorke' (Hall,
251). Cf. 192 below.

182. *Via!*] Forward! Away!
amain] at full speed.

185. *turn back*] turn our backs; see
I. iv. 4 and n.

186. *methinks*] it seems to me.

187. *a sunshine day*] Cf. Spenser, *Sh.
Cal.*, January, 3; *R 2*, IV. i. 221; Kyd,
S.P., I. iv. 136.

190. *fall'st*] corresponds to 'fall',
191; an i/l misprint, or imperfect correction of Q 'faints'; cf. *1 H 6*, II. i. 31;
and *2 H 6*, IV. ii. 33, for the same error.

Must Edward fall, which peril heaven forfend!
War. No longer Earl of March, but Duke of York:
    The next degree is England's royal throne;
    For King of England shalt thou be proclaim'd
    In every borough as we pass along;   19
    And he that throws not up his cap for joy
    Shall for the fault make forfeit of his head.
    King Edward, valiant Richard, Montague,
    Stay we no longer, dreaming of renown,
    But sound the trumpets, and about our task.   20
Rich. Then, Clifford, were thy heart as hard as steel,
    As thou hast shown it flinty by thy deeds,
    I come to pierce it, or to give thee mine.
Edw. Then strike up, drums! God and Saint George for us!

Enter a Messenger.

War. How now! what news?   20
Mess. The Duke of Norfolk sends you word by me,
    The Queen is coming with a puissant host;
    And craves your company for speedy counsel.
War. Why then it sorts; brave warriors, let's away.   *Exeun.*

---

204. S.D.] *Q,F.*   209. S.D. *Exeunt.*] *Edd.; Exeunt Omnes.* / *Q1,2,F; Exeu omnes* / *Q3.*

193. *degree*] step; rung of a ladder—the obsolete L. sense; *OED.* 1.

194. *proclaim'd*] Hall, 254, side-note, 'Kyng Edward the iiii proclaimed king of Englande'.

196. *throws . . . cap for joy*] Hall, 372, describing the proclamation of Richard III, 'one Nashfeelde and other belongynge to the protectoure with some prentices and laddes . . . began sodainly . . . to crye out as lowde as they could, kynge Richard, king Richar and there *threwe vp their cappes* in toke of *ioye*'. Cf. *R 3,* III. vii. 34–5, 'Son followers of mine own / At the low end of the hall hurl'd up their caps'.

197. *fault*] default; neglect; *OED.*

207. *The Queen is coming*] The pr posal to 'march amain' to London cancelled by this news; Hall, 253.

puissant] powerful (Fr.).

209. *it sorts*] it is fitting; *OED.* 18

[SCENE II.—*Before York.*]

Flourish. Enter KING HENRY, QUEEN MARGARET, *the* PRINCE
OF WALES, CLIFFORD, *and* NORTHUMBERLAND, *with drum and
trumpets.*

Q. Mar. Welcome, my lord, to this brave town of York.
    Yonder's the head of that arch-enemy
    That sought to be encompass'd with your crown:
    Doth not the object cheer your heart, my lord?
K. Hen. Ay, as the rocks cheer them that fear their wrack: 5
    To see this sight, it irks my very soul.
    Withhold revenge, dear God! 'tis not my fault,
    Nor wittingly have I infring'd my vow.
Clif. My gracious liege, this too much lenity
    And harmful pity must be laid aside.   10
    To whom do lions cast their gentle looks?
    Not to the beast that would usurp their den.
    Whose hand is that the forest bear doth lick?
    Not his that spoils her young before her face.
    Who scapes the lurking serpent's mortal sting?   15

Scene II

SCENE II] *Capell; not in* F.   S.D. *Flourish*] F; *not in* Q.   *Enter* . . . *Northumber-
and,*] Edd.; *Enter the King, the Queene, Clifford, Northum-* | *and Yong Prince,* | F;
Enter the King *and* Queene, Prince *Edward, and the Northerne Earles,* Q.
trumpets] F; *Souldiers* Q.   2. *Yonder's*] F3; *Yonders* Q,F1,2.   5. *wrack*]
Q,F; *wreck Theobald + most edd.*

The source is Hall, 252. Note that
the King reappears with the dissatisfied lords (I. i. 180 ff.), the Queen, and
the Prince.

    2. *the head*] scil. of York, ordered to
be set on York gates, I. iv. 179–80.

    4. *object*] anything presented to the
eye; sight.

    7. *Withhold revenge*] Henry is the only
opponent of the revenge principle in
the play, which is a kind of inclusive
revenge tragedy—father for son (Clif-
ord), as in *The Spanish Tragedy*; and
son for father (Richard, II. i. 86, 164),
as in *Hamlet*.

    8. *my vow*] See I. i. 197–8; and cf. 81,

89, and II. i. 175; Hall, 253, 'contrary
to his othe'.

    9. *lenity*] Clifford's reproach of
Henry's 'harmful pity', I. i. 62—a vice
in kings.

    13. *forest*] untamed; wild.

    13–14.] The fierceness of the wild
bear was proverbial; cf. Hos., xiii. 8,
'I will meete them as a beare that is
robbed of her whelpes, . . . and I will
devoure them' (Carter).

    14. *spoils*] carries off as prey.

    15. *lurking serpent's mortal sting*] Cf.
Lucr., 362–4, 'Who sees the lurking
serpent steps aside; / But she . . . / Lies
at the mercy of his mortal sting.'

Not he that sets his foot upon her back.
The smallest worm will turn being trodden on,
And doves will peck in safeguard of their brood.
Ambitious York did level at thy crown,
Thou smiling while he knit his angry brows: 20
He, but a duke, would have his son a king,
And raise his issue like a loving sire;
Thou, being a king, bless'd with a goodly son,
Didst yield consent to disinherit him,
Which argued thee a most unloving father.   25
Unreasonable creatures feed their young;
And though man's face be fearful to their eyes,
Yet, in protection of their tender ones,
Who hath not seen them, even with those wings
Which sometime they have us'd with fearful flight,   30
Make war with him that climb'd unto their nest,
Offering their own lives in their young's defence?
For shame, my liege, make them your precedent!
Were it not pity that this goodly boy
Should lose his birthright by his father's fault,   35
And long hereafter say unto his child,
'What my great-grandfather and grandsire got
My careless father fondly gave away'?
Ah, what a shame were this! Look on the boy;
And let his manly face, which promiseth   40
Successful fortune, steel thy melting heart
To hold thine own and leave thine own with him.

K. Hen. Full well hath Clifford play'd the orator,
      Inferring arguments of mighty force.
      But, Clifford, tell me, didst thou never hear   4

17–18, 26 ff.] probably suggested by
Warwick's speech (Hall, 270), 'What
worme is touched, and will not once
turne againe? What beast is striken
that will not rore or sound? What innocent child is hurte that will not crye?
If the poore vnreasonable beastes: If
the sely babes . . .'
      19. *level*] aim; cf. *2 H 6*, III. i. 160.
      26. *Unreasonable*] lacking the faculty
of reason. For the source see n. to 17–
18.

27. *fearful*] full of fear; causing fea[r]
      28. *tender*] (a) young, (b) preciou[s]
dear.
      30. *sometime*] sometimes, or at oth[er]
times.
      35. *birthright*] a recollection of Esau
      38. *fondly*] in the Elizabethan sen[se]
= foolishly.
      41. *melting*] softened by gentle [or]
tender passion (Schmidt).
      44. *Inferring*] alleging; adducing; i[n]
the L. sense = bringing in.

That things evil got had ever bad success?
And happy always was it for that son
Whose father for his hoarding went to hell?
I'll leave my son my virtuous deeds behind;
And would my father had left me no more!　　　50
For all the rest is held at such a rate
As brings a thousand-fold more care to keep
Than in possession any jot of pleasure.
Ah, cousin York, would thy best friends did know
How it doth grieve me that thy head stands here!　　　55

Q. Mar.　My lord, cheer up your spirits; our foes are nigh,
And this soft courage makes your followers faint.
You promis'd knighthood to our forward son:
Unsheathe your sword, and dub him presently.
Edward, kneel down.　　　60

K. Hen.　Edward Plantagenet, arise a knight;
And learn this lesson: Draw thy sword in right.

Prince.　My gracious father, by your kingly leave,
I'll draw it as apparent to the crown,
And in that quarrel use it to the death.　　　65

Clif.　Why, that is spoken like a toward prince.

Enter a Messenger.

Mess.　Royal commanders, be in readiness;

46. evil] *Q1,2;* ill *Q3,F.*　53.] *F;* Then maie the present profit counteruaile. *Q.*
55. stands] *Q;* is *F.*　66. S.D.] *Q,F.*

46. *things evil got*] from Hall, 377
(reign of Richard III), 'as the thynge
iuill gotten is neuer well kept'; cf.
Tilley, G301, 305.
　success] result; outcome—without
reference to its desirability.
　47–8.] proverbial, e.g. 'Happy is the
chylde whose father goeth to the
Deuyll', Latimer, *Seven Sermons* (Arber,
47); Tilley, C305; 'happy' = fortunate.
　51. *at such a rate*] at such expense.
There is a suggestion of interest to be
paid at a high rate—'a thousand-fold'.
　55. *stands*] a typical F sophistication;
cf. *R 2,* III. iii. 191; *R 3,* III. i. 196;
H 6, v. iv. 80.

57. *soft courage*] soft-heartedness (L.
cor = heart). Hudson compares *F.Q.,*
II. v. 5, on the 'coward courage' of a
'Disleall Knight'.
　58. *forward*] promising; precocious.
　59. *dub him*] 'Between the kneeling
and the rising, the king bestowed the
knighthood by the accolade, or tap
of the naked sword on the shoulder,
which we call dubbing' (Rothery).
See Hall, 252.
　presently] immediately—the normal
Elizabethan sense.
　62. *right*] justice.
　64. *apparent*] i.e. heir apparent.
　66. *toward*] bold; promising.
　67–9.] Hall, 252–3.

For with a band of thirty thousand men
Comes Warwick, backing of the Duke of York;
And in the towns, as they do march along,   70
Proclaims him king, and many fly to him.
Darraign your battle, for they are at hand.

Clif. I would your highness would depart the field:
The Queen hath best success when you are absent.

Q. Mar. Ay, good my lord, and leave us to our fortune.   75

K. Hen. Why, that's my fortune too: therefore I'll stay.

North. Be it with resolution then to fight.

Prince. My royal father, cheer these noble lords,
And hearten those that fight in your defence.   79
Unsheathe your sword, good father: cry, 'Saint George'.

March. Enter EDWARD, GEORGE, RICHARD, WARWICK,
NORFOLK, MONTAGUE, *and Soldiers.*

Edw. Now, perjur'd Henry, wilt thou kneel for grace,
And set thy diadem upon my head;
Or bide the mortal fortune of the field?

Q. Mar. Go rate thy minions, proud insulting boy!
Becomes it thee to be thus bold in terms   85
Before thy sovereign and thy lawful king?

Edw. I am his king, and he should bow his knee:
I was adopted heir by his consent:
Since when his oath is broke; for, as I hear,
You that are king, though he do wear the crown,   90
Have caus'd him by new Act of Parliament
To blot out me, and put his own son in.

---

72. are] *F;* be *Q.*   80. S.D. *March.*] *F; not in* Q.   Enter ... Soldiers.] *F (subst.);*
Enter the house of *Yorke. |* Q.   89. Since] *F2; George.* Since *Q; Cla.* Since *F1.*

71. *Proclaims*] Cf. II. i. 194 ff.
Darraign] set in order; prepare. Hereford and Norfolk (in the reign of Richard II) 'were ready to darraine the batteill' (Hall, 4). Cf. *F.Q.,* I. iv. 40; I. vii. 11.
74. *success*] result; cf. 46.
80. S.D.] It may be significant that Montague is mute in this scene, as in II. i. His speeches may have been allocated to some other character, as Falconbridge's were to him; cf. n. to I. i. 14.

81. *perjur'd Henry*] having broken his oath regarding the succession; cf. 89 below.
83. *mortal*] involving death.
84. *minions*] a man's—especially a king's or a prince's—male favourites; not necessarily homosexuals (*Sh. Bawdy*).
89.] F has been affected by Q copy, in the retention of *Cla.* (Q *George.*).
91. *new Act*] Cf. I. i. 256–7; II. i. 117–19, 172–6; and Hall, 234, 249.

Clif. And reason too:

    Who should succeed the father but the son?

Rich. Are you there, butcher? O, I cannot speak!   95

Clif. Ay, Crook-back, here I stand to answer thee,

    Or any he, the proudest of thy sort.

Rich. 'Twas you that kill'd young Rutland, was it not?

Clif. Ay, and old York, and yet not satisfied.

Rich. For God's sake, lords, give signal to the fight.   100

War. What say'st thou, Henry, wilt thou yield the crown?

Q. Mar. Why, how now, long-tongu'd Warwick! dare you speak?

    When you and I met at St Albans last,

    Your legs did better service than your hands.

War. Then 'twas my turn to flee, and now 'tis thine.   105

Clif. You said so much before, and yet you fled.

War. 'Twas not your valour, Clifford, drove me thence.

North. No, nor your manhood that durst make you stay.

Rich. Northumberland, I hold thee reverently.

    Break off the parley; for scarce I can refrain   110

    The execution of my big-swoln heart

    Upon that Clifford, that cruel child-killer.

Clif. I slew thy father: call'st thou him a child?

Rich. Ay, like a dastard and a treacherous coward,

    As thou didst kill our tender brother Rutland;   115

---

105. flee] *Q1,2;* fly(e) *Q3,F.*   110. parley] *Q,F* (parlie)*; parle Reed (1803).* for scarce] *Q,F;* scarce *Hanmer.*   112. that cruel] *F;* there, that cruel *Q;* cruel, *conj. this edn.*

95. *butcher*] referring to his murder of Rutland and York; cf. 112. The term is ironical coming from Richard; cf. v. v. 75.

97. *sort*] set.

103. *St Albans*] the second battle, reported at II. i. 111 ff.

104. *legs . . . hands*] alluding 'to the old proverb that one pair (of legs) is worth two pairs of hands' (Grey, *Notes in Shakespeare*, ii. 40).

105. *flee*] F took 'fly' from the Q3 copy.

110. *refrain*] used transitively = give up (something); *OED.* I. 5, or, more probably, restrain (L. refreno), *OED.* I.

111. *execution*] giving practical effect to (a passion); *OED.* I. b.

112.] F 'that' may be due to imperfect correction of Q; deletion of Q 'there' should perhaps have been extended to 'that'. Note (a) the gutturals in the line; (b) the irony of the sentiment, coming from Richard; cf. 95.

cruel child-killer] Hall, 385, 'bloud supper and child kyller'; *Mirror*, 189 (l. 136), 'That cruell Clifford'.

113. *I slew thy father*] Clifford's fixed idea again—the refrain of the first half of the play.

115. *tender*] see 28 above.

But ere sun set I'll make thee curse the deed.

K. Hen. Have done with words, my lords, and hear me speak.

Q. Mar. Defy them then, or else hold close thy lips.

K. Hen. I prithee give no limits to my tongue:

  I am a king, and privileg'd to speak.   120

Clif. My liege, the wound that bred this meeting here

  Cannot be cur'd by words; therefore be still.

Rich. Then, executioner, unsheathe thy sword.

  By Him that made us all, I am resolv'd

  That Clifford's manhood lies upon his tongue. 125

Edw. Say, Henry, shall I have my right or no?

  A thousand men have broke their fasts to-day

  That ne'er shall dine unless thou yield the crown.

War. If thou deny, their blood upon thy head;

  For York in justice puts his armour on.   130

Prince. If that be right which Warwick says is right,

  There is no wrong, but every thing is right.

Rich. Whoever got thee, there thy mother stands;

  For well I wot thou hast thy mother's tongue.

Q. Mar. But thou art neither like thy sire nor dam, 135

  But like a foul misshapen stigmatic,

  Mark'd by the Destinies to be avoided,

  As venom toads, or lizards' dreadful stings.

---

116. sun set] *Q;* Sunset *F.* 133. *Rich.*] *Q, Pope+Edd.; War. | F.*

116.] Cf. II. iv; II. vi. 40.

117, 119.] Henry asks twice to be heard: it is typical of the slight respect in which he is universally held that he is allowed to say no more throughout the scene.

122. *still*] silent.

124. *By Him . . .*] Cf. *Sp. Tr.,* II. ii. 89, 'I sweare to both, by Him that made us all'. The Devil again cites Scripture for his purpose.

resolv'd] satisfied; convinced; cf. *1 H 6,* III. iv. 20; *OED.* 24a.

128. *ne'er shall dine*] Cf. *R 3,* III. iv. 79, where the phrase is used in its proper context, from Hall, 360 (the arrest of Hastings), 'I wyll not dyne tyll I se thy head of'.

129. *deny*] refuse.

133. *Whoever got thee*] a reflection of the doubts as to Prince Edward's parentage, and the Queen's affair with Suffolk. Edward's 'mother susteyned not a little slaunder and obloguye of the common people, saying that the kyng was not able to get a chyld, and that this was not his sonne, with many slaunderous woordes, to the quenes dishonor', Hall, 230 ('got' = begot). The implication is continued in 146–8.

136. *foul . . . stigmatic*] The words have already been applied to Richard in *2 H 6,* v. i. 215, referring, of course, to his being 'stamped' with a hunch-back (Gk. *stigma* = a brand).

137. *Mark'd*] branded.

138. *venom*] noun as adjective; cf. *R 3,* I. iii. 291; *Lucr.,* 850.

Rich. Iron of Naples, hid with English gilt,
        Whose father bears the title of a king   140
        As if a channel should be call'd the sea—
        Sham'st thou not, knowing whence thou art
              extraught,
        To let thy tongue detect thy base-born heart?

Edw. A wisp of straw were worth a thousand crowns
        To make this shameless callet know herself.   145
        Helen of Greece was fairer far than thou,
        Although thy husband may be Menelaus;
        And ne'er was Agamemnon's brother wrong'd
        By that false woman as this king by thee.
        His father revell'd in the heart of France,   150
        And tam'd the King, and made the Dauphin stoop;
        And had he match'd according to his state,
        He might have kept that glory to this day;
        But when he took a beggar to his bed
        And grac'd thy poor sire with his bridal day,   155
        Even then that sunshine brew'd a shower for him
        That wash'd his father's fortunes forth of France
        And heap'd sedition on his crown at home.
        For what hath broach'd this tumult but thy pride?

---

142. Sham'st] *Q2,3,F;* Shames *Q1.*   152. to] *F;* till *Q.*

lizards' . . . stings] Cf. *2 H 6*, III. ii.
325. Both the venom and the stings
were popular beliefs, quite unfounded.

139. *gilt*] a pun?

141. *channel*] or kennel = gutter;
drain; cf. *2 H 6*, IV. i. 71.

142. *extraught*] extracted; derived.
The phrase seems to be imitated in
T.R., i. 351, 404.

143. *detect*] expose; betray.

144. *A wisp of straw*] a twist or figure
of straw for a scold to rail at; *OED.*
2b.

145. *callet*] scold; strumpet; cf. *2 H 6*,
II. iii. 81.

147. *Menelaus*] Thersites calls Menelaus 'the goodly transformation of
Jupiter there, his brother, the bull,—
the primitive state and oblique memorial of cuckolds' (*Troil.*, v. i. 51).
He was the brother of Agamemnon,

and the husband of Helen, whose rape
by Paris was the cause of the Trojan
war. Cf. 146–8.

150. *His father*] i.e. Henry's father,
Henry V. The passage 'reads like a
memory of *H 5*, I. ii. 252–66' (Wilson).

revell'd] made merry; acted at his
pleasure.

152. *state*] condition; social standing; Fr. *état.*

154–5. *beggar . . . / . . . poor sire*] Cf.
I. iv. 121–7; v. vii. 38–40; *2 H 6*, I. i.
106–7.

155. *grac'd . . . day*] made a present
to your father of the expenses of the
wedding—a gibe at the conditions of
the marriage, namely, that Margaret
'be sent over of the King of England's
own proper cost and charges, without
any dowry', *2 H 6*, I. i. 57–8.

Hadst thou been meek, our title still had slept;   160

And we, in pity of the gentle King,

Had slipp'd our claim until another age.

Geo. But when we saw our sunshine made thy spring,

And that thy summer bred us no increase,

We set the axe to thy usurping root;   165

And though the edge have something hit ourselves,

Yet know thou, since we have begun to strike,

We'll never leave till we have hewn thee down,

Or bath'd thy growing with our heated bloods.

Edw. And in this resolution I defy thee;   170

Not willing any longer conference,

Since thou deniest the gentle King to speak.

Sound trumpets! let our bloody colours wave!

And either victory, or else a grave.

Q. Mar. Stay, Edward.   175

Edw. No wrangling woman, we'll no longer stay:

These words will cost ten thousand lives this day. *Exeunt.*

---

166. have] *Q*; hath *F.*   172. deniest] *Q, Warburton+Edd.*; denied'st *F.*   175

Edward] *Edward, staie. Q, conj. this edn.*   177. S.D.] *Edd.; Exeunt Omnes.* | *Q1,2;*

Exeunt omnes. | *Q3,F.*

160–2.] an important admission of Margaret's responsibility for the civil wars.

160. *still*] Eliz. sense = always.

our title . . . had slept] York's title or claim (to the crown) would have remained dormant. The phrase appears in the 1563 edition of *The Mirror for Magistrates*, 398–9, 'Some haply here wyl move a farder doubt, / And for Yorkes parte allege an elder right, / O braynles heades that so run in and out. / Whan length of time a state hath firmely pyght: / And good accorde hath put all stryfe to flyght, / Were it not better such *titles should slepe*, / Than all a realme for theyr tryall to wepe?' In the 1571–87 editions, the phrase was altered to 'tytles still to slepe' (H. F. B.).

162. *slipp'd*] passed over; left unasserted.

164. *increase*] crop; produce.

165. *the axe . . . root*] Cf. Luke, iii. 9, 'Now also is the axe laid unto the root of the tree'; and the barren fig-tree a xiii. 6, 7: 'He came and sought fruite thereon and found none. Then sayde He . . . cut it downe; why keepeth i also the grounde barren' (Carter) This is another metaphor from the geneaological tree.

usurping] a reference to the origina usurpation of Henry IV.

166. *have*] subjunctive, sophisticatec in F to the indicative.

something] somewhat.

171. *conference*] the commonest Elizabethan sense—conversation; discussion; *OED.* 4.

172. *deniest*] forbiddest.

177. *words*] i.e. high words; recriminations.

[SCENE III.—*A field of battle between Towton and Saxton,
in Yorkshire.*]

Alarum. Excursions. Enter WARWICK.

War. Forspent with toil, as runners with a race,
       I lay me down a little while to breathe;
       For strokes receiv'd, and many blows repaid,
       Have robb'd my strong-knit sinews of their strength,
       And spite of spite needs must I rest awhile.   5

Enter EDWARD, *running.*

Edw. Smile, gentle heaven, or strike, ungentle death;
       For this world frowns, and Edward's sun is clouded.
War. How now, my lord! What hap? What hope of good?

Enter GEORGE.

Geo. Our hap is loss, our hope but sad despair,
       Our ranks are broke, and ruin follows us.   10
       What counsel give you? Whither shall we fly?
Edw. Bootless is flight, they follow us with wings;
       And weak we are, and cannot shun pursuit.

Enter RICHARD.

Rich. Ah, Warwick, why hast thou withdrawn thyself?
        Thy brother's blood the thirsty earth hath drunk,   15

Scene III

SCENE III] *Capell; not in* F.   *A field ... Yorkshire.*] *Malone; not in* F.   *Alarum.*]
F; *Alarmes.* / Q.   *Excursions.*] F; *not in* Q.   *Enter Warwick*] Q,F.   1. For-
pent] F (Fore-spent); Sore spent Q.   5. S.D. *Enter Edward*] Q,F.   *running*]
F; Q, *at* 13. S.D.   8. S.D.] Q,F.   13. S.D.] F; Enter *Richard* running Q.
15-22.] F; *for* Q, *see App.* 4.

Source: Hall, 254–6. Lancaster
scores an initial success, which is later
reversed by Warwick's resolution after
the death of Salisbury, for whose iden-
tity see n. to 15.

   1. *Forspent*] exhausted. 'For' is intensive.
   2. *breathe*] rest.
   5. *spite of spite*] come what may; no
matter what worse may happen.

   6. *ungentle*] ignoble.
   7. *sun*] Edward's badge; cf. II. i. 25.
   8. *hap ... hope*] the pun has already
occurred at I. i. 19–20.
   12. *Bootless*] useless.
   15.] Cf. Gen., iv. 10, 'The voyce of
thy brother's blood cryeth unto me
from the earth' (Carter).
      brother] See Intro., xxii. The Q ver-
sion, which reads 'father', must be

Broach'd with the steely point of Clifford's lance;
And in the very pangs of death he cried,
Like to a dismal clangor heard from far,
'Warwick, revenge! Brother, revenge my death!'
So, underneath the belly of their steeds,   20
That stain'd their fetlocks in his smoking blood,
The noble gentleman gave up the ghost.

War. Then let the earth be drunken with our blood;
I'll kill my horse because I will not fly.
Why stand we like soft-hearted women here,   25
Wailing our losses, whiles the foe doth rage;
And look upon, as if the tragedy
Were play'd in jest by counterfeiting actors?
Here on my knee I vow to God above
I'll never pause again, never stand still,   30
Till either death hath clos'd these eyes of mine,
Or fortune given me measure of revenge.

Edw. O Warwick, I do bend my knee with thine;
And in this vow do chain my soul to thine!
And ere my knee rise from the earth's cold face,   35
I throw my hands, mine eyes, my heart to Thee,
Thou setter up and plucker down of kings,
Beseeching Thee, if with Thy will it stands,
That to my foes this body must be prey,

original, since it confuses old Salisbury with his son, Warwick's brother. The mistake could easily have arisen through the ambiguity of Hall's phrase, 'the Bastard *of* Salisbury'. After the possible elimination of Salisbury from the cast (see n. to I. i. 245, and headnote to I. ii), this passage, essential to explain Warwick's fury and success in the battle, must have been revised and the error put right in the process.

The 'brother' is wrongly identified by French, 207, and Dover Wilson (n. to II. iii. 15) with Sir Thomas Neville, who was indeed a brother of Warwick, but was killed at Wakefield (Hall, 250); the Bastard Salisbury was killed at Towton (Hall, 253).

18. *dismal*] ill-boding; sinister.

19. *revenge*] still another relative t· be avenged!

23. *the earth ... blood*] Cf. Judith, vi. (Geneva version), 'the mountains shal be drunken with their blood' (Noble)

25. *stand*] delay.

26. *Wailing our losses*] Cf. v. iv. 1.

27. *look upon*] look on; cf. e.g. *R 2 Q*, IV. i. 237.

36. *I throw ... my heart*] Cf. Ps. xxv. 1 'I lift my heart to thee' (*SH*).

37.] Apparently addressed to th· Deity, whereas at III. iii. 157 it is ap plied, with one slight modification, t· Warwick, the 'King-maker'.

For the origin of the line, cf. Dan. ii. 21, 'he taketh away kings, hee se· teth up kings'; Ps. lxxv. 7, 'he puttet· down one, and setteth up another'.

38. *stands*] agrees.

Yet that Thy brazen gates of heaven may ope,   40
And give sweet passage to my sinful soul!
Now, lords, take leave until we meet again,
Where'er it be, in heaven or in earth.

Rich. Brother, give me thy hand; and, gentle Warwick,
Let me embrace thee in my weary arms: 45
I, that did never weep, now melt with woe
That winter should cut off our spring-time so.

War. Away, away! Once more, sweet lords, farewell.

Geo. Yet let us all together to our troops,
And give them leave to fly that will not stay,   50
And call them pillars that will stand to us;
And if we thrive, promise them such rewards
As victors wear at the Olympian games.
This may plant courage in their quailing breasts;
For yet is hope of life and victory.   55
Forslow no longer; make we hence amain.   *Exeunt.*

[SCENE IV.—*Another part of the field.*]

Excursions. Enter RICHARD *and* CLIFFORD.

Rich. Now, Clifford, I have singled thee alone.

49. all together] *Rowe;* altogether *F.*   56. Forslow] *F* (Foreslow).   56. S.D.]
F; Exeunt Omnes. | Q.

Scene IV

SCENE IV] *Capell; not in Q,F.   Another . . . field.*] *Steevens; not in Q,F.   S.D.*
Excursions . . . Clifford.] *F;* Alarmes, and then enter *Richard* at one dore and *Clifford*
at the other. *Q.*   1. *Rich.* Now] *F; Rich.* A *Clifford* a *Clifford. | Clif.* A *Richard*
a *Richard. | Q.*

40. *brazen*] imperishable; everlasting; difficult of entry or exit (Hart).
Cf. Horace, *Odes,* III. xxx. 1, 'monu-
mentum aere perennius'; and Ps.
xxiv. 7, 'ye gates . . . ye everlasting
doors'.

brazen gates] Cf. *F.Q.,* I. xii. 3; Kyd,
Sp. Tr., III. vii. 9; Peele, *Ed. 1,* I. i. 1;
T.R., ii. 91.

42–3.] Cf. *R 3,* III. iii. 24–5.

46. *that did never weep*] a point to be
noted in the building up of Richard's
character.

50–2.] Hall, 255.

51. *stand to*] support.

53. *Olympian*] 'vaguely classical'
(J. A. K. Thomson, *Sh. and the Classics*).

56. *Forslow*] delay; cf. 1 above.

Scene IV

The scene is created out of the suggestion in Hall, 255 (App. I), of Warwick's fury against Clifford at the
death of his Bastard brother Salisbury,
described in Scene ii above.

1, 12. *singled*] 'When he (the hart)

Suppose this arm is for the Duke of York,
And this for Rutland; both bound to revenge,
Wert thou environ'd with a brazen wall.

Clif. Now, Richard, I am with thee here alone.   5
This is the hand that stabb'd thy father York,
And this the hand that slew thy brother Rutland;
And here's the heart that triumphs in their death
And cheers these hands, that slew thy sire and brother,
To execute the like upon thyself;   10
And so, have at thee!

They fight. WARWICK *comes.* CLIFFORD *flies.*

Rich. Nay, Warwick, single out some other chase;
For I myself will hunt this wolf to death.   *Exeunt*

[SCENE V.—*Another part of the field.*]

Alarum. Enter KING HENRY *alone.*

K. Hen. This battle fares like to the morning's war,

11, 13. S.DD.] *F;* Alarmes. They fight, and then enters *Warwike* and rescue
Richard, & then *exeunt omnes.* | *Q.*

Scene v

SCENE V] *Capell; not in Q,F.*   Another . . . field.] *Steevens; not in Q,F.*   S.D
Alarum . . . alone.] *F;* Alarme still, and then enter *Henry solus.* | *Q.*

is hunted and doth first leave the
hearde, we say he is syngled' (Turber-
vile); Madden, 32; *OED.* v.[1] 2.

3. *bound to revenge*] The revenge
theme goes on accumulating. Cf.
Ham., I, v. 6–7.

4. *brazen*] impenetrable; cf. II. iii.
40 and n.

8. *triumphs*] exults.

11. *have at thee*] I attack you.

12. *chase*] quarry; that which is
hunted.

Scene v

Henry stands aloof from, and provides a point of contrast with, the
general atmosphere of blood, chaos,
and revenge. He has protested before,
mildly and ineffectually. It is here tha
Hall, 256, refers to this *unnatural* con
flict, and emphasizes the disruption o
all normal relations (App. I).

Henry had been hunted by Edward
but reached the safety of Berwic
(128).

Hart calls this 'a stop-gap' scene. I
is in fact a scene that might have com
straight from the Morality plays, wit
types as characters; and its moralizin
makes it almost a Chorus in which (u
to 124) the characters comment on th
action and theme of the play.

It may be part of the comment tha
Henry sits down, ironically enough, o
the same (stage) mole-hill on whic
York had been set.

When dying clouds contend with growing light,
What time the shepherd, blowing of his nails,
Can neither call it perfect day nor night.
Now sways it this way, like a mighty sea   5
Forc'd by the tide to combat with the wind;
Now sways it that way, like the self-same sea
Forc'd to retire by fury of the wind.
Sometime the flood prevails, and then the wind;
Now one the better, then another best;   10
Both tugging to be victors, breast to breast;
Yet neither conqueror nor conquered.
So is the equal poise of this fell war.
Here on this molehill will I sit me down. — Cf York
To whom God will, there be the victory!   15
For Margaret my queen, and Clifford too,
Have chid me from the battle, swearing both
They prosper best of all when I am thence.
Would I were dead, if God's good will were so!
For what is in this world but grief and woe?   20
O God! methinks it were a happy life
To be no better than a homely swain;
To sit upon a hill, as I do now,
To carve out dials quaintly, point by point,
Thereby to see the minutes how they run—   25
How many makes the hour full complete,

---

10. another] *F;* the other *conj. Daniel.*   15. there] *F;* theirs *conj. Capell.*   26.
makes] *F;* make *Q, Hanmer.*

---

3. *What time*] L. construction = at
the time when.

blowing . . . nails] from idleness or
cold; cf. *LLL.,* v. ii. 900.

6. *tide*] The simile was probably suggested by Hall's description (256) of
the battle 'some time flowyng, and
sometime ebbyng'. Cf. Ovid, *Metam.,*
viii. 614 ff., 'Utque carina, / Quam
ventus ventoque rapit contrarius
aestus, / Vim geminam sentit, paret-
que incerta duobus'; and iv. iii. 59.

with] against; cf. i. iv. 21, and
Mirror (Gloucester, l. 96), 'euen (as
who sayeth) to striue with the streame'.

13. *equal poise*] equal weight, as in

the scales of a balance; cf. *Meas.,* ii.
iv. 68, 'equal poise of sin and charity'.

14. *molehill*] an ironic reminder of
York's death in i. iv. Hart refers to the
old saying, 'king of a molehill'.

18. *They prosper*] Hall, 252, 'where
his person was present, there victory
fled'. Cf. ii. ii. 74.

19. *Would I were dead*] Cf. *Mirror,*
213, 'Would he had neuer been born'
(Henry the Sixth); and 95 below
(H. F. B.).

22. *swain*] shepherd.

24. *quaintly*] with ingenious art;
OED. 2.

26. *hour*] disyllabic.

How many hours brings about the day,
How many days will finish up the year,
How many years a mortal man may live.
When this is known, then to divide the times—　　30
So many hours must I tend my flock;
So many hours must I take my rest;
So many hours must I contemplate;
So many hours must I sport myself;
So many days my ewes have been with young;　　35
So many weeks ere the poor fools will ean;
So many years ere I shall shear the fleece:
So minutes, hours, days, weeks, months, and years,
Pass'd over to the end they were created,
Would bring white hairs unto a quiet grave.　　40
Ah, what a life were this! how sweet! how lovely!
Gives not the hawthorn bush a sweeter shade
To shepherds looking on their silly sheep,
Than doth a rich embroider'd canopy
To kings that fear their subjects' treachery?　　45
O yes, it doth; a thousand-fold it doth.
And to conclude, the shepherd's homely curds,
His cold thin drink out of his leather bottle,
His wonted sleep under a fresh tree's shade,
All which secure and sweetly he enjoys,　　50
Is far beyond a prince's delicates—
His viands sparkling in a golden cup,

27. brings] *F*; bring *Edd.*　　30. times] *F*; time *Theobald.*　　38. weeks] *Rowe*; not in *Q,F.*

27. *brings about*] completes.

34. *sport*] divert; disport.

36. *poor fools*] a term of endearment or pity.
ean] yean = to bring forth (lambs).

39. *the end they . . .*] the end or purpose for which they were made.

40. *white hairs . . . grave*] a recollection of Gen., xlii. 38, Jacob's 'then shall ye bring down my gray hairs with sorrow to the grave'. Cf. *2 H 6,* II. iii. 19, and v. i. 162 ff.

41 ff.] Cf. *Mirror, Add.,* 409, 'The sheepheardes life is better then the kinges' (H. F. B.).

43. *silly*] simple; helpless.

44. *canopy*] the covering carried over the sovereign on state occasions; the covering above a four-poster bed (suggested by 49 and 53).

47 ff.] Cf. Eccles., v. 12, 'The sleep of a labouring man is sweet, whether he eat little or much; but the abundance of the rich will not suffer him to sleep' (Carter).

48. *leather bottle*] black jack, such as may still be seen in Anne Hathaway's cottage.

50. *secure*] L. sense = free from care.

51. *delicates*] luxuries; delicacies.

His body couched in a curious bed,
When Care, Mistrust, and Treason waits on him.

Alarum. Enter a Son that hath kill'd his Father,
with the body in his arms.

Son. Ill blows the wind that profits nobody.   55
This man whom hand to hand I slew in fight
May be possessed with some store of crowns;
And I, that haply take them from him now,
May yet ere night yield both my life and them
To some man else, as this dead man doth me.   60
Who's this? O God! it is my father's face,
Whom in this conflict I unwares have kill'd.
O heavy times, begetting such events!
From London by the King was I press'd forth;
My father, being the Earl of Warwick's man,   65
Came on the part of York, press'd by his master;
And I, who at his hands receiv'd my life,
Have by my hands of life bereaved him.
Pardon me, God, I knew not what I did:
And pardon, father, for I knew not thee.   70
My tears shall wipe away these bloody marks;
And no more words till they have flow'd their fill.

54. S.D. *Alarum.*] F; *not in* Q.   *Enter . . . Father*] F (*Enter . . . Father, at one doore:*
and a Father that hath kill'd his Sonne at another doore.) ; Enter a souldier Q.   *with . . .*
rms] Q (*with a dead man in his armes*) ; *not in* F.   60. doth me] F; to me *Hanmer*.

53. *curious*] elaborate; exquisite.

54. *waits on*] attends; see Franz, 497,
or the syntax.

55. S.D. a Son] Cf. 78 '. . . a Father';
a piece of dramatic symbolism suggested no doubt by Hall, 256, on the unnatural conflict in which 'the son
ought against the father'. Joan Rees
in *NQ.*, cxcix (May 1954), suggests
Gorboduc, v. ii. 180 ff., as a more probable source than Hall, especially
201–33; cf. 'One kinsman shall be-
reave anothers life, / The father shall
unwitting slay the sonne, / The
sonne shall slay the sire and know
it not.' Cf. also the *Homily against Dis-*
obedience and Wilful Rebellion (1569)
as quoted in Tillyard, *SHP.*, p. 70.

57. *some store of crowns*] Cf. Kyd, *S.P.*,
II. i. 189, 212.

58. *haply*] by chance; as it hap-
pens.

62. *unwares*] unawares.

63. *O . . . times*] the Ciceronian 'O
tempora, O mores!' Cf. 73. Time is
thought of as the begetter of things to
come.

heavy] L. *gravis* = sad; serious;
unfortunate.

64, 66. *press'd*] taken by the press-
gang; compelled to enlist.

66. *part*] party; side.

69. *I knew not . . .*] A characteristic
Shakespearean recollection of the
Crucifixion; cf. the crowning of York,
I. iv. 94; and v. vii. 33–4.

K. Hen. O piteous spectacle! O bloody times!
 Whilst lions war and battle for their dens,
 Poor harmless lambs abide their enmity.   75
 Weep, wretched man; I'll aid thee tear for tear;
 And let our hearts and eyes, like civil war,
 Be blind with tears, and break o'ercharg'd with grief.

  Enter a Father that hath kill'd his Son, with the body
     in his arms.

Fath. Thou that so stoutly hath resisted me,
 Give me thy gold, if thou hast any gold,   80
 For I have bought it with an hundred blows.
 But let me see: is this our foeman's face?
 Ah, no, no, no; it is mine only son!
 Ah, boy, if any life be left in thee,
 Throw up thine eye! see, see, what showers arise, 85
 Blown with the windy tempest of my heart
 Upon thy wounds, that kills mine eye and heart!
 O, pity, God, this miserable age!
 What stratagems, how fell, how butcherly,
 Erroneous, mutinous, and unnatural,   90
 This deadly quarrel daily doth beget!
 O boy, thy father gave thee life too soon,
 And hath bereft thee of thy life too late!
K. Hen. Woe above woe! grief more than common grief!
 O that my death would stay these ruthful deeds! 95
 O pity, pity, gentle heaven, pity!
 The red rose and the white are on his face,

heraldic

78. S.D. *Enter . . . Son*] F (l. 54); *Enter Father* | F; Enter an other souldier C
with . . . *arms*] F (bearing of his Sonne); with a dead man Q. 87. kills] F
kill *Rowe*+*Edd.* 92, 93. soon / . . . late] F; late / . . . soon Q.

 75. *abide*] endure; face.

 77–8. *hearts . . . eyes* / *. . . blind . . .
break*] chiasmus (of the type called
Miltonic) = our hearts . . . break, . . .
our eyes . . . be blind(ed), (Vaughan,
ii. 486.)

 78. *blind*] the short form of the participle = blinded.

 81. *bought*] obtained; procured.

 89. *stratagems*] deeds of great violence; *OED*. 3.

 90. *Erroneous*] criminal, as strayir
from the path of virtue (L. *errare*).

 92–3. *too soon,* / *. . . too late!*] C
Lucr., 1801, 'I did give that life
Which she too early and too late hat
spill'd'.

 93. *late*] recently.

 94. *above*] upon; on top of.

 95.] Cf. *Mirror*, 213; and 19 abov
ruthful] demanding pity.

 97–102.] Cf. *1 H 6*, II. iv. 126, in tl

The fatal colours of our striving houses:
The one his purple blood right well resembles;
The other his pale cheeks, methinks, presenteth.   100
Wither one rose, and let the other flourish!
If you contend, a thousand lives must wither.

Son. How will my mother for a father's death
Take on with me and ne'er be satisfied!

Fath. How will my wife for slaughter of my son   105
Shed seas of tears and ne'er be satisfied!

K. Hen. How will the country for these woeful chances
Misthink the King and not be satisfied!

Son. Was ever son so rued a father's death?

Fath. Was ever father so bemoan'd his son?   110

K. Hen. Was ever king so griev'd for subjects' woe?
Much is your sorrow; mine, ten times so much.

Son. I'll bear thee hence, where I may weep my fill.

                                        Exit with the body.

Fath. These arms of mine shall be thy winding-sheet;
My heart, sweet boy, shall be thy sepulchre,   115
For from my heart thine image ne'er shall go.
My sighing breast shall be thy funeral bell;
And so obsequious will thy father be,
Even for the loss of thee, having no more,
As Priam was for all his valiant sons.   120
I'll bear thee hence; and let them fight that will,
For I have murder'd where I should not kill.

                                        Exit with the body.

113. S.D.] *Capell; not in F;* Exit with his father. *Q.*   119. Even] *Capell;* Men
F; Son Delius, Hart; Meet *Sisson.*   122. S.D.] *Capell;* Exit | *F;* Exit with his
sonne. *Q.*

scene where the 'contention' of York
and Lancaster begins in the Temple
Garden with the plucking of the
Roses.
   98. *fatal*] charged with fate or doom;
cf. 'fatal steeds', IV. ii. 21.
   100. *presenteth*] represents.
   103 ff.] The scene becomes more
and more formal and choric.
   104. *Take on with me*] 'go on'
madly and excitedly; make a great
outcry.

   108. *Misthink*] think ill of; cf. *Ant.*,
v. ii. 175.
   114. *These arms*] Cf. Marlowe, *Jew
of Malta,* 1193, 'These armes . . . thy
sepulchre.'
   118–20.] contradicted by Homer,
Iliad, xxiv. 239 ff.; Priam cared only
about Hector, not his fifty sons
(J. A. K. Thomson).
   118. *obsequious*] dutiful, especially
towards the dead; cf. *Ham.*, I. ii.
92.

K. Hen. Sad-hearted men, much overgone with care,
    Here sits a king more woeful than you are.

Alarums. Excursions. Enter QUEEN MARGARET, *the* PRINCE,
and EXETER.

Prince. Fly, father, fly! for all your friends are fled,   125
    And Warwick rages like a chafed bull.
    Away! for death doth hold us in pursuit.
Q. Mar. Mount you, my lord; towards Berwick post amain.
    Edward and Richard, like a brace of greyhounds
    Having the fearful-flying hare in sight,   130
    With fiery eyes sparkling for very wrath,
    And bloody steel grasp'd in their ireful hands,
    Are at our backs; and therefore hence amain.
Exe. Away! for vengeance comes along with them.
    Nay, stay not to expostulate; make speed,   135
    Or else come after: I'll away before.
K. Hen. Nay, take me with thee, good sweet Exeter:
    Not that I fear to stay, but love to go
    Whither the Queen intends. Forward; away!   *Exeunt*

124. S.D. *Alarums . . . Exeter.*] F (*. . . the Queen . . .*); Alarmes and enter the *Queene
. . .* Enter prince *Edward. . . .* Enter *Exeter. | Q.*   128. Berwick] *Q,F* (Barwicke)
130. fearful-flying] *This edn, conj. Vaughan;* fearefull flying *F.*   139. S.D.] *F
not in Q.*

123. *overgone*] overcome; exhausted.
126. *Warwick rages*] 'like a man de-
sperat' (Hall, 255). Shakespeare regu-
larly associates the wild sea with wild
animals; cf. *Tit.*, IV. ii. 138; *Shr.*, I. ii.
199; *Ven.*, 662.

chafed] irritated; angered.
132. *steel*] swords.
135. *expostulate*] discuss; set forth
one's views.
139. *intends*] is about to go; direct
her course; *OED.* 6; cf. *Per.*, I. ii. 116

[SCENE VI.—*Another part of the field.*]

A loud alarum. Enter CLIFFORD *wounded, with an arrow in his neck.*

Clif. Here burns my candle out; ay, here it dies,
    Which, whiles it lasted, gave King Henry light.
    Oh, Lancaster, I fear thy overthrow
    More than my body's parting with my soul.
    My love and fear glu'd many friends to thee;   5
    And, now I fall, thy tough commixture melts,
    Impairing Henry, strengthening misproud York.
    The common people swarm like summer flies;
    And whither fly the gnats but to the sun?
    And who shines now but Henry's enemies?   10
    O Phoebus, hadst thou never given consent
    That Phaëthon should check thy fiery steeds,
    Thy burning car never had scorch'd the earth!
    And, Henry, hadst thou sway'd as kings should do,
    Or as thy father, and his father did,   15
    Giving no ground unto the house of York,
    They never then had sprung like summer flies;
    I, and ten thousand in this luckless realm

Scene VI

SCENE VI] *Capell; not in* Q,F.   *Another . . . field.*] *Dyce; not in* Q,F.   S.D. *A loud alarum.*] F; *not in* Q.   *Enter . . . wounded*] Q,F.   *with . . . neck.*] Q; *not in* F.
6. fall, thy] *Rowe;* fall. Thy F; *die, that* Q.   commixture] Q; Commixtures F.
8.] Q, *Theobald* + *Edd.; not in* F.   9. fly] F; flies Q, *conj. this edn.*   12. Phaëthon] Q,F (*Phaeton*).

S.D. with an arrow . . .] Q has reported correctly; the arrow is in Hall, 255, and *Mirror*, 191.
    5. *My love and fear*] love and fear of me.
    glu'd] attached.
    6. *commixture*] compound.
    7. *misproud*] arrogant; wrongly proud.
    8.] The Q line could be a recollection of 17 and IV. ii. 2, 'The common people by numbers swarme to vs'. Vaughan thinks it disturbs the coherence between 7 and 9, 'the latter of which manifestly alludes to the York Coat of Arms, which was a Sun'; and there is no room for both Q and F versions ('a barren repetition'). Many editors, however, have followed Theobald in adopting both; 17 seems to imply some previous reference.
    11, 12. *Phoebus . . . Phaëthon*] See n, to I. iv. 33.
    12. *check*] control.
    14. *sway'd*] wielded power; ruled.

Had left no mourning widows for our death;
And thou this day hadst kept thy chair in peace.   20
For what doth cherish weeds but gentle air?
And what makes robbers bold but too much lenity?
Bootless are plaints, and cureless are my wounds;
No way to fly, nor strength to hold our flight:
The foe is merciless and will not pity;   25
For at their hands I have deserv'd no pity.
The air hath got into my deadly wounds,
And much effuse of blood doth make me faint.
Come, York and Richard, Warwick and the rest;
I stabb'd your fathers' bosoms: split my breast.   30

[He faints.]

Alarum and retreat. Enter EDWARD, GEORGE, RICHARD,
MONTAGUE, WARWICK, *and Soldiers.*

Edw. Now breathe we, lords: good fortune bids us pause
And smooth the frowns of war with peaceful looks.
Some troops pursue the bloody-minded Queen,
That led calm Henry, though he were a king,
As doth a sail, fill'd with a fretting gust,   35
Command an argosy to stem the waves.
But think you, lords, that Clifford fled with them?
War. No, 'tis impossible he should escape;
For, though before his face I speak the words,

24. our] *Q1,2, Warburton;* out *Q3,F.*   30. S.D. *He faints.] Rowe; not in Q,F.*
Alarum and retreat.] F; not in Q.   Enter . . . Soldiers.] F (Enter Edward, Warwicke
Richard, and Soldiers, Montague, & Clarence.); Enter Edward, Richard and Warwicke
and Souldiers. Q.

19. *mourning widows*] widows mourning.

20. *kept thy chair*] (*a*) passed a quiet
old age; cf. *2 H 6*, v. ii. 48, 'in thy
. . . chair-days'; (*b*) retained your
throne.

23. *cureless*] incurable.

24. *our*] The F 'out' is due to Q3
copy; see Intro., xxiv; and cf. *Rom.*, III.
i. 190 and v. iii. 192, for the same
error.

28. *effuse*] verb or noun; cf. 'depart',
2 H 6, I. i. 2.

30. *I stabb'd*] Clifford's final state-

ment of his one theme, with a difference.

S.D. retreat] call to retreat by bugle
and drums.

31. *breathe we*] let us rest.

35. *fretting*] a double reference to
(*a*) the wind, blowing in gusts, and
(*b*) a woman nagging.

36. *Command*] force; compel.

argosy] merchant ship of the largest
size, especially Venetian.

37–45. *Clifford*] Note the dramatic
irony, especially in 'before his face'
'he's surely dead' and 'be gently us'd'

Your brother Richard mark'd him for the grave;   40
And, wheresoe'er he be, he's surely dead.

Clifford groans and dies.

Rich. Whose soul is that which takes her heavy leave?
A deadly groan, like life and death's departing.
See who it is.

Edw.   And now the battle's ended,
If friend or foe, let him be gently us'd.   45

Rich. Revoke that doom of mercy, for 'tis Clifford,
Who, not contented that he lopp'd the branch
In hewing Rutland when his leaves put forth,
But set his murdering knife unto the root
From whence that tender spray did sweetly spring—   50
I mean our princely father, Duke of York.

Var. From off the gates of York fetch down the head,
Your father's head, which Clifford placed there;
Instead whereof let this supply the room;
Measure for measure must be answered.   55

Edw. Bring forth that fatal screech-owl to our house,
That nothing sung but death to us and ours:
Now death shall stop his dismal threatening sound,
And his ill-boding tongue no more shall speak.

Var. I think his understanding is bereft.   60
Speak, Clifford, dost thou know who speaks to thee?
Dark cloudy death o'ershades his beams of life,
And he nor sees, nor hears us, what we say.

---

41. *be*] *Q; is F.*   S.D.] *Steevens; Clifford grones and then dies. Q; Clifford grones |
.   42–4.*] *F; Edw. Harke, what soule . . . | Rich. A deadlie grone . . . | Ed. See
'ho it is, and now . . . Q.*

40. *mark'd him for the grave*] See II. ii.
16; cf. II. iv; 'mark'd' = destined.

41. *be*] F sophisticates.

42. *heavy*] sad; sorrowful.

43. *departing*] parting; separation;
. 'Till death us depart', in the Mariage Service, till 1662; *OED*. vb. 3.

45. *If*] whether.

gently] nobly; with honour; like a
entleman.

46. *doom*] judgment; sentence.

47–50. *lopp'd . . . spray*] regular
hakespearean imagery from the
enealogical tree.

54. *room*] place.

55. *Measure for measure*] This sums up
the revenge theme of the play so far.
Cf. Mark, iv. 24, 'With what measure
ye mete, with the same shall it be
measured to you again'; and Tilley,
M800, 801.

answered] returned, requited.

56. *the fatal screech-owl to our house*]
i.e. the screech-owl fatal to our house;
see Abbott, 419(a); and cf. *1 H 6*, IV.
ii. 15.

58. *dismal*] ill-boding; sinister.

60. *bereft*] taken from him; impaired.

Rich. O, would he did! and so, perhaps, he doth:
    'Tis but his policy to counterfeit,   6₅
    Because he would avoid such bitter taunts
    Which in the time of death he gave our father.
Geo. If so thou think'st, vex him with eager words.
Rich. Clifford, ask mercy, and obtain no grace.
Edw. Clifford, repent in bootless penitence.   7₀
War. Clifford, devise excuses for thy faults.
Geo. While we devise fell tortures for thy faults.
Rich. Thou didst love York, and I am son to York.
Edw. Thou pitied'st Rutland, I will pity thee.
Geo. Where's Captain Margaret, to fence you now?   7₅
War. They mock thee, Clifford; swear as thou wast wont.
Rich. What, not an oath? Nay, then the world goes hard
    When Clifford cannot spare his friends an oath.
    I know by that he's dead; and, by my soul,
    If this right hand would buy but two hours' life,   8₀
    That I in all despite might rail at him,
    This hand should chop it off, and with the issuing blood
    Stifle the villain whose unstaunched thirst
    York and young Rutland could not satisfy.
War. Ay, but he's dead. Off with the traitor's head,   8₅
    And rear it in the place your father's stands.
    And now to London with triumphant march,
    There to be crowned England's royal king;
    From whence shall Warwick cut the sea to France,

---

67. Which] *F*; As *Q, Pope.*   72. While] *F*; Whilst *Q.*   80. buy but] *Q, Capell;* buy *F.*

65. *policy*] craft; cunning device.

66-7. *such . . . taunts / Which . . .*] The reference is to I. iv. Cooper defines 'sarcasmos' as 'A bitinge Taunte or scoffe' (Baldwin, *Sm. Lat.*, ii. 145).

68. *vex*] harass; torment; cf. Job, xix. 1, and Hall, 225.

   eager] L. sense = sharp; bitter. Cf. Homilies, 'An Exhortation concerning good order': 'bitter and eager words'.

75. *Captain*] Hall, 298, 'take vpon her, the name of capitain'.

   fence] protect.

82. *This hand*] i.e. his left hand.

83. *unstaunched*] insatiable.

84. *Rutland could not satisfy*] Cf. II. i 99, 'and yet not satisfied'. The empha sis is on the blood (cf. 82), not the pe sons; cf. I. iii. 21, 23, 49-51; iv. 7₉ II. i. 127.

86. *the place*] Cf. 52 ff. In Hall, 25 Clifford's head is not mentione among those that replaced York' The touch was added by Shakespea to reinforce the pattern of irony.

89. *cut the sea*] Cf. 'Sulcare mari *Vir.* To cutte the seas' (Cooper).

89 ff.] preparing the way for the ne act—Warwick's mission to Franc Edward's marriage, and the cons

And ask the Lady Bona for thy queen.   90
So shalt thou sinew both these lands together;
And, having France thy friend, thou shalt not dread
The scatter'd foe that hopes to rise again;
For though they cannot greatly sting to hurt,
Yet look to have them buzz to offend thine ears.   95
First will I see the coronation;
And then to Brittany I'll cross the sea
To effect this marriage, so it please my lord.

Edw. Even as thou wilt, sweet Warwick, let it be;
For in thy shoulder do I build my seat,   100
And never will I undertake the thing
Wherein thy counsel and consent is wanting.
Richard, I will create thee Duke of Gloucester;
And George, of Clarence; Warwick, as ourself,
Shall do and undo as him pleaseth best.   105

Rich. Let me be Duke of Clarence, George of Gloucester,
For Gloucester's dukedom is too ominous.

War. Tut, that's a foolish observation:
Richard, be Duke of Gloucester. Now to London,
To see these honours in possession.   *Exeunt.* 110

110. S.D.] *F; Exeunt Omnes. | Q.*

quences—the theme of the remaining half of the play.

The whole passage is strewn with irony, especially (*a*) Edward's declaration (100–1) of trust in Warwick, and (*b*) Richard's creation as Gloucester, and Warwick's 'foolish observation'.

91. *sinew*] join together strongly, as with sinews.

93. *scatter'd*] with the sense '*cast down upon the ground*', of 'objects which in some higher position have been collected together'; hence 'rise again' (Vaughan).

95. *buzz*] spread false rumours.

100. *shoulder*] emblem of supporting strength.

seat] throne.

103 ff. *create . . . Gloucester*] Hall, 258–9.

104. *ourself*] Edward assumes the royal 'We'.

107. *ominous*] Hall, 209, remarks on the bad luck attached to the title, with reference to Humphrey of Gloucester.

110. *possession*] Read as four syllables.

[ACT III

SCENE I.—*A chase in the north of England.*]

Enter two Keepers, with cross-bows in their hands.

1 Keep. Under this thick-grown brake we'll shroud ourselves,
For through this laund anon the deer will come;
And in this covert will we make our stand,
Culling the principal of all the deer.

ACT III

Scene 1

ACT III SCENE I] *Rowe; not in Q,F.* A chase ... England.] *Alexander; Hanmer*
(*A forest ...*); *Theobald* (*A wood ...*); *not in Q,F.* S.D.] *Malone; Enter Sinklo,
and Humfrey, with ... hands.* | *F;* Enter two keepers with bow and arrowes. *Q.*
1. *1 Keep.*] *Malone; Sink.* | *F (and throughout the scene); Keeper.* | *Q.* thick-grown]
Pope; thicke growne *F.*

The scene is an embroidery on a
theme suggested by Hall, 257 and 261
(App. I), 'Henry . . . disguised . . .
entered . . . Englande.' The triumph
of Edward of York, now on his way to
coronation in London, is contrasted
with the plight of Henry of Lancaster;
the prevailing atmosphere of blood
and revenge with the religious quiet-
ism (note the prayer-book, 12 S.D.) of
Henry; and the pastoral scene with the
field of battle.

The scene serves also as a kind of
chorus which takes up some of the
main general themes of the play—the
divine right of kings, the uses of adversity, the inwardness of Content, the
fickleness of men, the sanctity of oaths.

S.D. *chase*] This does not quite
amount to Hanmer's 'forest' or Theobald's 'wood'. It is a 'laund' (l. 2), that
is, open grass-lands or 'lawns', with a
'brake' and a 'covert', and in the hills.

keepers] The F names 'Sinklo' and
'Humfrey', here and in the speech-
prefixes throughout the scene may be

due to one of several causes. The names
are almost certainly those of the actors
who played the 'keepers' (cf. Gabriel,
I. ii. 47, and John Holland in *2 H 6,*
IV. ii. 1). Sinklo is reasonably identified
with John Sincler, who appears in the
cast of *2 Seven Deadly Sins,* and in *The
Taming of the Shrew,* Ind., i. 88. Humfry
is probably Humphrey Jeffes, a member of the Pembroke company of 1597.
(See further Intro., xix f.) The names
may be either Shakespeare's own or
the insertion of the prompter or book-
keeper.

cross-bows] heavy bows set cross-
wise on a stock, firing a 'bolt' rather
noisily (6).

1. *shroud*] conceal; shelter.

2. *laund*] an early form of 'lawn',
glade; cf. Fr. *lande* = heath, moor; an
open space of grass among trees.

anon] soon, straightway.

3. *stand*] hiding-place constructed in
the 'brake' (cf. Madden, 236). Cf.
Cym., III. iv. 107–8; II. iii. 70.

4. *Culling*] picking out (Fr. *cueillir*).

2 *Keep.* I'll stay above the hill, so both may shoot. 5

1 *Keep.* That cannot be; the noise of thy cross-bow
Will scare the herd, and so my shoot is lost.
Here stand we both, and aim we at the best;
And, for the time shall not seem tedious,
I'll tell thee what befell me on a day 10
In this self place where now we mean to stand.

2 *Keep.* Here comes a man; let's stay till he be past.

Enter KING HENRY, *disguised, with a prayer-book.*

K. Hen. From Scotland am I stol'n, even of pure love,
To greet mine own land with my wishful sight.
No, Harry, Harry, 'tis no land of thine; 15
Thy place is fill'd, thy sceptre wrung from thee,
Thy balm wash'd off wherewith thou wast anointed:
No bending knee will call thee Caesar now,
No humble suitors press to speak for right,
No, not a man comes for redress of thee: 20
For how can I help them and not myself?

Keep. Ay, here's a deer whose skin's a keeper's fee:
This is the quondam king; let's seize upon him.

K. Hen. Let me embrace thee, sour Adversity,
For wise men say it is the wisest course. 25

2 *Keep.*] *Malone; Hum. | F.*   12. 2 *Keep.*] *Malone; Sink. | F.*   S.D.] *Malone;
Enter the King with a Prayer booke. | F;* Enter king *Henrie* disguisde. *Q.*   13, 24,
8. *K. Hen.*] *F* (*Hen.*).   17. wast] *F3;* was *F1,2.*   24. thee, sour Adversity]
inger, conj. Dyce; the sower Aduersaries, *F.*

7. *shoot*] shot; discharge (of arrows).
8. *at the best*] as well as we can.
9. *for*] so that; cf. III. ii. 154; see
ranz, 573.
11. *self*] same.
12. S.D.] See head-note.
14. *wishful*] longing—transferred
pithet.
16–17.] Cf. *R2*, III. ii. 55, 'wash the
alm off from an anointed king'. The
omission of these lines may have
ensorial implications.
18–20. *No bending knee ... Caesar ... |
o humble suitors press to speak ... | ... re-
ess*] Cf. *Caes.*, III. i. 27–8, 'Let him go |
nd presently prefer his *suit* to Caesar';
, 'He is address'd: *press* near and

second him'; 31–2, 'What is now
amiss / That Caesar and his senate
must *redress*?'; 34–5, 'Metellus Cimber
throws before thy seat / An *humble*
heart'; 45, 'If thou dost *bend*'; 75, 'Doth
not Brutus bootless *kneel*?' Cf. v. i. 81
below, 'Et tu, Brute! Wilt thou stab
Caesar too!' and *Massacre at Paris*,
1005 ff., 'Yet Caesar shall goe forth. /
Let mean consaits, and baser men
feare death, / ... Thus Caesar did goe
foorth, and thus he dyed'.
19. *right*] justice.
20. *of*] from.
23. *quondam*] former (L.).
24. *Adversity*] Cf. *AYL.*, II. i. 12,
'Sweet are the uses of adversity'.

2 Keep. Why linger we? let us lay hands upon him.
1 Keep. Forbear awhile; we'll hear a little more.
K. Hen. My queen and son are gone to France for aid;
        And, as I hear, the great commanding Warwick
        Is thither gone, to crave the French King's sister   3(
        To wife for Edward. If this news be true,
        Poor queen and son, your labour is but lost;
        For Warwick is a subtle orator
        And Lewis a prince soon won with moving words.
        By this account, then, Margaret may win him,   3!
        For she's a woman to be pitied much:
        Her sighs will make a battery in his breast;
        Her tears will pierce into a marble heart;
        The tiger will be mild whiles she doth mourn;
        And Nero will be tainted with remorse,   4(
        To hear and see her plaints, her brinish tears.
        Ay, but she's come to beg, Warwick to give;
        She on his left side craving aid for Henry:
        He on his right, asking a wife for Edward.
        She weeps, and says her Henry is depos'd: 4.
        He smiles, and says his Edward is install'd;
        That she, poor wretch, for grief can speak no more;
        Whiles Warwick tells his title, smooths the wrong,
        Inferreth arguments of mighty strength,

26. *2 Keep.*] *Malone; Hum.* / F (*and throughout the scene*).

28. *gone to France*] Hall, 253; and III.
iii.

33. *a subtle orator*] There is no sign of
this in the Chronicles, or in Warwick's
character; but *Mirror*, 223, speaks of
his 'crafty-filed tounge'.

36 ff.] an interesting sidelight on
Margaret's character, and Henry's.
Margaret's melancholy after the battle
of Barnet (Hall, 297–8; v. iv) is omitted by Shakespeare, who is concerned
to build up the 'she-wolf' and 'tiger's
heart' side of her nature. This, the
only reference to her sorrow in the
play, strikes a rather ironical note,
especially the allusion to the 'tiger'
in 39.

37. *battery*] assault; bombardment;
breach; cf. *Ven.*, 426.

38. *tears . . . marble*] Cf. 'Much rai
wears the marble', III. ii. 50; and *Lucr*
560, 'Tears . . . through marble wea
with raining'; Tilley, D618.

38–9.] Cf. Ariosto, *Orlando Furios*
I. xl, 'cominciò . . . a lamentarsi
soavemente, / ch'avrebbe di piet
spezzato un sasso, / una tigre crud
fiatta clemente.'

40. *Nero*] the type of hard-hearte
ness and cruelty; cf. *John*, v. ii. 15
'You bloody Neroes'; and *1 H 6*, I. i
95.

tainted with remorse] improperly o
unnaturally touched with pity.

47. *That*] with the result that.

48. *smooths*] glosses over.

49. *Inferreth*] alleges; adduce:
brings forward; cf. II. ii. 44.

And in conclusion wins the King from her   50
With promise of his sister, and what else,
To strengthen and support King Edward's place.
O Margaret, thus 'twill be; and thou, poor soul,
Art then forsaken, as thou went'st forlorn.

2 Keep. Say, what art thou that talk'st of kings and queens?

K. Hen. More than I seem, and less than I was born to: 56
A man at least, for less I should not be;
And men may talk of kings, and why not I?

2 Keep. Ay, but thou talk'st as if thou wert a king.

K. Hen. Why, so I am, in mind; and that's enough.   60

2 Keep. But if thou be a king, where is thy crown?

K. Hen. My crown is in my heart, not on my head;
Not deck'd with diamonds and Indian stones,
Nor to be seen: my crown is call'd content;
A crown it is that seldom kings enjoy.   65

2 Keep. Well, if you be a king crown'd with content,
Your crown content, and you, must be contented
To go along with us; for, as we think,
You are the king King Edward hath depos'd;
And we his subjects, sworn in all allegiance,   70
Will apprehend you as his enemy.

K. Hen. But did you never swear, and break an oath?

2 Keep. No, never such an oath; nor will not now.

K. Hen. Where did you dwell when I was King of England?

2 Keep. Here in this country, where we now remain.   75

K. Hen. I was anointed king at nine months old;
My father and my grandfather were kings,
And you were sworn true subjects unto me:
And tell me then, have you not broke your oaths?

2 Keep. No, we were subjects but while you were king.   80

K. Hen. Why, am I dead? do I not breathe a man?

5. that] *Q, Rowe; not in* F.   56. *K. Hen.*] F (*King.*), *and throughout the scene.*
o. No, we] *Pope;* No, for we F.

51. *what else*] anything more; cf.
what beside', II. i. 175.
  69.] Cf. the ambiguous prophecy in
H 6, I. iv. 30, 'The duke yet lives that
Henry shall depose', of which this is
an adaptation.
  75. *country*] region; district.

76.] Hall, 414–15. Shakespeare frequently refers to Henry's proclamation
as king in 1422, 'at nine months old',
but combines it with his actual coronation (Hall, 422) in 1431, e.g. I. i. 112;
1 H 6, I. i. 169; *2 H 6,* I. i. 89; IV. ix. 4;
R 3, II. iii. 17.

Ah, simple men, you know not what you sware.
Look, as I blow this feather from my face,
And as the air blows it to me again,
Obeying with my wind when I do blow,   85
And yielding to another when it blows,
Commanded always by the greater gust,
Such is the lightness of you common men.
But do not break your oaths; for of that sin
My mild entreaty shall not make you guilty.   90
Go where you will, the King shall be commanded;
And be you kings; command, and I'll obey.

1 Keep. We are true subjects to the king, King Edward.

K. Hen. So would you be again to Henry,
    If he were seated as King Edward is.   95

1 Keep. Therefore we charge you, in God's name, and the
        king's,
    To go with us unto the officers.

K. Hen. In God's name, lead; your king's name be obey'd:
    And what God will, that let your king perform;
    And what he will, I humbly yield unto.   *Exeunt.* 100

---

82. sware] *This edn, conj. Delius;* sweare *F.*   96. Therefore we] *This edn;* An
therefore we *Q;* We *F.*   and the] *Q,F;* and in the *Rowe.*   100. S.D.] *F*
Exeunt Omnes. | Q.

82. *simple*] foolish.

   sware] The reference is to the
past, to the oath they had taken to
Henry on his accession (sworn, 70;
were sworn, 78; have . . . broke, 79),
and not to oaths in general. The same
F sophistication, taking 'sweare' for
'sware', occurs in *H 5*, v. i. 83 (Q
sweare; F swore). Cf. also II. i. 172 and
n., and Intro., xxxiv–xl, especially
xxxvii.

   83–8. *this feather . . . common men*] Cf.
2 H 6, IV. viii. 54, 'Was ever feather so

lightly blown to and fro as this multi
tude?'

   85. *with*] instrumental—by mean
of, in the direction dictated by; c
Holinshed, 'the common people bend
ing like a reed with every wind tha
blows' (Vaughan).

   wind] breath.

   87. *Commanded*] controlled; forced.

   88. *lightness*] with the implied sens
of 'fickleness'.

   90. *entreaty*] treaty; engagement
agreement—stated in 91.

[SCENE II.—*London. The Palace.*]

Enter KING EDWARD, RICHARD (DUKE OF GLOUCESTER),
GEORGE (DUKE OF CLARENCE), *and* LADY ELIZABETH GREY.

K. Edw. Brother of Gloucester, at St Albans field
　　　This lady's husband, Sir John Grey, was slain,
　　　His lands then seiz'd on by the conqueror.
　　　Her suit is now to repossess those lands;
　　　Which we in justice cannot well deny,　　　　　　5
　　　Because in quarrel of the house of York

Scene II

SCENE II] *Pope; not in* Q,F.　　　London. The Palace.] *Edd.; not in* Q,F.　　　S.D.]
(subst.); Enter king *Edward,* Clarence, *and* Gloster, Montague, Hastings, *and the
Lady Gray. | Q.　　　2.* John] *Pope;* Richard Q,F.　　　3. lands] *Capell;* Land F.

Source: Hall, 252, 264–5, 365–6.
The Chronicles duplicate the account
of Edward's courtship. The second
(365–6) is from Sir Thomas More's
History of Richard III, which Hall in-
corporates: and it is to this fuller account that Shakespeare is mainly indebted, e.g. St Albans field, 1; lands,
.; give us leave, 33; to tell thee plain,
69–70; children, 26 ff., 100 ff.; and
v. i. 69.

The scene is similar to one in the
anonymous *Edward III*. It emphasizes
Edward's weakness, already antici-
pated by the clear-sighted Richard at
. i. 41–2; Hall speaks of Edward (345)
as 'giuen to fleshly wantonness'. This
weakness leads to another 'fatal marriage', involving, like Henry's (*1 H 6*,
. v; *2 H 6*, I. i), a breach of faith, besides the aggravation of civil dissension
resulting from the disgrace of Warwick, and the alienation of France.

The courtship incident leads to the
first of Richard's long soliloquies, expressing his cynical self-centred character, ambitions, and plans.

2. *Sir John Grey*] He is called John in
the Chronicles. 'Richard' is probably
due to F use of Q copy, uncorrected.
Cf. Sir *John* Montgomery, for *Richard*,
t IV. vii. 40.

4. *repossess*] regain possession of.
5, 9. *deny*] refuse.
6. *in quarrel ... York*] Hall, 252, gives
the main account of Grey. The later
account, Hall, 365, shows that he was
really a Lancastrian; and the references to *lands* being *seized*, and the object of the widow's *suit*, show that
Shakespeare also used this account,
but only the end of it, i.e. he might
have missed the reference. Hall's account here (252) might easily mislead
as to Grey's side in the quarrel. At St
Albans the King was with one army
(Warwick's), the Queen led the other.
Afterwards Henry made two sets of
knights—on the one hand Grey, with
twelve more; on the other, Prince
Edward 'with 30 other persons,
which in the morning fought on the
quenes side, *against his parte*'. The
inference could be drawn that the
first group were on Henry's part or
side; or alternatively, since they
are mentioned immediately after
two Yorkist knights who stayed behind to look after the King and were
taken prisoners, that they also were
Yorkists.

Shakespeare gives the correct version in *R 3*, I. iii. 127–30, based on
Hall, 365–6.

The worthy gentleman did lose his life.

Rich. Your Highness shall do well to grant her suit;
　　It were dishonour to deny it her.

K. Edw. It were no less; but yet I'll make a pause.　　　　10

Rich. [*Aside to Geo.*] Yea, is it so?
　　I see the lady hath a thing to grant,
　　Before the King will grant her humble suit.

Geo. [*Aside to Rich.*] He knows the game: how true he keeps
　　the wind!

Rich. [*Aside to Geo.*] Silence!　　　　　　　　　　　15

K. Edw. Widow, we will consider of your suit;
　　And come some other time to know our mind.

L. Grey. Right gracious lord, I cannot brook delay:
　　May it please your Highness to resolve me now;
　　And what your pleasure is shall satisfy me.　　　　　20

Rich. [*Aside to Geo.*] Ay, widow? then I'll warrant you all
　　your lands,
　　And if what pleases him shall pleasure you.
　　Fight closer or, good faith, you'll catch a clap.

Geo. [*Aside to Rich.*] I fear her not, unless she chance to fall.

Rich. [*Aside to Geo.*] Marry, Godsforbot! for he'll take
　　vantages.　　　　　　　　　　　　　　　　　　2[5]

K. Edw. How many children hast thou, widow, tell me.

11, 15, 25, 28. *Aside to Geo.*] Capell; *not in* Q,F.　　11.] *F;* I, is the wind in tha[t]
doore? Q; Yea, is it so? In that door sits the wind? *conj. this edn.*　　18. *L. Grey*]
Edd.; La. | Q; Wid. | F (*and throughout the scene*).　　23. clap] Q; blow F.　　2[5]
Marry, Godsforbot] Q; God forbid that F.

11.] This could be a case of a MS.
addition to Q being taken by the compositor as an alternative.

For the 'wind', cf. 14. The line
should probably read as conjectured.

14. *game . . . wind*] The comparison
is to a dog in pursuit of quarry, with a
quibble on 'the game'. Cf. *Ham.*, III. ii.
337, 'Why do you go about to recover
the wind of me?'

keeps the wind] keeps the quarry on
the windward side, so as to maintain
the scent; cf. Madden, 53 and n.

18. *brook*] endure.

19. *resolve*] satisfy; free from doubt.

23. *closer*] (a) nearer to the enemy;
for fear of a blow or thrust (*OED.* 14b);

(b) leaving no opening in the defenc[e]
(*OED.* 4); the antithesis of 'fight t[o]
open'. Cf. *Rom.*, I. i. 105.

a clap] F sophisticates. There is [a]
pun on the senses of (a) gonorrhoe[a]
(b) a blow or stroke (*OED.* 5b[1]. 5[)]
with a possible reference to (c) a pa[s]-
toral staff (*OED.* 12), like the 'crut[ch]
(Q crouch) of 35.

24. *fear her not*] do not fear for her[.]

25.] F sophisticates. 'The old "God[s]
forbot" was formerly very commo[n]
and is found in Golding's *Ovid* (xi
891). It is used by Nashe (*Have wi[th]
you, etc.*), and by Nicholas Bret[on]
(several times)' (Hart).

vantages] opportunities.

Geo. [*Aside to Rich.*] I think he means to beg a child of her.

Rich. [*Aside to Geo.*] Nay, whip me then; he'll rather give her
    two.

L. Grey. Three, my most gracious lord.

Rich. [*Aside.*] You shall have four, and you'll be rul'd by him.

K. Edw. 'Twere pity they should lose their father's lands. 31

L. Grey. Be pitiful, dread lord, and grant it then.

K. Edw. Lords, give us leave; I'll try this widow's wit.

Rich. [*Aside.*] Ay, good leave have you; for you will have leave
    Till youth take leave and leave you to the crutch. 35

                              [*Rich. and Geo. retire.*]

K. Edw. Now tell me, madam, do you love your children?

L. Grey. Ay, full as dearly as I love myself.

K. Edw. And would you not do much to do them good?

L. Grey. To do them good, I would sustain some harm.

K. Edw. Then get your husband's lands, to do them good. 40

L. Grey. Therefore I came unto your Majesty.

K. Edw. I'll tell you how these lands are to be got.

L. Grey. So shall you bind me to your Highness' service.

K. Edw. What service wilt thou do me if I give them?

L. Grey. What you command that rests in me to do. 45

K. Edw. But you will take exceptions to my boon.

L. Grey. No, gracious lord, except I cannot do it.

K. Edw. Ay, but thou canst do what I mean to ask.

L. Grey. Why, then I will do what your Grace commands.

---

28. whip me then] *Q*; then whip me *F*.
not in *Q,F*.   30. and] *Q1,2*; if *Q3,F*.
Johnson (. . . to the other side.); not in *Q,F*.

30, 34. S.D. *Aside.*] *Johnson and Capell*;
32. then] *F*; them *Q*.   35. S.D.]

---

27. *beg*] with the further (legal)
sense of 'petition [the Court of Wards]
for the custody of a minor' (*OED.*
5a).

28. *whip me*] treat me as a rogue or
vagabond—a mild oath.

30. *and*] commonly sophisticated to
'if' in *Q3* and *F*.

33. *give us leave*] excuse us, scil. by
standing aside.

wit] intelligence; understanding—
the normal Elizabethan sense.

34. *good leave have you*] we leave you
alone; cf. Kyd, *Sp. Tr.*, III. xi. 2.

you will have leave] you will take liberties, use licence.

35. *crutch*] a pun on the senses (*a*) the
human 'fork', (*b*) an invalid's crutch,
or clap (cf. 23).

36 ff.] Hart notes the stichomythia
—dialogue in alternate, balanced lines
—due to the Elizabethan vogue of
Seneca.

38, 40. *do them good*] advance their
interests.

44. *service*] Wilson notes the equi-
vocal sense.

45. *rests in me*] remains in my power.

Rich. [*Aside to Geo.*] He plies her hard; and much rain wears
    the marble.   50

Geo. [*Aside to Rich.*] As red as fire! Nay, then, her wax must
    melt.

L. Grey. Why stops my lord? Shall I not hear my task?

K. Edw. An easy task; 'tis but to love a king.

L. Grey. That's soon perform'd, because I am a subject.

K. Edw. Why, then, thy husband's lands I freely give thee. 55

L. Grey. I take my leave with many thousand thanks.

Rich. [*Aside to Geo.*] The match is made; she seals it with a
    curtsy.

K. Edw. But stay thee—'tis the fruits of love I mean.

L. Grey. The fruits of love I mean, my loving liege.

K. Edw. Ay, but, I fear me, in another sense.   60
    What love think'st thou I sue so much to get?

L. Grey. My love till death, my humble thanks, my prayers;
    That love which virtue begs, and virtue grants.

K. Edw. No, by my troth, I did not mean such love.

L. Grey. Why, then, you mean not as I thought you did.   65

K. Edw. But now you partly may perceive my mind.

L. Grey. My mind will never grant what I perceive
    Your Highness aims at, if I aim aright.

K. Edw. To tell thee plain, I aim to lie with thee.

L. Grey. To tell you plain, I had rather lie in prison.   70

K. Edw. Why, then thou shalt not have thy husband's
    lands.

L. Grey. Why, then mine honesty shall be my dower;
    For by that loss I will not purchase them.

K. Edw. Therein thou wrong'st thy children mightily.

L. Grey. Herein your Highness wrongs both them and me;   75
    But, mighty lord, this merry inclination

50, 82, 107. S.D. *Aside to Geo.*] *Dyce; Aside | Capell; not in Q,F.*   51, 83, 108
S.D. *Aside to Rich.*] *Dyce; Aside | Capell; not in Q,F.*

50. *rain . . . marble*] proverbial; cf.
'gutta cavat lapidem' (Ovid). Richard
begins to show his gnomic turn of
speech.

58. *the fruits of love*] Cf. Kyd, *Sp. Tr.*,
II. iv. 55, 'I thus and thus: these are
the fruits of love'; and *2 T R.*, viii. 118,
'This is the fruit of Popery'.

66. *perceive my mind*] grasp my meaning; also, my inclination or desire.

68. *aim*] guess. Note the continued
thread of double meaning.

72. *honesty*] chastity.

73. *purchase*] obtain, otherwise than
by inheritance—the legal sense.

76. *inclination*] disposition.

Accords not with the sadness of my suit:
Please you dismiss me, either with ay or no.

K. Edw. Ay, if thou wilt say ay to my request;
No, if thou dost say no to my demand.   80

L. Grey. Then, no, my lord. My suit is at an end.

Rich. [*Aside to Geo.*] The widow likes him not, she knits her
    brows.

Geo. [*Aside to Rich.*] He is the bluntest wooer in Christendom.

K. Edw. [*Aside.*] Her looks doth argue her replete with
      modesty;
Her words doth show her wit incomparable;   85
All her perfections challenge sovereignty:
One way or other, she is for a king;
And she shall be my love, or else my queen.—
Say that King Edward take thee for his queen?

L. Grey. 'Tis better said than done, my gracious lord: 90
I am a subject, fit to jest withal,
But far unfit to be a sovereign.

K. Edw. Sweet widow, by my state I swear to thee
I speak no more than what my soul intends;
And that is to enjoy thee for my love.   95

L. Grey. And that is more than I will yield unto.
I know I am too mean to be your queen,
And yet too good to be your concubine.

K. Edw. You cavil, widow, I did mean my queen.

L. Grey. 'Twill grieve your Grace my sons should call you
   father.   100

K. Edw. No more than when my daughters call thee mother.
Thou art a widow, and thou hast some children;
And by God's mother, I, being but a bachelor,
Have other some. Why, 'tis a happy thing
To be the father unto many sons.   105

---

04. *other some*] *Q;* other-some *F.*

---

77. *sadness of my suit*] seriousness of
my request.
   83. *bluntest*] rudest; most unpolished.
   86. *challenge*] lay claim to; demand
as due; cf. IV. vi. 6.
   90. *better*] easier.
   91. *subject*] (*a*) citizen, (*b*) matter.

93. *state*] majesty; royal status.
   97–8.] Hall, 366; Wilson says Holinshed only.
   97. *mean*] of low rank; humble.
   99. *mean*] The equivocation continues.
   104. *other some*] others; another set.

Answer no more, for thou shalt be my queen.

Rich. [*Aside to Geo.*] The ghostly father now hath done his
    shrift.

Geo. [*Aside to Rich.*] When he was made a shriver, 'twas for
    shift.

K. Edw. Brothers, you muse what chat we two have had.

Rich. The widow likes it not, for she looks vex'd.   110

K. Edw. You'd think it strange if I should marry her.

Geo. To who, my lord?

K. Edw.   Why, Clarence, to myself.

Rich. That would be ten days' wonder at the least.

Geo. That's a day longer than a wonder lasts.

Rich. By so much is the wonder in extremes.   115

K. Edw. Well, jest on, brothers: I can tell you both
    Her suit is granted for her husband's lands.

Enter a Nobleman.

Nob. My gracious lord, Henry your foe is taken
    And brought your prisoner to your palace gate.

K. Edw. See that he be convey'd unto the Tower: 120
    And go we, brothers, to the man that took him,
    To question of his apprehension.
    Widow, go you along. Lords, use her honourably.

Exeunt all but Richard

Rich. Ay, Edward will use women honourably.

110. vex'd] *This edn, conj.* Vaughan; very sad *F; not in* Q.   117. S.D.] *F;* Ente
a Messenger. Q.   119. your] *F; as* Q, *conj. this edn.*   123. honourably] Q
honourable *F.*   S.D.] *F* (*Exeunt. | Manet Richard.*); *Exeunt Omnes, | Manet Gloste*
and speakes. *Q.*

106. *my queen*] Hart quotes Johnson
on the dialogue that closes here, 'very
lively and spritely; the reciprocation
is quicker than is common in Shakespeare'.

107. *ghostly*] spiritual.
  father] priest.
  shrift] confession, and absolution.

108. *shriver*] father confessor.
  shift] (*a*) a trick, (*b*) smock, chemise;
cf. *1 H 6*, I. ii. 119, 'Doubtles she shrives
this woman to her smock'.

109. *muse*] wonder.

110. *vex'd*] angry; annoyed—much
stronger than now; cf. *Cym.*, I. i. 13
(vexation). Q's 'very sad' spoils th
metre, and is less effective than 'vex'd'
of which it would be an easy misread
ing; cf. box/boy, *Troil.*, V. i. 13.

113. *ten days' wonder*] referring to th
proverbial 'nine days' wonder'.

115. *in extremes*] of the highest degree

122. *apprehension*] seizure; arrest.

124 ff.] Richard's first plain declara
tion of his ambition; contrast wit
Henry's speech at II. v. 1–54.

Would he were wasted, marrow, bones, and all,   125
That from his loins no hopeful branch may spring,
To cross me from the golden time I look for!
And yet, between my soul's desire and me—
The lustful Edward's title buried—
Is Clarence, Henry, and his son young Edward,   130
And all the unlook'd for issue of their bodies,
To take their rooms ere I can plant myself—
A cold premeditation for my purpose!
Why then I do but dream on sovereignty;
Like one that stands upon a promontory   135
And spies a far-off shore where he would tread,
Wishing his foot were equal with his eye;
And chides the sea, that sunders him from thence,
Saying he'll lade it dry to have his way:
So do I wish the crown, being so far off;   140
And so I chide the means that keeps me from it;
And so I say I'll cut the causes off,
Flattering me with impossibilities.
My eye's too quick, my heart o'erweens too much,
Unless my hand and strength could equal them.   145
Well, say there is no kingdom then for Richard;
What other pleasure can the world afford?
I'll make my heaven in a lady's lap,

32. plant] Q; place F.

125. *wasted*] scil. with disease, in
keeping with 'lustful', 129; cf. *Mirror*,
39 (Eleanor, 201), 'The Deuil him
naw both body, blood and bones'.

126-7. *loins . . . branch . . . cross*] Till-
ard, *SHP.*, 196, notes the probable
religious reference to the tree of Jesse;
and suggests that 'cross' is 'a physical
image suggested by the efficient mas-
iveness of the stem that springs in the
works of art from the loins of the re-
umbent Jesse.' Cf. 'plant' at 132. Cf.
TR., viii. 109, 'From out these loins
hall spring a Kingly branch'. Cross =
ebar.

131. *unlook'd for*] (a) unexpected,
(b) undesired.

132. *plant*] stronger than F 'place',
which would be an easy misreading;

and an appropriate continuation of
the 'tree of Jesse' imagery; cf. 126-
7.

133. *cold*] comfortless; gloomy;
hopeless.

139. *lade*] load or carry water in
buckets; drain; bale out.

143.] Tillyard suggests a dash after
'with'. 'The pause between preposi-
tion and noun both defines the rhythm
and adds a wealth of implication to the
noun' (*SHP.*, 196).

144. *quick*] Elizabethan sense—
alive; impatient.

o'erweens] is too arrogant or presumptuous.

148.] I'll 'womanize', or 'devote myself to love-making' (*Sh. Bawdy*).

148 ff.] Cf. *R 3*, I. i. 16 ff., on the

And deck my body in gay ornaments,
And 'witch sweet ladies with my words and looks.   15
O miserable thought! and more unlikely,
Than to accomplish twenty golden crowns.
Why, Love forswore me in my mother's womb:
And, for I should not deal in her soft laws,
She did corrupt frail Nature with some bribe,   15
To shrink mine arm up like a wither'd shrub;
To make an envious mountain on my back,
Where sits Deformity to mock my body;
To shape my legs of an unequal size;
To disproportion me in every part,   16
Like to a chaos, or unlick'd bear-whelp
That carries no impression like the dam.
And am I then a man to be belov'd?
O monstrous fault to harbour such a thought!
Then, since this earth affords no joy to me   16
But to command, to check, to o'erbear such
As are of better person than myself,
I'll make my heaven to dream upon the crown;
And, whiles I live, t'account this world but hell,
Until my misshap'd trunk that bears this head   17
Be round impaled with a glorious crown.
And yet I know not how to get the crown,
For many lives stand between me and home:
And I,—like one lost in a thorny wood,
That rents the thorns and is rent with the thorns,   17

161. or] *F3;* or an *F1,2.*   175. rents] *F;* rends *Pope+Edd.*

same contrasted themes of love and power, and below, at v. vi. 68 ff., for Richard's self-description.

150. *'witch*] bewitch.
152. *accomplish*] gain; obtain.
153. *forswore*] abjured.
154. *for*] so that; cf. III. i. 9.
157. *envious*] transferred epithet = spiteful; malicious.
161. *chaos*] formless mass.
or] F 'an' is a normal scribal or compositorial insertion.
unlick'd bear-whelp] Hart quotes Golding, Ovid, xv. 416–19, 'The Bear whelp . . . like an euill fauored lump of flesh alyue dooth lye./The dam b licking shapeth out his membe orderly'.

162. *impression*] form or shape (such as might be imposed by pressure).
164. *monstrous*] like a monster; u natural.
fault] error.
166. *check*] rebuke.
167. *person*] appearance.
171. *impaled*] encircled as by a pa or fence.
175. *rents*] rends; *OED.* v². I.

Seeking a way, and straying from the way;
Not knowing how to find the open air,
But toiling desperately to find it out—
Torment myself to catch the English crown:
And from that torment I will free myself,   180
Or hew my way out with a bloody axe.
Why, I can smile, and murder whiles I smile,
And cry 'Content!' to that that grieves my heart,
And wet my cheeks with artificial tears,
And frame my face to all occasions.   185
I'll drown more sailors than the Mermaid shall;
I'll slay more gazers than the basilisk;
I'll play the orator as well as Nestor,
Deceive more slily than Ulysses could,
And, like a Sinon, take another Troy.   190
I can add colours to the chameleon,
Change shapes with Proteus for advantages,
And set the murderous Machiavel to school.

83. that that] *Q1,2;* that which *Q3,F.*   193. murderous Machiavel] *F;* aspiring
talin / *Q.*

183. *that that*] F sophisticates, after
3.
184. *artificial*] not natural; feigned;
se.
186. *Mermaid*] Vaughan refers to
olland's Pliny, bk xxix, ch. i, where
e mermaids are mentioned in com-
nation, as here, with Proteus, and
e clearly identified with the Homeric
rens, who, by their songs, charmed
ilors to shipwreck on the rocks and
owning. See *Odyssey,* xii. 39–54 and
5. Cf. *Err.,* III. iii. 47, 'Mermaide ... /
drowne me in . . . teares: / Sing
ren for thy selfe'; *Tit.,* II. i. 2–5, 'This
ren, that will charm . . . / And see
s shipwracke'; and 162, 'Ile stop
ine eares against the Mermaids
ng'; and Spenser, *F.Q.,* II. xii. 17, 30.
187. *basilisk*] a fabulous serpent,
pposed to kill by its look.
188. *Nestor*] His eloquence is noted
Homer, but only later is it insisted
, e.g. Ovid, *Metam.,* xiii. 63.
190. *Sinon*] *Aeneid,* ii; not in Homer.

He persuaded the Trojans to take in
the wooden horse, by means of which
the city was captured. Cf. *Lucr.,*
1501–68, and Prince's n. in the new
Arden edn of the *Poems.*
191. *chameleon*] a type of lizard that
changes its colour to blend with its en-
vironment; cf. Ovid, *Metam.,* xv. 411–
12, 'id quoque, quos ventis animal nu-
tritur et aura, / protinus adsimulat,
tetigit quoscumque colores.'
192. *Proteus*] the prophetic old man
of the sea, who could change his shape
at will.
for advantages] to serve his turn.
193. *set . . . to school*] Cf. *Mirror,* 382,
'and settes vs all to scoole'.
Machiavel] the famous Italian author
of *The Prince* (1513), Niccolò Machia-
velli, whose political writings elaborated the theme that all actions, no
matter how immoral, were justified by
the good of the state, or 'Prince'. His
work was known to the Elizabethans
chiefly through his French mis-inter-

    Can I do this, and cannot get a crown?
    Tut! were it further off, I'll pluck it down.   *Exit.* 19

[SCENE III.—*France. The King's Palace.*]

Flourish. Enter LEWIS *the French King, his sister* BONA, *his Admiral*
called BOURBON; PRINCE EDWARD, QUEEN MARGARET, *and th*
EARL OF OXFORD. LEWIS *sits, and riseth up again.*

K. Lew. Fair Queen of England, worthy Margaret,
    Sit down with us: it ill befits thy state
    And birth that thou should'st stand while Lewis doth si
Q. Mar. No, mighty King of France: now Margaret
    Must strike her sail, and learn awhile to serve
    Where kings command. I was, I must confess,
    Great Albion's Queen in former golden days;
    But now mischance hath trod my title down
    And with dishonour laid me on the ground,
    Where I must take like seat unto my fortune   1
    And to my humble state conform myself.

Scene III

SCENE III] *Capell; not in Q,F*   *France ... Palace.*] *Edd.; not in Q,F.*   S.1
Flourish.] *F; not in Q.*   *Enter ... again.*] *F;* Enter king *Lewis* and the ladie *Bon*
and *Queene | Margaret, Prince Edward,* and *Oxford |* and others. *Q.*   1. *K. Lew*
Edd.; Lewis *| Q,F (throughout).*   4. *Q. Mar.] Edd.;* Marg. *| F;* Queen. *| Q (throug*
out).   11. state] *Dyce, conj. Walker;* seat *F.*

preter, Gentillet, so that his theories became synonymous with atheism, equivocation, and murder for political reasons.

Scene III

Source: Hall, 257, 261, 265, 365.

The scene is imaginary, created from hints such as Warwick's 'letters' (Hall, 261). Shakespeare's amalgamation of Warwick's two visits to France is directly suggested, and facilitated, by Hall's treatment. The return from his first visit (1461) and the return, in rebellion, from his second (1470) are linked at the second point, where the first visit is recapitulated (Hall, 365) at more length.

5. *strike her sail*] humble herself Margaret is humble and gracious f the moment; cf. her first appearanc before Henry, in *2 H 6,* I. i. Cf. *Mirr* 143, 'to strike the sayle'.

7. *golden days*] one of Shakespeare most felicitous and suggestive image cf. golden time, III. ii. 127; *I H 6,* I. v 31; golden lads, *Cym.,* IV. ii. 263—in plying at the same time richness, pr eminence, colour, and sunshine.

8. *mischance*] misfortune; ill fortun

11. *state*] Cf. *stand ... sit ... state* lines 2–3, balanced by *seat ... state* 10–11. The F repetition of 'seat'— homonym of 'state' at that time— could be scribal or compositoria under the influence of 10. This kir

K. Lew. Why, say, fair Queen, whence springs this deep
  despair?

Q. Mar. From such a cause as fills mine eyes with tears
  And stops my tongue, while heart is drown'd in cares.

K. Lew. Whate'er it be, be thou still like thyself, 15
  And sit thee by our side. [*Seats her by him*] Yield not thy
   neck
  To Fortune's yoke, but let thy dauntless mind
  Still ride in triumph over all mischance.
  Be plain, Queen Margaret, and tell thy grief;
  It shall be eas'd, if France can yield relief. 20

Q. Mar. Those gracious words revive my drooping thoughts
  And give my tongue-tied sorrows leave to speak.
  Now, therefore, be it known to noble Lewis
  That Henry, sole possessor of my love,
  Is, of a king, become a banish'd man, 25
  And forc'd to live in Scotland a forlorn;
  While proud ambitious Edward, Duke of York,
  Usurps the regal title and the seat
  Of England's true-anointed lawful King.
  This is the cause that I, poor Margaret, 30
  With this my son, Prince Edward, Henry's heir,
  Am come to crave thy just and lawful aid;
  And if thou fail us, all our hope is done.
  Scotland hath will to help, but cannot help;
  Our people and our peers are both misled, 35
  Our treasure seiz'd, our soldiers put to flight,
  And, as thou seest, ourselves in heavy plight.

K. Lew. Renowned Queen, with patience calm the storm,
  While we bethink a means to break it off.

Q. Mar. The more we stay, the stronger grows our foe. 40

---

of error is frequent in *1 H 6*. F, of course, can be interpreted as it stands to mean that Margaret takes a lowly seat, to which she must 'conform herself'.

 16. *sit thee*] be seated; seat thyself.

 17. *dauntless mind*] This 'refers, not to her present condition, but to her famous character' (Hart).

 25. *of*] from being.

26. *in Scotland*] Margaret is naturally ignorant of Henry's capture, in England.

 forlorn] a forlorn person; *OED*. B1.

 37. *heavy*] sad; sorrowful.

 39. *While*] until—the common Elizabethan sense, still current provincially.

 break it off] mitigate (Vaughan).

 40, 41. *stay*] delay.

K. Lew. The more I stay, the more I'll succour thee.

Q. Mar. O, but impatience waiteth on true sorrow.
And see where comes the breeder of my sorrow.

Enter WARWICK.

K. Lew. What's he approacheth boldly to our presence?

Q. Mar. Our Earl of Warwick, Edward's greatest friend.   45

K. Lew. Welcome, brave Warwick! What brings thee to
France?

He descends. She ariseth.

Q. Mar. Ay, now begins a second storm to rise;
For this is he that moves both wind and tide.

War. From worthy Edward, King of Albion,
My lord and sovereign, and thy vowed friend,   50
I come, in kindness and unfeigned love,
First, to do greetings to thy royal person,
And then to crave a league of amity,
And lastly to confirm that amity
With nuptial knot, if thou vouchsafe to grant   55
That virtuous Lady Bona, thy fair sister,
To England's King in lawful marriage.

Q. Mar. [*Aside.*] If that go forward, Henry's hope is done.

War. (*To Bona*) And, gracious madam, in our king's behalf,
I am commanded, with your leave and favour,   60
Humbly to kiss your hand, and with my tongue
To tell the passion of my sovereign's heart;
Where Fame, late entering at his heedful ears,
Hath plac'd thy beauty's image and thy virtue.

Q. Mar. King Lewis and Lady Bona, hear me speak   65

---

43. S.D.] *Q,F.*   45. Our] *Q,F;* Proud *conj. Vaughan.*   46. S.D.] *F; not in Q.*
58. S.D. *Aside*] *Capell; not in Q,F.*   59. S.D.] *F* (Speaking to Bona.).

43. *breeder*] author.

45. *Edward's . . . friend*] a touch of
dramatic irony, from more than one
point of view, in the light of 163 ff. and
III. i.

47. *second storm*] The first was, of
course, that mentioned in 38.

48. *moves . . . wind and tide*] possibly
suggested by Hall, 232; see n. to 157.

51. *unfeigned love*] 2 Cor., vi. 6,
'By kindnesse, by love unfeigned'
(Carter).

58. *go forward*] come to pass; take
place; cf. Kyd, *Sp. Tr.*, II. iii. 18, 'in
case the match go forward'.

62. *passion*] still has much of the
original L. sense of 'suffering'.

63. *Fame*] report; rumour (L. *fama*).

Before you answer Warwick. His demand
Springs not from Edward's well-meant honest love,
But from Deceit, bred by Necessity;
For how can tyrants safely govern home
Unless abroad they purchase great alliance?   70
To prove him tyrant this reason may suffice,
That Henry liveth still; but were he dead,
Yet here Prince Edward stands, King Henry's son.
Look, therefore, Lewis, that by this league and marriage
Thou draw not on thy danger and dishonour;   75
For though usurpers sway the rule awhile,
Yet heavens are just, and time suppresseth wrongs.

War. Injurious Margaret!

Prince.   And why not Queen?

War. Because thy father Henry did usurp;
And thou no more art prince than she is queen.   80

Oxf. Then Warwick disannuls great John of Gaunt,
Which did subdue the greatest part of Spain;
And after John of Gaunt, Henry the Fourth,
Whose wisdom was a mirror to the wisest;
And after that wise prince, Henry the Fifth,   85
Who by his prowess conquered all France:
From these our Henry lineally descends.

War. Oxford, how haps it in this smooth discourse
You told not how Henry the Sixth hath lost
All that which Henry the Fifth had gotten?   90
Methinks these peers of France should smile at that.

---

5. thy] *F;* thee *Johnson, Hudson.*   78. Prince.] *Edd.; Edw. | F; Prince Ed. | Q*
Edw. | Q3).   88. it] *F;* that *Q.*   90. that which] *F;* that that *Q.*

69, 71. *tyrant*] usurper.

70. *purchase*] obtain; gain.

76. *sway*] wield; control.

77. *heavens are just*] ironical, coming from Margaret; in Kyd, *S.P.,* II. i. 122, 124, 126, 128.

78. *Injurious*] insulting, offensive, *OED.* 2.

81. *disannuls*] makes null and void; brings to nothing; cancels.

81–2. *John of Gaunt . . .*] Hart quotes Kyd, *Sp. Tr.,* I. v. 51–2, 'He with a puissant armie came to Spaine, / And

tooke our King of Castile prisoner'. Brooke refers to the licensing (14 May 1594) of 'the famous historye of Iohn of Gaunte . . . with his conquest of Spaine and marriage of his Twoo daughters to the Kinges of Castile and Portugale'. See also n. in *R 2* (New Arden), xl.

82. *Which*] used for 'Who', as in our version of the Lord's Prayer.

89–90. *hath lost | All that*] a sore point with Warwick, from the beginning of *2 H 6;* cf. I. i. 110.

But for the rest: you tell a pedigree
Of threescore and two years—a silly time
To make prescription for a kingdom's worth.

Oxf. Why, Warwick, canst thou speak against thy liege,   95
Whom thou obeyed'st thirty and six years,
And not bewray thy treason with a blush?

War. Can Oxford, that did ever fence the right,
Now buckler falsehood with a pedigree?
For shame! leave Henry, and call Edward king.   100

Oxf. Call him my king by whose injurious doom
My elder brother, the Lord Aubrey Vere,
Was done to death? and more than so, my father,
Even in the downfall of his mellow'd years,
When Nature brought him to the door of Death?   105
No, Warwick, no; while life upholds this arm,
This arm upholds the house of Lancaster.

War. And I the house of York.

K. Lew. Queen Margaret, Prince Edward, and Oxford,
Vouchsafe at our request to stand aside,   110
While I use further conference with Warwick.

They stand aloof

Q. Mar. Heavens grant that Warwick's words bewitch him
not!

K. Lew. Now, Warwick, tell me, even upon thy conscience,
Is Edward your true king? for I were loath

102. My] *F;* Mine *Q.*   106. while] *F;* whilst *Q.*   109. Oxford] *F;* Lor
Oxford *Hanmer.*   111. S.D.] *F; not in Q.*

92. *tell*] (*a*) recount; relate, (*b*) count, as in 'bank-teller'.

93. *threescore and two years*] from the accession of Henry IV (1399) to that of Edward IV (1461).

silly] scanty; meagre; trifling; *OED.* 2d.

94. *prescription*] a legal term = claim founded on long use.

96. *thirty and six years*] Warwick was attainted by the Lancastrian Parliament at Coventry, in 1459, and his allegiance was merely formal after the attempt made on his life ten months previously (Boswell-Stone). Warwick was, however, born in 1428

and was now thirty-six years old

97. *bewray*] alternative form of 'betray' = reveal.

98. *fence*] protect.

99.] Hall, 258.

101. *injurious doom*] unjust judgment

104. *downfall . . . mellow'd years*] a his mature years passed away, like rip fruit falling from a tree, or the sun set ting. Cf. 'From Hyperion's rising in th east until his very *downfall* in the sea *Tit.*, v. ii. 57.

111. *conference*] discussion; conversa tion—the Elizabethan sense.

112. *bewitch*] Cf. III. i. 33, wher Warwick is 'a subtle orator'.

      To link with him that were not lawful chosen.   115

War. Thereon I pawn my credit and mine honour.

K. Lew. But is he gracious in the people's eye?

War. The more that Henry was unfortunate.

K. Lew. Then further: all dissembling set aside,
      Tell me for truth the measure of his love   120
      Unto our sister Bona.

War.   Such it seems
      As may beseem a monarch like himself.
      Myself have often heard him say, and swear,
      That this his love was an eternal plant,
      Whereof the root was fix'd in Virtue's ground,   125
      The leaves and fruit maintain'd with Beauty's sun,
      Exempt from envy, but not from disdain,
      Unless the Lady Bona quite his pain.

K. Lew. Now, sister, let us hear your firm resolve.

Bona. Your grant, or your denial, shall be mine: 130
      (*To Warwick*) Yet I confess that often ere this day,
      When I have heard your king's desert recounted,
      Mine ear hath temper'd judgment to desire.

K. Lew. Then, Warwick, thus: our sister shall be Edward's.
      And now forthwith shall articles be drawn   135
      Touching the jointure that your king must make,
      Which with her dowry shall be counterpois'd.

---

124. *eternall Q*; *externall F.*   128. quite] *Q1,2*; quit *Q3,F.*   131. S.D.] *F*
(*Speaks to War.*), *after the line; not in Q.*   133. temper'd] *This edn, conj. Vaughan;*
tempted *Q,F.*

115, 117. *lawful chosen . . . people's eye*]
referring to (*a*) Edward's claim by descent, (*b*) his approval by the people
(Hall, 253). Both were necessary; a
fact still recognized in the Coronation
ceremony.

116. *pawn*] pledge.

117. *gracious . . . eye*] Cf. Kyd, *S.P.*,
II. i. 143, 'disgracious in thine eye';
finding favour.

124. *eternal*] perennial (Hudson).

127. *envy*] malice; hate. The line
qualifies 'love', 124.

disdain] indignation; vexation.

128. *quite*] requite his sorrow or
trouble; satisfy him (Hart). F follows
Q3.

133. *temper'd*] No question of 'temp-
tation' arises here. Judgment does not
itself desire; judgment and desire are
both present, and have to be modified
or adjusted in order to meet and agree;
cf. *Rom.*, II. i. Prol. 14, 'Temp'ring ex-
tremities with extreme sweete'; and
'temper with their stars', at IV. vi. 29
below. Cf. *R 3*, I. i. 65, where Q1
'tempers' becomes 'tempts' in the suc-
ceeding Qq and in F.

135. *articles*] terms of agreement.

136. *Touching*] regarding.

jointure] marriage settlement, or allowance given to a bride.

137. *counterpois'd*] made equal; balanced.

Draw near, Queen Margaret, and be a witness
That Bona shall be wife to the English king.
Prince. To Edward, but not to the English king.   140
Q. Mar. Deceitful Warwick, it was thy device
By this alliance to make void my suit:
Before thy coming Lewis was Henry's friend.
K. Lew. And still is friend to him and Margaret:
But if your title to the crown be weak,   145
As may appear by Edward's good success,
Then 'tis but reason that I be releas'd
From giving aid which late I promised.
Yet shall you have all kindness at my hand
That your estate requires and mine can yield.   150
War. Henry now lives in Scotland, at his ease,
Where having nothing, nothing can he lose.
And as for you yourself, our quondam queen,
You have a father able to maintain you,
And better 'twere you troubled him than France.   155
Q. Mar. Peace, impudent and shameless Warwick, peace,
Proud setter up and puller down of kings!
I will not hence till with my talk and tears,
Both full of truth, I make King Lewis behold
Thy sly conveyance and thy lord's false love;   160
For both of you are birds of self-same feather.

Post blowing a horn within.

156. peace,] *F2 + Edd.; not in F1.*   161. S.D.] *F (after 160)*; Sound for a post within. *Q.*

138. *be a witness*] Note the dramatic irony.

146. *good success*] 'success' still had the general meaning of 'result, outcome', whether good or bad.

150. *estate*] condition; state (Fr. *état*).

151. *in Scotland*] See n. to 26 above.
at his ease] free from solicitude—more dramatic irony.

153. *quondam*] former (L.).

154. *a father able*] Margaret's father, with his grand titles but slender means, is always a sore point; cf. II. ii. 154, 'a beggar', and v. vii. 38–9. The allusion here was probably suggested by Hall's comment, 'hauing as muche

profites of the . . . stile . . . as rents' (263).

157. *Proud setter up . . .*] Cf. II. iii. 37. Hall, 232, says of Warwick, 'the common people . . . iudged hym able to do all thynges . . . whiche way he bowed, that waie ran the streame'.

160. *conveyance*] (a) legal term for transfer of property, here applied to Lewis's friendship, alliance, and aid, for which Margaret had sued and which she had been promised; (b) underhand dealing; trickery; *OED*. 11b.

161. *birds . . . feather*] The proverb is also referred to at II. i. 170.

K. Lew. Warwick, this is some post to us or thee.

Enter the Post.

Post. (*To War.*) My lord ambassador, these are for you,
　　　Sent from your brother, Marquess Montague;
　　　(*To Lewis*) These from our King unto your Majesty: 165
　　　(*To Margaret*) And, madam, these for you; from whom
　　　　I know not.　　　　　*They all read their letters.*

Oxf. I like it well that our fair Queen and mistress
　　　Smiles at her news, while Warwick frowns at his.

Prince. Nay, mark how Lewis stamps as he were nettled:
　　　I hope all's for the best.　　　　　170

K. Lew. Warwick, what are thy news? and yours, fair Queen?

Q. Mar. Mine, such as fill my heart with unhop'd joys.

War. Mine, full of sorrow and heart's discontent.

K. Lew. What? has your king married the Lady Grey?
　　　And now, to soothe your forgery and his,　　　175
　　　Sends me a paper to persuade me patience?
　　　Is this th'alliance that he seeks with France?
　　　Dare he presume to scorn us in this manner?

Q. Mar. I told your Majesty as much before:
　　　This proveth Edward's love and Warwick's honesty. 180

War. King Lewis, I here protest in sight of heaven,
　　　And by the hope I have of heavenly bliss,
　　　That I am clear from this misdeed of Edward's—
　　　No more my king, for he dishonours me,
　　　But most himself, if he could see his shame.　　　185
　　　Did I forget that by the house of York

162. S.D.] *F; not in Q.*　163. S.D.] *F* (*Speakes to Warwick.*), *after the line.*　these]
This edn; these Letters *F;* this letter *Q.*　165. S.D.] *F, after the line.*　166.
S.D. *To Margaret.*] *F* (*And Madam,* these for you: *To Margaret* / From whom . . .).
They . . . letters.] *F; not in Q.*　169. Prince] *Edd.; Pr. Ed.* | *Q; Prince Ed.* | *F.*
169–70.] *As Rowe; as prose* | *F.*　175. soothe] *F;* smooth *Rann, conj. Heath.*

　162. *post*] express messenger.
　163. *these*] the F 'letters'.
　172. *unhop'd*] unexpected.
　175. *soothe*] smooth or gloss over (an
offence), *OED.* 6; a sense also exempli-
fied in Fletcher, etc., *Rollo Duke of Normandy*, III. i. 173–6. But cf. 'smooths the
wrong', III. i. 48.

forgery] deceit.
　180. *proveth*] in the older sense, surviving in the doublet 'probe', of 'test',
as much as in the sense (here ironical)
of 'shows to be true'. Cf. *1 H 6*, II.
ii. 58, 'I mean to prove this Lady's
courtesy'.
　186. *by*] by means of.

My father came untimely to his death?
Did I let pass th'abuse done to my niece?
Did I impale him with the regal crown?
Did I put Henry from his native right?   190
And am I guerdon'd at the last with shame?
Shame on himself! for my desert is honour;
And to repair my honour lost for him
I here renounce him and return to Henry.
My noble Queen, let former grudges pass,   195
And henceforth I am thy true servitor.
I will revenge his wrong to Lady Bona,
And replant Henry in his former state.

Q. Mar. Warwick, these words have turn'd my hate to love;
And I forgive and quite forget old faults,   200
And joy that thou becom'st King Henry's friend.

War. So much his friend, ay, his unfeigned friend,
That if King Lewis vouchsafe to furnish us
With some few bands of chosen soldiers,
I'll undertake to land them on our coast   205
And force the tyrant from his seat by war.
'Tis not his new-made bride shall succour him;
And as for Clarence, as my letters tell me,
He's very likely now to fall from him
For matching more for wanton lust than honour   210
Or than for strength and safety of our country.

Bona. Dear brother, how shall Bona be reveng'd
But by thy help to this distressed queen?

Q. Mar. Renowned Prince, how shall poor Henry live
Unless thou rescue him from foul despair?   215

---

187. *My father . . .*] the Earl of Salisbury, taken prisoner at Wakefield, and
executed by the Lancastrians at Pomfret (Hall, 251).

untimely] before his time; early.

188. *abuse*] wrong; injury.

my niece] The 'abuse' is described in
Hall, 265.

189. *impale*] circle; surround (his
brows); cf. III. ii. 171.

190. *native right*] the right (to the
crown) he was born to (L. *natus*).

196. *servitor*] servant.

198. *replant*] a repetition of the 'Plantagenet' pun, as at I. i. 48, etc.

state] royal position.

199.] Cf. Kyd, *S.P.*, II. i. 152, 'And
all my former love is turned to hate';
F.Q., I. v. 37, 'Her love she turnd to
hate'.

200. *forgive . . . forget*] proverbial;
Tilley, F597.

206. *tyrant*] usurper.

seat] throne.

209. *fall from*] desert.

210. *wanton*] unrestrained, *OED.* 1.

Bona. My quarrel and this English queen's are one.

War. And mine, fair Lady Bona, joins with yours.

K. Lew. And mine with hers, and thine, and Margaret's.
Therefore at last I firmly am resolv'd
You shall have aid.   220

Q. Mar. Let me give humble thanks for all at once.

K. Lew. Then, England's messenger, return in post
And tell false Edward, thy supposed king,
That Lewis of France is sending over maskers
To revel it with him and his new bride.   225
Thou seest what's past, go fear thy king withal.

Bona. Tell him, in hope he'll prove a widower shortly,
I'll wear the willow garland for his sake.

Q. Mar. Tell him my mourning weeds are laid aside,
And I am ready to put armour on.   230

War. Tell him from me that he hath done me wrong,
And therefore I'll uncrown him ere't be long.
There's thy reward; be gone.   *Exit Post.*

K. Lew.   But, Warwick,
Thou and Oxford, with five thousand men,
Shall cross the seas and bid false Edward battle;   235
And, as occasion serves, this noble Queen
And Prince shall follow with a fresh supply.
Yet, ere thou go, but answer me one doubt:
What pledge have we of thy firm loyalty?

War. This shall assure my constant loyalty: 240
That if our Queen and this young Prince agree,

---

228. I'll] *Q; I F.*   229. are] *F;* be *Q.*   233. S.D.] *F; Exit Mes. | Q3; not in*
Q1,2.

---

222. *in post*] in great haste.

224–5. *maskers . . .*] performers or actors in a mask, or theatrical show. For the idea, cf. *H 5*, I. ii. 250 ff. (the tun of tennis balls).

226. *fear*] intimidate; make afraid.
withal] with that.

228. *I'll*] Cf. IV. i. 99, where both Q and F have 'I'll'.
willow garland] emblem of disappointed love; cf. *F.Q.*, I. i. 9, 'The willow worne of forlorne Paramours'; *Oth.*, IV. iii. 39 ff.

230. *armour*] Here Margaret is again the successor of Joan of Arc. Steevens notes that the practice was then not unusual: Queen Elizabeth appeared in armour at Tilbury.

233. *thy reward*] largess, or money.

234–43.] Warwick's two visits to the French court (1461 and 1470) are skilfully amalgamated (Hall, 265, 280–1).

236. *serves*] is favourable, opportune.

237. *supply*] reinforcements.

I'll join mine eldest daughter and my joy
To him forthwith in holy wedlock's bands.

Q. Mar. Yes, I agree, and thank you for your motion.
    Son Edward, she is fair and virtuous,   245
    Therefore delay not, give thy hand to Warwick;
    And with thy hand thy faith irrevocable
    That only Warwick's daughter shall be thine.

Prince. Yes, I accept her, for she well deserves it;
    And here, to pledge my vow, I give my hand.   250
                     He gives his hand to Warwick.

K. Lew. Why stay we now? These soldiers shall be levied,
    And thou, Lord Bourbon, our High Admiral,
    Shalt waft them over with our royal fleet.
    I long till Edward fall by war's mischance
    For mocking marriage with a dame of France.   255
                     Exeunt all but Warwick.

War. I came from Edward as ambassador,
    But I return his sworn and mortal foe:
    Matter of marriage was the charge he gave me,
    But dreadful war shall answer his demand.
    Had he none else to make a stale but me?   260
    Then none but I shall turn his jest to sorrow.
    I was the chief that rais'd him to the crown,
    And I'll be chief to bring him down again:

---

242. mine eldest] *Q,F;* my youngest *Theobald.*   243. wedlock's] *Q1,2;* wed-
locke *Q3,F.*   250. S.D.] *F; not in Q.*   253. Shalt] *F2+Edd.;* Shall *Q,F.*
255. S.D.] *Edd.;* Exeunt. Manet Warwicke. / *F; not in Q.*   263. to . . . down again]
Q,F; again to . . . down *conj. this edn.*

242-3. *I'll join . . . in holy wedlock's
bands*] Cf. *Mirror*, 432, 'with me to
ioyne in wedlockes bande'; F follows
Q3.

242. *eldest*] Cf. iv. i. 118; ii. 12.
The facts are given correctly in Hall,
271-2, and in *R 3*, i. i. 153. The confusion could be Shakespeare's, but
alternatively the Q reporters', perpetuated in F.

244. *motion*] proposal; offer.

251. *stay*] delay.

253. *waft*] convey by sea.

254. *long till*] desire earnestly that;
am impatient for.

255. *mocking*] applies in the double
sense—to the marriage, and to the lady
(Vaughan); pretending marriage, and
making a mock of Lady Bona.

258. *Matter*] a question.

260. *stale*] (*a*) tool, (*b*) dupe; cf. *Tit.,*
i. i. 304-5.

263. *to . . . down again*] The F reading
is from Q, and may have the authority
only of that reported text (though
Warwick's part is well reported). The
conjecture supposes a familiar type of
error, the ironing-out of an inversion.
If it is correct, the scene would end
(like some others in Shakespeare) with

Not that I pity Henry's misery,
But seek revenge on Edward's mockery.　　　*Exit.* 265

265. S.D.] *Q,F.*

two rhyming couplets; and 262–3 would have an even better rhetorical balance
than in Q's report.

[ACT IV

SCENE I.—*London, The Palace.*]

Enter RICHARD, GEORGE, SOMERSET, *and* MONTAGUE.

Rich. Now tell me, brother Clarence, what think you
    Of this new marriage with the Lady Grey?
    Hath not our brother made a worthy choice?
Geo. Alas, you know 'tis far from hence to France!
    How could he stay till Warwick made return?   5
Som. My lords, forbear this talk; here comes the King.

Flourish. Enter KING EDWARD [*attended*]; LADY GREY[, *as
Queen*]; PEMBROKE, STAFFORD, HASTINGS[, *and others*].
Four stand on one side and four on the other.

Rich. And his well-chosen bride.
Geo. I mind to tell him plainly what I think.
K. Edw. Now, brother of Clarence, how like you our choice,

ACT IV
Scene 1

ACT IV SCENE I] *Rowe; not in Q,F.*   London. The Palace.] *Edd.; not in Q,F.*
Enter . . . Montague.] *F; Enter king* Edward, *the* Queene *and* Clarence, *and* Gloster,
and Montague, *and* Hastings, *and* Penbrooke, *with souldiers.* Q.   1. *Rich.*] *F*
(*throughout*); *Glo.* | *Q* (*throughout*).   6. S.D.] *F* (*subst.*); *not in* Q.   *attended*]
Capell; not in F.   *as Queen*] *Rowe; not in* F.   *and others*] *Capell (subst.); not in* F.

Source: Hall, 271 (not in Holinshed), 365. Warwick's interview with
Clarence is transferred to Edward himself.

S.D. Somerset] Shakespeare knew
that three Dukes of Somerset were
killed in the Wars of the Roses. The
first is mentioned at I. i. 16. The present Somerset is a compound of the
other two—Henry Beaufort, the third
duke, who abandoned the Lancastrians, then changed sides again, and

was beheaded by the Yorkists after the
battle of Hexham in 1464; and his
brother, the fourth duke, always a
staunch Lancastrian; it is he who appears on the Lancastrian side throughout Act V. Shakespeare has made one
dramatic Somerset of the two brothers.
See Boswell-Stone, 320 and 335; and
French, 181.
    6. S.D.] Four . . . four] F preserves
the element of symmetry so natural
and characteristic on the apron-stage

That you stand pensive, as half malcontent? 10

Geo. As well as Lewis of France or the Earl of Warwick,
 Which are so weak of courage and in judgment
 That they'll take no offence at our abuse.

K. Edw. Suppose they take offence without a cause;
 They are but Lewis and Warwick: I am Edward, 15
 Your King and Warwick's, and must have my will.

Rich. And you shall have your will, because our King:
 Yet hasty marriage seldom proveth well.

K. Edw. Yea, brother Richard, are you offended too?

Rich. No, God forfend that I should wish them sever'd 20
 Whom God hath join'd: ay, and 'twere pity
 To sunder them that yoke so well together.

K. Edw. Setting your scorns and your mislike aside,
 Tell me some reason why the Lady Grey
 Should not become my wife and England's Queen. 25
 And you too, Somerset and Montague,
 Speak freely what you think.

Geo. Then this is my opinion: that King Lewis
 Becomes your enemy for mocking him
 About the marriage of the Lady Bona. 30

Rich. And Warwick, doing what you gave in charge,

13. our] *F;* your *Capell.* 17. you] *Rowe; not in Q,F.* 20. forfend] *Q;* forbid *F.*
20–2. No . . . together] *This edn, conj. Vaughan (subst.);* Not I: no: / . . . wish . . .
seuer'd, / Whom God . . . ioyn'd together: / I, . . . pittie, . . . them, / That . . .
together. *F;* Once gaine saie your highnesse pleasure, / I, & twere a pittie to
sunder them that yoake so wel togither. *Q.* 26–7.] *F;* Speake freelie *Clarence,*
Gloster, / *Montague,* and *Hastings.* / *Q.* 28. my] *Q1,2;* mine *Q3,F.* 28–30.]
As Pope; . . . opinion: / . . . Enemie, / . . . Marriage / . . . Bona. *F;* . . . opinion: /
That *Warwike* being dishonored in his embassage, / Doth seeke reuenge to quite
his iniuries. *Q.*

10. *malcontent*] dissatisfied.

11–13.] ironical, of course.

12. *Which*] Abbott, 226, for the usage.

13. *abuse*] deception—the frequent Elizabethan sense—rather than ill-treatment (as given by Schmidt). It refers to the breach of faith over Edward's marriage.

16. *must have my will*] typical of Edward's character.

18. *hasty*] rash; precipitate.

20–2.] The F 'corrector' has combined sophistication of the older 'forfend' with carelessness in eliminating memorial matter from the Q copy. Vaughan notes that 'together' is not in the marriage service. See Intro., xxxix.

20. *God forfend*] the ironical devil, Richard, citing Scripture for his purpose.

22. *yoke*] are coupled, especially in marriage, like oxen under the yoke.

29. *mocking*] Cf. III. iii. 255, and n.

   Is now dishonour'd by this marriage.

K. Edw. What if both Lewis and Warwick be appeas'd
   By such invention as I can devise?

Mont. Yet to have join'd with France in such alliance 35
   Would more have strengthen'd this our commonwealth
   'Gainst foreign storms than any home-bred marriage.

Hast. Why, knows not Montague that of itself
   England is safe, if true within itself?

Mont. But the safer when 'tis back'd with France. 40

Hast. 'Tis better using France than trusting France.
   Let us be back'd with God and with the seas
   Which he hath given for fence impregnable,
   And with their helps only defend ourselves:
   In them and in ourselves our safety lies. 45

Geo. For this one speech Lord Hastings well deserves
   To have the heir of the Lord Hungerford.

K. Edw. Ay, what of that? it was my will and grant;
   And for this once my will shall stand for law.

Rich. And yet, methinks, your Grace hath not done well 50
   To give the heir and daughter of Lord Scales
   Unto the brother of your loving bride;
   She better would have fitted me, or Clarence:
   But in your bride you bury brotherhood.

Geo. Or else you would not have bestow'd the heir 55
   Of the Lord Bonville on your new wife's son,
   And leave your brothers to go speed elsewhere.

K. Edw. Alas, poor Clarence! is it for a wife
   That thou art malcontent? I will provide thee.

Geo. In choosing for yourself you show'd your judgment, 60
   Which being shallow, you shall give me leave

---

32. this] *This edn;* this new F.

32.] F 'new' looks like a duplication, from a marginal correction, of 'now'; or a scribal recollection of 2 above.

 34. *invention*] plan; device.

 39. *England . . . itself*] an old sentiment, very common in Elizabethan literature; cf. *John,* v. vii. 117–18, and *2 T R.,* ix. 45–6, 'Let England liue but true within it selfe, / And all

the world can neuer wrong her state'.

 43. *fence*] defence.

 44. *only*] alone.

 48–9.] Cf. n. to 16.

 51. *the heir*] the rich heiress Elizabeth, daughter of the Lord Scales of *2 H 6* (French).

 57. *speed*] succeed.

 58.] Note the fatuity of Edward, in face of his brothers' discontent.

To play the broker in mine own behalf;
And to that end I shortly mind to leave you.

K. Edw. Leave me, or tarry, Edward will be King,
And not be tied unto his brother's will.   65

Q. Eliz. My lords, before it pleas'd his Majesty
To raise my state to title of a queen,
Do me but right, and you must all confess
That I was not ignoble of descent;
And meaner than myself have had like fortune.   70
But as this title honours me and mine,
So your dislikes, to whom I would be pleasing,
Doth cloud my joys with danger and with sorrow.

K. Edw. My love, forbear to fawn upon their frowns:
What danger or what sorrow can befall thee   75
So long as Edward is thy constant friend
And their true sovereign whom they must obey?
Nay, whom they shall obey, and love thee too,
Unless they seek for hatred at my hands;
Which if they do, yet will I keep thee safe,   80
And they shall feel the vengeance of my wrath.

Rich. [*Aside.*] I hear, yet say not much, but think the more.

Enter a Post.

K. Edw. Now, messenger, what letters or what news
From France?

Post. My sovereign liege, no letters, and few words, 85

65. brother's] *Rowe;* Brothers *F;* brothers' *conj. anon.*   will] *F;* wils *Q.*   82.
82. side.] *Johnson; not in* Q,F.   S.D.] *F;* Enter a Messenger. *Q (after 83).*   83.
messenger] *F;* sirrah *Q.*

62. *play the broker*] act as agent or go-
between.
63. *mind*] intend.
66 ff.] The Queen, after listening
in silence to the remarks of George
and Richard, affecting her family and
position, at last makes a dignified
reply.
69. *not ignoble of descent*] Hall, 365,
says she was 'borne of noble bloude,
specially by her mother, which was
Duchesse of Bedforde, and she was
maried to sir Richard Wooduile lorde
Riuers, her father . . .' The Duchess

was sister-in-law to Henry V, whose
brother Bedford was. Cf. Kyd, *Sp. Tr.*,
i. i. 5–6, 'my discent, / Though not
ignoble'.
70. *meaner*] people of lowlier descent
or rank.
72. *dislikes*] disapproval; antipathy.
to whom] The antecedent is contain-
ed in the subjective 'your' = 'of you'.
82.] proverbial, as is common with
Richard; cf. 'I see much, but I say
little and do less', and 'I say little but
I think the more' (*Proverbs*, ed. J. Shar-
man, 1546, 72, 98).

But such as I, without your special pardon,
Dare not relate.

K. Edw. Go to, we pardon thee: therefore, in brief,
Tell me their words as near as thou canst guess them.
What answer makes King Lewis unto our letters?   90

Post. At my depart, these were his very words:
'Go tell false Edward, thy supposed king,
That Lewis of France is sending over maskers
To revel it with him and his new bride.'

K. Edw. Is Lewis so brave? Belike he thinks me Henry.   95
But what said Lady Bona to my marriage?

Post. These were her words, utter'd with mild disdain:
'Tell him, in hope he'll prove a widower shortly,
I'll wear the willow garland for his sake.'

K. Edw. I blame not her; she could say little less;   100
She had the wrong. But what said Henry's queen?
For I have heard that she was there in place.

Post. 'Tell him,' quoth she, 'my mourning weeds are done,
And I am ready to put armour on.'

K. Edw. Belike she minds to play the Amazon.   105
But what said Warwick to these injuries?

Post. He, more incens'd against your Majesty
Than all the rest, discharg'd me with these words:
'Tell him from me that he hath done me wrong,
And therefore I'll uncrown him ere't be long.'   110

K. Edw. Ha! durst the traitor breathe out so proud words?
Well, I will arm me, being thus forewarn'd:
They shall have wars and pay for their presumption.
But say, is Warwick friends with Margaret?   114

Post. Ay, gracious sovereign, they are so link'd in friendship

88-9.] *Capell;* ... thee: / ... words, / ... them. *F.*   92. thy] *Q, Rowe;* the *F*
103. are] *F;* be *Q.*

88. *Go to*] Come.

91. *At my depart*] Cf. II. i. 110, and
2 *H 6,* I. i. 2, for this use of verb as
noun.

99. *willow garland*] in sign of disappointed love; cf. III. iii. 228.

102. *in place*] a Gallicism (Steevens)
= present.

103. *done*] Her mourning is ended

and her widow's weeds (garments) pu[t]
off.

106. *injuries*] insults; calumnies—th[e]
common Elizabethan usage.

108. *discharg'd*] dismissed.

112. *arm ... forewarn'd*] alluding t[o]
the proverb, 'Forewarned is fore[-]
armed', a translation of L. *praemonitus
praemunitus.* Cf. 126, and Tilley, F54

That young Prince Edward marries Warwick's daughter.
Geo. Belike the elder; Clarence will have the younger.
　　　Now, brother king, farewell, and sit you fast,
　　　For I will hence to Warwick's other daughter;
　　　That, though I want a kingdom, yet in marriage　　120
　　　I may not prove inferior to yourself.
　　　You that love me and Warwick, follow me.
　　　　　　　　　　　Exit George, and Somerset follows.
Rich. [*Aside.*] Not I: my thoughts aim at a further matter;
　　　I stay not for the love of Edward, but the crown.
K. Edw. Clarence and Somerset both gone to Warwick!　125
　　　Yet am I arm'd against the worst can happen,
　　　And haste is needful in this desperate case.
　　　Pembroke and Stafford, you in our behalf
　　　Go levy men and make prepare for war;
　　　They are already, or quickly will be, landed:　　130
　　　Myself in person will straight follow you.
　　　　　　　　　　　Exeunt Pembroke and Stafford.
　　　But, ere I go, Hastings and Montague,
　　　Resolve my doubt. You twain, of all the rest,
　　　Are nearest to Warwick by blood and by alliance:
　　　Tell me if you love Warwick more than me.　　135
　　　If it be so, then both depart to him;
　　　I rather wish you foes than hollow friends.
　　　But if you mind to hold your true obedience,
　　　Give me assurance with some friendly vow,
　　　That I may never have you in suspect.　　　140
Mont. So God help Montague as he proves true!
Hast. And Hastings as he favours Edward's cause!
K. Edw. Now, brother Richard, will you stand by us?

117. elder ... younger] *Q,F;* younger ... elder *Theobald.*　122. S.D.] *F; Exit Clarence* and *Summerset. | Q.*　123. *Aside.*] *Rowe; not in Q,F.*　123–4.] *As Pope; Not I: / My ... matter: / I ... F; Not I; / My ... I / Stay ... Capell.*　124. the love] *F;* love *Pope.*　126. arm'd] *F;* warn'd *conj. Vaughan.*　131. S.D.] *F; not in Q.*　134. nearest] *Q1,2;* neere *Q3,F.*

117. *Belike*] presumably.

　elder ... younger] Cf. III. iii. 242. Both passages are in Q; and it is possible that the error (for 'younger ... elder') is memorial; the allocation is given correctly in *R 3*, and Hall, 281.

118. *sit you fast*] keep your posi-

tion firmly; George was the next heir.

120. *want*] lack.

129. *prepare*] preparation; cf. 'depart' at 91 above.

131. *straight*] immediately.

134. *nearest*] F here follows Q3 copy.

140. *in suspect*] under suspicion.

Rich. Ay, in despite of all that shall withstand you.
K. Edw. Why, so! then am I sure of victory.   145
       Now, therefore, let us hence, and lose no hour
       Till we meet Warwick with his foreign power.   *Exeunt.*

       [SCENE II.—*A plain in Warwickshire.*]

Enter WARWICK *and* OXFORD *in England, with French Soldiers.*

War. Trust me, my lord, all hitherto goes well;
       The common people by numbers swarm to us.

              Enter GEORGE *and* SOMERSET.

       But see where Somerset and Clarence comes.
       Speak suddenly, my lords: are we all friends?
Geo. Fear not that, my lord.   5
War. Then, gentle Clarence, welcome unto Warwick;
       And welcome Somerset. I hold it cowardice
       To rest mistrustful where a noble heart

147. S.D.] *F; Exeunt Omnes. | Q.*

                    Scene II
SCENE II] *Capell; not in Q,F.   A plain in Warwickshire.] Capell; not in Q,F.*
S.D.] *F; Enter ... Oxford,* with souldiers. *Q.*   2. by numbers swarm to us] *Q,F;*
swarm by numbers to us *Pope;* swarm to us by numbers *Hudson.*   2. S.D.] *F;*
not in Q.   5. Fear] *Q,F; Oh! fear Hanmer; Fear you conj. this edn.*

145. *so!*] good!
147. *power*] army.

       Scene II
Source: Hall, 272, 275, leading up
to the battle of Banbury Field in Scene
iii. The French soldiers, however, are
the result of telescoping this series of
events with those that later led to the
battle of Tewkesbury (v. iv, v), where
Margaret did have the help of French
troops.
       S.D. in England, with French Sol-
diers] 'This S.D. almost suggests patri-
otic indignation' (Wilson). It further
suggests the author's hand.
       1–18.] set up from Q copy uncor-
rected; cf. 2, 12, 15. See McKerrow

in *RES.*, xiii. 66–7; and Intro., xxiii.
       1.] Cf. Kyd, *S.P.*, II. i. 291, 'Hetherto
all goes well'; and *Sp. Tr.*, III. x. 1,
'thus farre things goe well'.
       2.] The word-order is memorially
contaminated in Q, and seems doubtful in F.
       3. *comes*] For the verb inflection in
's' with two singular subjects, see
Abbott, 336.
       4. *suddenly*] without preparation; ex-
tempore.
       5. *Fear not that*] you may be certain
of that; cf. *Rom.*, III. v. 87; *2 H 4*, IV. i.
185; *2 H 6*, II. iv. 56.
       6. *gentle*] noble—normal Elizabeth-
an sense.
       8. *rest*] remain (Fr. *rester*).

Hath pawn'd an open hand in sign of love;
Else might I think that Clarence, Edward's brother,   10
Were but a feigned friend to our proceedings.
But come, sweet Clarence; my daughter shall be thine.
And now what rests but, in night's coverture,
Thy brother being carelessly encamp'd,
His soldiers lurking in the towns about,   15
And but attended by a simple guard,
We may surprise and take him at our pleasure?
Our scouts have found the adventure very easy:
That, as Ulysses and stout Diomede
With sleight and manhood stole to Rhesus' tents,   20
And brought from thence the Thracian fatal steeds,
So we, well cover'd with the night's black mantle,
At unawares may beat down Edward's guard,
And seize himself—I say not, slaughter him,
For I intend but only to surprise him.   25
You that will follow me to this attempt,
Applaud the name of Henry with your leader.

They all cry 'Henry!'

---

2. come] *This edn;* welcome *Q,F.*   15. towns] *Theobald+Edd.;* towne *Q,F.*
7. S.D.] *F; not in Q.*

---

9. *pawn'd*] pledged.

12. *come*] The QF 'welcome' is prob-ably a memorial repetition from 6 and 7, uncorrected; cf. i. ii. 63: Q welcome, come.

my daughter] 'he married the Lady Isabell', Hall, 272. See iii. iii. 242, and v. i. 116–17 and n.

13. *coverture*] shade; cover.

14. *carelessly*] without due care or precautions.

15. *towns*] The Q reading is a memorial or transmission error, uncorrected in F; cf. iv. iii. 13.

16. *simple*] mere; nothing else but.

18. *adventure*] hazard; venture.

19. *Ulysses . . . Diomede*] identified with sleight and manhood respective-ly.

stout] valiant.

20. *sleight*] trickery; cunning.

21. *Thracian fatal steeds*] 'The oracle had declared that Troy could not be taken if the horses of Rhesus once drank of the Xanthus and grazed on the Trojan plains. The Greeks there-fore sent Diomede and Ulysses to inter-cept the Thracian prince when he came to bring help to Priam [Prince of Troy]; and they killed him on the night of his arrival and carried off the horses' (Hart). See Ovid, *Metam.*, xiii. 247–54; *Heroides*, i. i; *Amores*, i. x. 23–4; and Virgil, *Aeneid*, i. 469–73: 'ardentis-que avertit equos in castra, prius-quam / pabula gustassent Troiae Xanthumque bibissent'. The story ultimately derives from *Iliad*, x; and is the subject of Euripides' *Rhesus*.

fatal] fraught with destiny.

22. *night's black mantle*] Cf. Spenser, *F.Q.*, i. i. 39, 'Whiles sad Night ouer him her mantle black doth spred.'

25. *surprise*] capture unawares.

> Why, then, let's on our way in silent sort,
> For Warwick and his friends, God and St George! *Exeunt*

[SCENE III.—EDWARD's *camp near Warwick*.]

Enter three Watchmen to guard the King's tent.

1 Watch. Come on, my masters, each man take his stand:
  The King by this is set him down to sleep.
2 Watch. What, will he not to bed?
1 Watch. Why, no; for he hath made a solemn vow
  Never to lie and take his natural rest
  Till Warwick or himself be quite suppress'd.
2 Watch. To-morrow then belike shall be the day,
  If Warwick be so near as men report.
3 Watch. But say, I pray, what nobleman is that
  That with the King here resteth in his tent?
1 Watch. 'Tis the Lord Hastings, the King's chiefest friend.
3 Watch. O, is it so? But why commands the King
  That his chief followers lodge in towns about him,
  While he himself keeps in the cold field?
2 Watch. 'Tis the more honour because more dangerous.

---

28. Why] *F; Cla.* Why *Q.*

Scene III

SCENE III] *Capell; not in Q,F.   Edward's. . . . Warwick.*] *Capell; not in Q,*
S.D.]*F; not in Q.*   13. about him] *F; not in Q; about conj. this edn.*   14. keeps
F; keepeth Theobald; keeps here Hanmer; keeps out conj. Vaughan.   15. mor
dangerous] *F; dangerous Hanmer.*

---

28. *sort*] manner.

Scene III

Source: as for IV. ii. Edward's two
separate defeats are merged: (*a*) 1469,
before Warwick's reconciliation with
Henry, and Henry's capture, and (*b*)
1470, Warwick's transfer to the Lancastrian cause when in France, and his
landing at Dartmouth. In both cases
French troops were involved.
  The scene is mainly Shakespeare's
creation, though imitated from Kyd,

Sp. Tr., III. iii, of which 16 is echoed i
the first line of III. ii.
  2. *set him down*] settled down.
  13–14.] See IV. ii. 15. For the po
sible editorial addition of 'him' in I
cf. *R 2,* IV. i. 237 (Q look vpon; F loo
vpon me); and Hall, 290, 'the towne
rounde aboute'.
  13. *lodge*] lie; sleep.
  about] round about.
  14. *keeps*] lives; dwells.
  15. *honour . . . dangerous*] proverbia
cf. Beaumont and Fletcher, *Rule*

₃ Watch. Ay, but give me worship and quietness;
  I like it better than a dangerous honour.
  If Warwick knew in what estate he stands,
  'Tis to be doubted he would waken him.
₂ Watch. Unless our halberds did shut up his passage. 20
₂ Watch. Ay, wherefore else guard we his royal tent
  But to defend his person from night-foes?

  Enter WARWICK, GEORGE, OXFORD, SOMERSET,
    and French Soldiers, silent all.

War. This is his tent; and see where stand his guard.
  Courage, my masters! Honour now or never!
  But follow me, and Edward shall be ours. 25
Watch. Who goes there?
Watch. Stay, or thou diest.

  Warwick and the rest cry all, 'Warwick! Warwick!' and
  set upon the guard, who fly, crying, 'Arm! Arm!',
  Warwick and the rest following them.

The drum playing and the trumpet sounding, enter WARWICK,
SOMERSET, and the rest, bringing the KING *out in his gown, sitting*
in a chair. RICHARD *and* HASTINGS *fly over the stage.*

Som. What are they that fly there?
War. Richard and Hastings; let them go;
  Here is the Duke.
K. Edw.   Why, Warwick, when we parted, 30

---

22. S.D.] *F; not in* Q. 27. S.D.] *F* (*. . . flyes . . .*); *All*. A *Warwike*. | Alarmes,
and Gloster and Hastings flies. Q. 29–30. Richard . . . go; / Here . . . Duke.]
this edn; Richard . . . Duke. Q,F; Richard . . . is / The duke. *Pope.* 30. Why]
this edn; The duke, why Q; The Duke? / Why F.

---

ife, IV. i. 42, 'The more the danger,
ll the more the honour'; and Tilley,
35.
16. *worship*] ease and dignity.
19. *doubted*] feared; cf. IV. viii. 37;
ll so used provincially.
20. *halberds*] battle-axes on long
poles.
shut up] bar.
29–30.] F has been contaminated by
copy; see Intro., xvii.
30.] The Q repetition of 'The Duke'

probably originated from the cue in
Edward's 'part', as written or remem-
bered (cf. I. iii. 47, and III. ii. 111–12,
and Intro., xvii) and was thence incorporated in F. It is metrically superfluous.
  It might be argued that it represents
the immediate retort of surprise and
hot indignation, and gives the point a
necessary initial emphasis. This, however, was not Edward's way. He is
much more casual; and what emphasis

Thou call'dst me King.

War.   Ay, but the case is alter'd.
When you disgrac'd me in my embassade,
Then I degraded you from being King,
And come now to create you Duke of York.
Alas, how should you govern any kingdom   3�:
That know not how to use ambassadors,
Nor how to be contented with one wife,
Nor how to use your brothers brotherly,
Nor how to study for the people's welfare,
Nor how to shroud yourself from enemies?   4⁰

K. Edw. Yea, brother of Clarence, art thou here too?
Nay, then I see that Edward needs must down.
Yet, Warwick, in despite of all mischance,
Of thee thyself and all thy complices,
Edward will always bear himself a king.   4⁵
Though Fortune's malice overthrow my state,
My mind exceeds the compass of her wheel.

War. Then, for his mind, be Edward England's king;
                                 Takes off his crown
But Henry now shall wear the English crown
And be true King indeed; thou but the shadow.   5⁰
My lord of Somerset, at my request,
See that forthwith Duke Edward be convey'd
Unto my brother, Archbishop of York.
When I have fought with Pembroke and his fellows,

---

32. embassade] *F;* embassage *Q.*   34. now to create] *F;* to new create *con.*
Johnson.   36. know] *F;* knowes *Q.*   37.] *F; not in Q.*   45. a] *Q; as F*
48. S.D.] *F; not in Q.*

is required is provided by the position
of 'King'. The same balance may be
seen, between Warwick and Richard,
at v. i. 28–9.
   31.] Cf. Kyd, *S.P.,* ii. i. 292, 'the
case is altered'.
   32. *embassade*] Hall, 278 = embassage; the only example in Shakespeare.
   36. *know*] For the Q syntax, see
Abbott, 247.
   37.] not in Q; possibly censored.
   40. *shroud*] shelter; conceal.
   42. *must down*] scil. with the wheel of
Fortune, 46–7; cf. iv. iv. 28.

46. *state*] sovereignty.
47. *compass*] circle; range.
52. *Duke*] Note the irony.
52–3. *convey'd / . . . York*] to Middleham Castle, in Yorkshire; Hall, 275.
53. *Archbishop of York*] George
Nevill; see App. II.
54. *fought with Pembroke*] This precedes the capture of Henry, in Hall,
273–5.
   Pembroke . . . fellows] perhaps a topi-
cal allusion to the company by whom
the play was acted—Pembroke's Men;
see Intro., xvi, xlv ff.

I'll follow you, and come and tell what answer   55
Lewis and the Lady Bona send to him.
Now, for a while, farewell, good Duke of York.

K. Edw. What fates impose, that men must needs abide;
It boots not to resist both wind and tide.

They lead him out forcibly.

Oxf. What now remains, my lords, for us to do   60
But march to London with our soldiers?

War. Ay, that's the first thing that we have to do,
To free King Henry from imprisonment
And see him seated in the regal throne.   *Exeunt.*

[SCENE IV.—*London. The Palace.*]

Enter QUEEN ELIZABETH *and* RIVERS.

Riv. Madam, what makes in you this sudden change?

Q. Eliz. Why, brother Rivers, are you yet to learn
What late misfortune is befall'n King Edward?

Riv. What, loss of some pitch'd battle against Warwick?

Q. Eliz. No, but the loss of his own royal person.   5

Riv. Then is my sovereign slain?

Q. Eliz. Ay, almost slain, for he is taken prisoner;

. come and] *Q; not in* F.   57–9. York. | *K. Edw.* What . . . tide. *They* . . .
cibly.] *This edn;* Yorke. *They leade him out forcibly.* | *K. Ed.* What . . . tide. *Exeunt.* |
Yorke. *Exeunt some with Edward.* | Q.   64. S.D.] F (*exit.*); *Exeunt Omnes.* | Q.

Scene IV

SCENE IV] *Capell; not in* Q,F.   *London. The Palace.*] *Capell + Theobald; not in*
F.   S.D.] *Malone; Enter Riuers, and Lady Gray.* | F; Enter *the Queene and the*
Lord Riuers. | Q (*after Scene v.*).   1. in you] *This edn, conj. Collier;* you *in* F+Edd.
Q. Eliz.] Edd.; *Gray.* | F; Queen. | Q (*and throughout the scene*).

59. *boots not*] is of no avail.
both wind and tide] For the source of the imagery in Ovid, see II. v. 6 and n.

Scene IV

The news of Edward's defeat has travelled fast!

1. *makes in you*] Most editors accept the F reading; but it has no parallel as a double accusative, with a preposi-

tional phrase as the second accusative (as taken by Schmidt). It is more likely to be the common type of inversion, to an apparently more usual order, by scribe or compositor. This interpretation is also more in keeping with the Queen's reply.

2. *Rivers*] Anthony Woodvile, the Queen's eldest brother; see above IV. i. 51–3.

Either betray'd by falsehood of his guard,
Or by his foe surpris'd at unawares:
And, as I further have to understand,   1
Is new committed to the Bishop of York,
Fell Warwick's brother, and by that our foe.

Riv. These news, I must confess, are full of grief;
Yet gracious madam, bear it as you may:
Warwick may lose that now hath won the day.   1

Q. Eliz. Till then, fair hope must hinder life's decay,
And I the rather wean me from despair
For love of Edward's offspring in my womb:
This is it that makes me bridle passion
And bear with mildness my misfortune's cross,   2
Ay, ay, for this I draw in many a tear
And stop the rising of blood-sucking sighs,
Lest with my sighs or tears I blast or drown
King Edward's fruit, true heir to th' English crown.

Riv. But, madam, where is Warwick then become?   2

Q. Eliz. I am inform'd that he comes towards London
To set the crown once more on Henry's head.
Guess thou the rest: King Edward's friends must down.
But to prevent the tyrant's violence—
For trust not him that hath once broken faith—   3
I'll hence forthwith unto the sanctuary
To save at least the heir of Edward's right.
There shall I rest secure from force and fraud.
Come, therefore, let us fly while we may fly:
If Warwick take us, we are sure to die.   *Exeunt.*   3

35. S.D.] *F; Exit. | Q.*

8. *falsehood*] treachery.

9. *surpris'd*] taken; captured; cf. IV.
ii. 17, 25.

10. *have to*] am given to.

12. *by that*] therefore; on that account; as a consequence of that.

19. *passion*] violent commotion of
mind, especially sorrow (Schmidt).

22. *blood-sucking sighs*] For the mistaken implication, cf. *2 H 6*, III. ii. 63;
Ham., IV. vii. 123; *MND.*, III. ii. 97;
etc.

23. *blast*] blight; wither; destroy.

25. *is . . . become*] has got to; cf. II.
10; and *F.Q.*, i. x. 16.

28. *down*] Cf. IV. iii. 42.

29. *prevent*] anticipate; forestall—th
common Elizabethan sense.

tyrant's] usurper's.

30.] Notice Elizabeth's justified di
trust of this oath-breaking society.

31. *sanctuary*] sacred place whic
conferred immunity from arrest.

32. *right*] title; just claim.

33. *secure from*] L. sense = free fro
the care caused by.

[SCENE V.—*A park near Middleham Castle in Yorkshire.*]

Enter RICHARD, LORD HASTINGS, SIR WILLIAM STANLEY,
[*and Others*].

Rich. Now, my Lord Hastings and Sir William Stanley
Leave off to wonder why I drew you hither
Into this chiefest thicket of the park.
Thus stands the case: you know our King, my brother,
Is prisoner to the Bishop here, at whose hands   5
He hath good usage and great liberty,
And often but attended with weak guard
Comes hunting this way to disport himself.
I have advertis'd him by secret means
That if about this hour he make this way,   10
Under the colour of his usual game,
He shall here find his friends with horse and men
To set him free from his captivity.

Enter KING EDWARD *and a Huntsman with him.*

Hunt. This way, my lord, for this way lies the game.
K. Edw. Nay, this way, man: see where the huntsmen stand.
Now, brother of Gloucester, Hastings, and the rest,   16
Stand you thus close to steal the Bishop's deer?
Rich. Brother, the time and case requireth haste;
Your horse stands ready at the park corner.

Scene v

CENE V] *Capell; not in* Q,F.   *A . . . Yorkshire.*] *Theobald; not in* Q,F.   S.D.]
,F (*subst.*).   *and Others*] *Capell; not in* Q,F.   4. *stands*] *Edd.; stand* F.
. *Comes*] *Edd.; Come* F.   13. S.D.] *F;* Enter *Edward and a Huntsman.* Q.
6. *Hastings*] *This edn;* Lord *Hastings* / F.

Source: Edward's two flights (Hall,
75 and 283) are amalgamated. The
resence of Hastings is unhistorical.
The escape stratagem, though in Hall,
apocryphal (Brooke).

  3. *thicket . . . park*] After Tewkesbury,
ome fled for succor in thyck of the
arke' (Hall, 300).

  park] 'a piece of ground enclosed and
ored with beasts of chase' (Schmidt).

  4, 18. *case*] circumstances; state of
ings; situation.

  9. *advertis'd*] The Latin sense is pre-
served=turned his attention to (something), *OED*. 4. The accent is on the
second syllable.

  11. *colour*] pretext; excuse—a legal
term.

  game] hunting; the chase.

  14. *game*] quarry; hunted animal.

  16. *Hastings*] F 'Lord' is probably a
scribal addition.

  17. *close*] concealed.

  19. *horse*] horses (Vaughan).

K. Edw. But whither shall we then?

Hast.   To Lynn, my lord?   20

    And ship from thence to Flanders?

Rich. Well guess'd, believe me; for that was my meaning.

K. Edw. Stanley, I will requite thy forwardness.

Rich. But wherefore stay we? 'tis no time to talk.

K. Edw. Huntsman, what say'st thou? wilt thou go along? 25

Hunt. Better do so than tarry and be hang'd.

Rich. Come then, away; let's ha' no more ado.

K. Edw. Bishop, farewell: shield thee from Warwick's
    frown,

    And pray that I may repossess the crown.   *Exeunt.*

[SCENE VI.—*London. The Tower.*]

Flourish. Enter KING HENRY, GEORGE, WARWICK, SOMERSET,
young RICHMOND, OXFORD, MONTAGUE, *and Lieutenant* [*of the
Tower*].

K. Hen. Master Lieutenant, now that God and friends
    Have shaken Edward from the regal seat
    And turn'd my captive state to liberty,
    My fear to hope, my sorrows unto joys,

20. lord?] *This edn;* Lord, F.   21. ship] *Camb.;* shipt F.   Flanders?] Q,
(Flanders.); Flanders, as I guess *conj. Vaughan.*   29. S.D.] F; *Exeunt Omnes.* | Q

Scene VI

SCENE VI] *Capell; not in* Q,F.   *London. The Tower.*] Pope + Theobald; *not in*
Q,F.   S.D.] F (. . . *Henry the sixt,* . . . *Warwicke, Somerset* . . . *Henry, Oxford* . .
Lieutenant.); Enter *Warwike* and *Clarence, with the Crowne and then king Henry*
and Oxford, and Summerset, and the yong Earle of Richmond. | Q (*after Scene vii*)
of the Tower] Rowe; *not in* Q,F.   1-37, 48-64.] F; *not in* Q.   1. Master] *Capell*
M.F.

20. *Lynn*] 'passed the washes and
came to . . . Lynne' (Hall, 283). Hastings does not know the plan (cf. 1-13,
especially 2), and can only be asking
or guessing (cf. 22).

23. *forwardness*] zeal.

24. *stay*] delay.

25. *go along*] go, or come, with us;
along = forward.

29. *repossess*] regain possession of.

Scene VI

The scene continues from IV. i
(Hall, 285-7). It bears a resem-
blance to the abdication scene i
Richard II, and it was presumably fo
this reason that 1-37 and 48-64 do no
appear in Q. The resignation of th
crown and the reference to determin
ing the succession would be ampl
grounds for censorship.

At our enlargement what are thy due fees? 5

Lieu. Subjects may challenge nothing of their sovereigns;
But, if an humble prayer may prevail,
I then crave pardon of your Majesty.

K. Hen. For what, Lieutenant? For well using me?
Nay, be thou sure, I'll well requite thy kindness, 10
For that it made my prisonment a pleasure;
Ay, such a pleasure as incaged birds
Conceive when, after many moody thoughts,
At last by notes of household harmony
They quite forget their loss of liberty. 15
But, Warwick, after God, thou set'st me free,
And chiefly therefore I thank God and thee;
He was the author, thou the instrument.
Therefore, that I may conquer Fortune's spite
By living low where Fortune cannot hurt me, 20
And that the people of this blessed land
May not be punish'd with my thwarting stars,
Warwick, although my head still wear the crown,
I here resign my government to thee,
For thou are fortunate in all thy deeds. 25

Var. Your Grace hath still been fam'd for virtuous,
And now may seem as wise as virtuous
By spying and avoiding Fortune's malice,
For few men rightly temper with the stars;

11. prisonment] *Hudson, conj. Lettson;* imprisonment *F.*

5. *enlargement*] liberation; setting at large.

6. *challenge*] demand as their due; cf. III. ii. 86. The idea is implicit in that of Divine Right and the Royal Prerogative.

11. *for that*] because; *OED.* 1.

prisonment] sophisticated by scribe or editor to 'imprisonment', especially as, with the retention of 'my', the metre would be unaffected. It occurs in *John,* III. iv. 161. The imagery and the idea (with 'incaged birds', 12) are those of *Cym.,* III. iii. 42–4, 'our *cage* / We make quire, as doth the *prison'd* bird, / And sing our bondage freely.'

13. *Conceive*] take into the mind; feel.

14. *notes ... harmony*] filling the house with song (Brooke).

18. *author*] first cause or creator.
instrument] agent.

19. *spite*] aphetic form of 'despite' = malice; ill-will.

20. *low*] in a humble position; cf. II. v. 21 ff., where Henry elaborates the same idea.

22. *my thwarting stars*] my bad luck; cf. II. ii. 74.

26. *fam'd*] reported as being; reputed; L. *fama.*

29. *temper*] not = 'accord or work in harmony', but = 'permit themselves to be moulded and managed by their allotted fortunes' (Vaughan). The

<blockquote>
Yet in this one thing let me blame your Grace,   3●

For choosing me when Clarence is in place.
</blockquote>

Geo. No, Warwick, thou art worthy of the sway,

To whom the heavens in thy nativity

Adjudg'd an olive branch and laurel crown,

As likely to be blest in peace and war;   3.

And therefore I yield thee my free consent.

War. And I choose Clarence only for Protector.

K. Hen. Warwick and Clarence, give me both your hands:

Now join your hands, and with your hands your hearts,

That no dissension hinder government.   4

I make you both Protectors of this land,

While I myself will lead a private life

And in devotion spend my latter days

To sin's rebuke and my Creator's praise.

War. What answers Clarence to his sovereign's will?   4

Geo. That he consents, if Warwick yield consent;

For on thy fortune I repose myself.

War. Why then, though loath, yet must I be content.

We'll yoke together, like a double shadow

To Henry's body, and supply his place;   5

I mean, in bearing weight of government,

While he enjoys the honour, and his ease.

And, Clarence, now then it is more than needful

Forthwith that Edward be pronounc'd a traitor

And all his lands and goods be confiscate.   5

Geo. What else? And that succession be determin'd.

War. Ay, therein Clarence shall not want his part.

K. Hen. But with the first of all your chief affairs

Let me entreat—for I command no more—

---

55. *be confiscate*] *Malone;* confiscate *F1;* confiscated *F2.*

verb is used passively, and 'with' is
instrumental.

   31. *in place*] present; available.

   32. *sway*] power; sovereignty.

   33. *nativity*] horoscope; stars or fortune governing his birth. It continues
the metaphor of 'stars'.

   42.] Cf. Arthur in *The Misfortunes of
Arthur,* III. i. 37, 'Let me be thrall, and
leade a priuate life'.

   43. *latter days*] last days of my lif
cf. Hall, 45.

   47. *repose myself*] rely.

   49. *yoke*] couple; join.

   50. *supply*] fill.

   55. *confiscate*] normal omission of t
participial ending after t; see Abbo
342.

   56. *What else?*] certainly.

   57. *want*] lack.

That Margaret your Queen and my son Edward   60
Be sent for to return from France with speed;
For till I see them here, by doubtful fear
My joy of liberty is half eclips'd.

Geo. It shall be done, my sovereign, with all speed.

K. Hen. My Lord of Somerset, what youth is that,   65
Of whom you seem to have so tender care?

Som. My liege, it is young Henry, Earl of Richmond.

K. Hen. Come hither, England's hope. *Lays his hand on his head.*
                  If secret powers
Suggest but truth to my divining thoughts,
This pretty lad will prove our country's bliss.   70
His looks are full of peaceful majesty;
His head by nature fram'd to wear a crown,
His hand to wield a sceptre; and himself
Likely in time to bless a regal throne.
Make much of him, my lords, for this is he   75
Must help you more than you are hurt by me.

Enter a Post.

War. What news, my friend?

Post. That Edward is escaped from your brother
And fled, as he hears since, to Burgundy.

War. Unsavoury news! But how made he escape?   80

Post. He was convey'd by Richard, Duke of Gloucester
And the Lord Hastings, who attended him
In secret ambush on the forest side
And from the Bishop's huntsmen rescu'd him;

68. S.D.] *F; not in* Q.   76. S.D.] *F;* Enter one with a letter to *Warwike.* | Q.

62. *doubtful*] full of doubt.

65 ff.] Hall, 287; preparation for *R 3.* Richmond was the grandson of Katherine, widow of Henry V, and her second husband, Owen Tudor. He 'appears under the "tender care" of the Duke of Somerset, his near kinsman, the last male of the Beauforts, through whom Henry founded his pretensions to the throne' (French, 195).

68. *England's hope*] The prophecy is apocryphal, though in the Chronicles.

69. *divining thoughts*] Ovid's 'divinante animo', *Tristia,* iv. vi. 29; cf. *Tit.,* ii. iii. 214, and Sonnet 106.

78–9. *Edward is escaped*] Edward's two historical flights are here amalgamated, as in iv. v.

81. *convey'd*] stolen away secretly.

82. *attended*] awaited (Fr. *attendre*)— the common Elizabethan sense.

83. *forest*] used possessively; Franz, 199.

        For hunting was his daily exercise.   85

War. My brother was too careless of his charge.

        But let us hence, my sovereign, to provide

        A salve for any sore that may betide.

                  Exeunt all but Somerset, Richmond, and Oxford.

Som. My lord, I like not of this flight of Edward's;

        For doubtless Burgundy will yield him help,   90

        And we shall have more wars before't be long.

        As Henry's late presaging prophecy

        Did glad my heart with hope of this young Richmond,

        So doth my heart misgive me, in these conflicts,

        What may befall him to his harm and ours.   95

        Therefore, Lord Oxford, to prevent the worst,

        Forthwith we'll send him hence to Brittany,

        Till storms be past of civil enmity.

Oxf. Ay, for if Edward repossess the crown,

        'Tis like that Richmond with the rest shall down.   100

Som. It shall be so: he shall to Brittany.

        Come, therefore, let's about it speedily.   *Exeunt.*

[SCENE VII.—*Before York.*]

Flourish. Enter KING EDWARD, RICHARD, HASTINGS, *and Soldiers.*

K. Edw. Now, brother Richard, Hastings, and the rest,

---

88. S.D. *Exeunt all but . . .*] F (*Exeunt. | Manet . . .*); *not in* Q.   102. S.D.] F; *not in* Q.

Scene VII

SCENE VII] *Capell; not in* Q,F.   *Before York.*] *Capell; not in* Q,F.   S.D.] F (*Enter Edward, . . .*); *Enter Edward and Richard, and Hastings with a troope of Hollanders.* Q.   1. Hastings] *Pope;* Lord Hastings F.

88. *A salve for any sore*] an Elizabethan commonplace; cf. *F.Q.,* III. ii. 36.

89. *like not of*] am not pleased by.

90. *Burgundy . . . help*] See below, vii. 6.

96. *prevent*] the normal Elizabethan sense = anticipate (L. *pre-venire*).

97. *to Brittany*] Hall, 302–3; this incident is brought forward from

an earlier series belonging to 1461

Scene VII

Source: Hall, 290–2. Edward's claim was actually made at Nottingham: at York he merely promised the inhabitants safety.

1.] Possibly the manuscript was misread, from abbreviations of 'Richard

Yet thus far Fortune maketh us amends,
And says that once more I shall interchange
My waned state for Henry's regal crown.
Well have we pass'd and now repass'd the seas,   5
And brought desired help from Burgundy;
What then remains, we being thus arriv'd
From Ravenspurgh haven before the gates of York,
But that we enter, as into our dukedom?

Rich. The gates made fast! Brother, I like not this;   10
For many men that stumble at the threshold
Are well foretold that danger lurks within.

C. Edw. Tush, man, abodements must not now affright us:
By fair or foul means we must enter in,
For hither will our friends repair to us.   15

Hast. My liege, I'll knock once more to summon them.

Enter, on the walls, the Mayor of York and his Brethren.

May. My lords, we were forewarned of your coming
And shut the gates for safety of ourselves,
For now we owe allegiance unto Henry.

C. Edw. But, Master Mayor, if Henry be your king,   20
Yet Edward, at the least, is Duke of York.

May. True, my good lord, I know you for no less.

C. Edw. Why, and I challenge nothing but my dukedom,
As being well content with that alone.

Rich. [*Aside.*] But when the fox hath once got in his nose,   25
He'll soon find means to make the body follow.

Hast. Why, Master Mayor, why stand you in a doubt?

---

16. S.D.] *F;* Enter the Lord Maior of *Yorke* vpon the wals. *Q.*   25. *Aside*] *Rowe;*
not in *Q,F.*

---

and 'Lord', as 'Rich. Ld.'; or F sophis-
cated as at IV. v. 16.

  3. *interchange*] exchange.

  8. *Ravenspurgh*] at the mouth of the
Humber, where Bolingbroke landed,
like York, merely to claim his own (see
3, 47). The site is now submerged
(Brooke).

  11. *stumble*] proverbial; cf. Tilley,
S259.

12. *foretold*] forewarned.

13. *abodements*] forebodings; omens
which cause foreboding.

15. *repair*] betake themselves.

16. S.D. on the walls] i.e. above.

23. *challenge*] claim; cf. IV. vi. 6; III.
ii. 86.

25. *fox . . . nose . . .*] typical proverbial, Aesopian, remarks from Richard;
cf. Tilley, F655.

Open the gates; we are King Henry's friends.

May. Ay, say you so? the gates shall then be open'd.

He descends.

Rich. A wise stout captain, and soon persuaded!   30

Hast. The good old man would fain that all were well
So 'twere not 'long of him; but being enter'd,
I doubt not, I, but we shall soon persuade
Both him and all his brothers unto reason.

Enter the Mayor and two Aldermen[, below].

K. Edw. So, Master Mayor: these gates must not be shut   35
But in the night or in the time of war.
What! fear not, man, but yield me up the keys;

Takes his keys.

For Edward will defend the town and thee
And all those friends that deign to follow me.

*March. Enter [*Sir John*] Montgomery, *with drum and Soldiers*

Rich. Brother, this is Sir John Montgomery,   40
Our trusty friend, unless I be deceiv'd.

K. Edw. Welcome, Sir John! But why come you in arms?

Montg. To help King Edward in his time of storm,
As every loyal subject ought to do.

K. Edw. Thanks, good Montgomery; but we now forget   45
Our title to the crown, and only claim
Our dukedom till God please to send the rest.

Montg. Then fare you well, for I will hence again:
I came to serve a king and not a duke.

---

29. S.D.] *F*; *Exit* Maire. *Q.*   34. S.D. *Enter . . . Aldermen*] *F*; The Maire open
the dore, and brings the keies in his hand. *Q.   below*] *Capell; not in Q,F.*   37
S.D.] *F; not in Q.*   39. S.D. *March.*] *F; not in Q.   Enter*] *Q; Enter Moun*
gomerie / *F.   with . . . Soldiers*] *Q,F.*   43. *Montg.*] *F (Mount.); Sir Iohn. | Q*
his] *F;* this *Q.*   45–7.] *Pope; . . . Mountgommerie: | . . . Crowne. | . . . Dukedome,
. . . rest. F;* Thankes braue *Mountgommery.* | But I onlie claime my Dukedom,
Vntil it please God to send the rest. *Q.*

30. *stout*] valiant; ironical, of course.
captain] trisyllabic, as often, e.g.
Mac., I. ii. 34.
32. *'long of*] on account of; because
of; = along of.
40. *John*] Holinshed gives 'Thomas'.

This could be an error of Shake
speare's, as 'Nell' for 'Meg' in *2 H 6*
it is more likely, however, to be a
memorial error carried over uncor
rected from Q; cf. 'Richard' for 'John
at III. ii. 2.

Drummer, strike up, and let us march away.   50
The drum begins to march.

K. Edw. Nay, stay, Sir John, a while; and we'll debate
By what safe means the crown may be recover'd.

Montg. What talk you of debating? In few words:
If you'll not here proclaim yourself our King,
I'll leave you to your fortune and be gone   55
To keep them back that come to succour you.
Why shall we fight, if you pretend no title?

Rich. Why, brother, wherefore stand you on nice points?
Resolve yourself, and let us claim the crown.

K. Edw. When we grow stronger, then we'll make our claim:
Till then 'tis wisdom to conceal our meaning.   61

Hast. Away with scrupulous wit! Now arms must rule.

Rich. And fearless minds climb soonest unto crowns.
Brother, we will proclaim you out of hand;
The bruit thereof will bring you many friends.   65

K. Edw. Then be it as you will; for 'tis my right,
And Henry but usurps the diadem.

Montg. Ay, now my sovereign speaketh like himself,
And now will I be Edward's champion.

Hast. Sound trumpet; Edward shall be here proclaim'd.   70
Come, fellow soldier, make thou proclamation.
[*Gives him a paper.*] *Flourish.*

Sold. Edward the Fourth, by the grace of God, King of
England and France, and Lord of Ireland, etc.

Montg. And whosoe'er gainsays King Edward's right,
By this I challenge him to single fight.   75
Throws down his gauntlet.

All. Long live Edward the Fourth!

---

50. S.D.] *F; not in Q.*   59.] *Q; not in F.*   71. S.D. *Gives . . . paper.*] *Capell* (subst.); *not in Q, F.*   *Flourish.*] *F (Flourish. Sound.); not in Q.*   75. S.D.] *F; not in Q.*

51. *stay*] wait; delay.

57. *pretend*] assert; claim.

58. *stand . . . on nice points*] be particular about fine distinctions.

59.] The Q line seems apt and necessary to Edward's reply; F may well have omitted.

62. *scrupulous*] hesitating; full of scruples.

wit] intellectual operations, or prudence.

63.] Richard speaks also for himself.

64. *out of hand*] immediately.

65. *bruit*] rumour; noising abroad (Fr. *bruit*).

69. *champion*] one who does battle for another, 'like the King's Champion at a Coronation' (Wilson).

K. Edw. Thanks, brave Montgomery, and thanks unto you
    all:
    If Fortune serve me, I'll requite this kindness.
    Now for this night let's harbour here in York,
    And when the morning sun shall raise his car   80
    Above the border of this horizon
    We'll forward towards Warwick and his mates;
    For well I wot that Henry is no soldier.
    Ah, froward Clarence, how evil it beseems thee
    To flatter Henry and forsake thy brother!   85
    Yet, as we may, we'll meet both thee and Warwick.
    Come on, brave soldiers: doubt not of the day,
    And, that once gotten, doubt not of large pay.   *Exeunt.*

[SCENE VIII.—*London. The Bishop's Palace.*]

Flourish. Enter KING HENRY, WARWICK, MONTAGUE, GEORGE,
OXFORD, *and* EXETER.

War. What counsel, lords? Edward from Belgia,

88. S.D.] *F; Exeunt Omnes. | Q.*

Scene VIII

SCENE VIII] *Capell; not in Q,F.   London . . . palace.] This edn, conj. Wright;
London The Palace. | Camb.; not in Q,F.   S.D.] F (subst.); not in Q.   Exeter]
Edd.; Somerset | F.*

78. *serve*] favour.

79. *harbour*] shelter; the original
meaning of finding shelter for troops.

80. *car*] the sun being thought of as
Phoebus.

81. *horizon*] accented on the first syl-
able; cf. Collins, *Greene*, i. 305.

84. *evil*] ill.

87. *day*] day of battle; victory.

Scene VIII

The scene takes place in the Bishop's
palace (Hall, 285; cf. v. i. 45). It con-
tains the preparation for the meeting
of the rival forces at Coventry, where,
however, no fighting occurs (Hall,
293). The capture of Henry (294) leads
up to Act V.

S.D. Exeter] Exeter is present (see
34, 48), and has two speeches (37, 51),
but his place is taken in the F S.D. by
Somerset, who does not speak. Somerset had actually gone with Richmond
to Brittany. The Cambridge Editors
note, correctly, that 'the mistake arose
from the Quartos in which Scene vi
and Scene viii form but one'. They
assumed, of course, that the Q influence operated through the revision of
Q to form F. Much more probable,
and with the same practical result, is
the use of corrected Q copy for F in
the printing-house. The S.D. to Q
Scene vi required little alteration;
but the presence of Somerset was overlooked. See Intro., xxix.

With hasty Germans and blunt Hollanders,
Is pass'd in safety through the Narrow Seas,
And with his troops doth march amain to London;
And many giddy people flock to him.   5

K. Hen. Let's levy men and beat him back again.

Geo. A little fire is quickly trodden out,
Which, being suffer'd, rivers cannot quench.

War. In Warwickshire I have true-hearted friends,
Not mutinous in peace, yet bold in war;   10
Those will I muster up, and thou, son Clarence,
Shalt stir in Suffolk, Norfolk, and in Kent,
The knights and gentlemen to come with thee:
Thou, brother Montague, in Buckingham,
Northampton, and in Leicestershire, shalt find   15
Men well inclin'd to hear what thou command'st:
And thou, brave Oxford, wondrous well-belov'd
In Oxfordshire, shalt muster up thy friends.
My sovereign, with the loving citizens,
Like to his island girt in with the ocean,   20
Or modest Dian circled with her nymphs,
Shall rest in London till we come to him.
Fair lords, take leave and stand not to reply.
Farewell, my sovereign.

K. Hen. Farewell, my Hector and my Troy's true hope.   25

Geo. In sign of truth, I kiss your Highness' hand.

K. Hen. Well-minded Clarence, be thou fortunate. |

3. Is] *Q;* Hath *F.*   6. *K. Hen.*] *F (King.); Oxf. | Malone.*   12. stir] *Pope;* tirre vp *Q,F.*   16. command'st] *F;* commands *Q.*   17–18. belov'd / In Oxfordshire shalt] *Hart;* belou'd, / In Oxfordshire shalt *F;* belou'd, / Shalt in thy countries *Q.*

2. *hasty*] rash.
blunt] rude; uncivilized.
3. *Is*] F sophisticates; cf. III. iii. 32; v. iii. 2.
5. *giddy*] fickle; inconstant.
8. *being suffer'd*] if left alone or unchecked.
11. *son*] son-in-law; see IV. ii. 12.
21. *circled*] Cf. Ovid, *Metam.,* ii. 441, 'suo comitata choro'.
23. *stand not*] do not delay.
25. *Hector . . . Troy's . . . hope*] Cf. II.

i. 51; and *Tit.,* IV. i. 89, 'sweete boy, the Romaine Hector's hope'; Hall, 277 (of Talbot), 'Thys English Hector'; *Mirror,* 314, 'Not worthy Hector . . . / Her hope, her ioye . . . / O Troy, Troy . . .'
26. *In sign of truth*] Note the irony, coming from the 'perjured' Clarence, who was quite unfamiliar with 'truth', or loyalty.
27. *Well-minded*] well-disposed; Hall, 295, applies to Montague.

Mont. Comfort, my lord; and so I take my leave.

Oxf. And thus I seal my truth and bid adieu.

K. Hen. Sweet Oxford, and my loving Montague,   30
     And all at once, once more a happy farewell.

War. Farewell, sweet lords; let's meet at Coventry.

                    Exeunt [all but King Henry and Exeter].

K. Hen. Here at the palace will I rest a while.
     Cousin of Exeter, what thinks your lordship?
     Methinks the power that Edward hath in field   35
     Should not be able to encounter mine.

Exe. The doubt is that he will seduce the rest.

K. Hen. That's not my fear; my meed hath got me fame:
     I have not stopp'd mine ears to their demands,
     Nor posted off their suits with slow delays;   40
     My pity hath been balm to heal their wounds,
     My mildness hath allay'd their swelling griefs,
     My mercy dried their water-flowing tears;
     I have not been desirous of their wealth,
     Nor much oppress'd them with great subsidies,   45
     Nor forward of revenge, though they much err'd.
     Then why should they love Edward more than me?
     No, Exeter, these graces challenge grace;
     And, when the lion fawns upon the lamb,
     The lamb will never cease to follow him.   50

                    Shout within, 'A York! A York!'

---

32. S.D.] Capell (*Exeunt War. Cla. Oxf. and Mon.*); *Exeunt.* | F; *Exeunt Omnes.* | Q
50. S.D. *A York! A York!*] Dyce, conj. Johnson; *A Lancaster, A Lancaster.* | F; not in Q

33. *palace*] of the Bishop of London, near St Paul's (Hall, 294).

35. *Methinks*] It seems to me.
power] army; force.

37. *doubt*] fear, as still used provincially; cf. IV. iii. 19.
seduce] lead astray from their loyalty —the L. sense.

40. *posted off*] put off till later (L. *post*); cf. *Tr. Tr. of R 3* (*Sh. Lib.*, v. 126), 'did post him off with many long delayes'.

41. *balm*] Cf. John Parkinson, *Paradisus Terrestris* (1629), 'good to heal green wounds being made into a salve'.

43. *water-flowing*] flowing like water;

cf. *F.Q.*, I. iii. 44, 'And all the way she wets with flowing teares'.

45. *subsidies*] taxes imposed by medieval rulers at irregular intervals, and levied at so much in the pound on property.

46. *forward of*] eager for; cf. Hall, 303, 'he neuer asked vengeaunce nor punishment'.
err'd] went astray, from the path of duty and obedience—the L. sense.

48. *challenge*] demand; lay claim to; cf. III. ii. 86; IV. vi. 6; IV. vii. 23.

50. S.D.] Either a slip of Shakespeare, or a mistaken alteration in the editing, influenced perhaps by the

Exe. Hark, hark, my lord! what shouts are these?

> *Enter* KING EDWARD, [RICHARD,] *and Soldiers.*

K. Edw. Seize on the shame-fac'd Henry, bear him hence;
　　　　And once again proclaim us King of England.
　　　　You are the fount that makes small brooks to flow:
　　　　Now stops thy spring; my sea shall suck them dry,　　55
　　　　And swell so much the higher by their ebb.
　　　　Hence with him to the Tower: let him not speak.
　　　　　　　　　　　Exeunt [*some*] *with King Henry.*
　　　　And, lords, towards Coventry bend we our course,
　　　　Where peremptory Warwick now remains.
　　　　The sun shines hot; and if we use delay,　　60
　　　　Cold biting winter mars our hop'd-for hay.
Rich. Away betimes, before his forces join,
　　　　And take the great-grown traitor unawares:
　　　　Brave warriors, march amain towards Coventry. *Exeunt.*

---

51. S.D. *Edward, Richard*] *Hanmer; Edward* | *Q,F.　　and Soldiers*] *F (and his Soul-diers); and his traine. Q.*　　57. S.D.] *F (Exit with ...); not in Q.　　some*] *Camb.; not in Q,F.*　　64. S.D.] *F; Exeunt Omnes.* | *Q.*

shouts for Lancaster in v. i. The shout is meant, of course, to announce the arrival of Edward.

　52. *shame-fac'd*] properly—shame-fast, or fixed in shame; modest; bashful.

　55. *Now stops thy spring ...*] now that thy spring (the fountain of small brooks) is stopped (in thy destruction) ...

　58. *Coventry*] where Warwick was collecting his forces; see 32.

　59. *peremptory*] determined; over-bearing.

[ACT V

SCENE I.—*Coventry.*]

Enter WARWICK, *the Mayor of Coventry, two Messengers, and Others upon the walles.*

War. Where is the post that came from valiant Oxford?
     How far hence is thy lord, mine honest fellow?
1 Mess. By this at Dunsmore, marching hitherward.
War. How far off is our brother Montague?
     Where is the post that came from Montague?   5
2 Mess. By this at Daintry, with a puissant troop.

Enter [SIR JOHN] SOMERVILLE.

War. Say, Somerville, what says my loving son?
     And by thy guess how nigh is Clarence now?
Som. At Southam I did leave him with his forces,
     And do expect him here some two hours hence.   10
                                        [*Drum heard.*]
War. Then Clarence is at hand; I hear his drum.
Som. It is not his, my lord; here Southam lies:
     The drum your honour hears marcheth from Warwick.

ACT V
Scene 1

ACT V SCENE I] *Pope; not in Q,F.*   *Coventry.*] *Camb.; not in Q,F.*   S.D.] *F;*
Enter *Warwike* on the walles. *Q.*   6. S.D.] *Capell; Enter* Someruile. *| F; not in Q.*
10. S.D.] *Capell; not in Q,F.*

Source: Hall, 294 ff. The events here recorded actually ended in a compromise, so that no fighting took place, and the enemies were reconciled. These events are linked by Shakespeare, rather perfunctorily, with the battle of Barnet, in the concluding lines of the scene. Hall does, however, include at this point the waverings of Clarence—'a false & a periured duke' (cf. 105, and v. v. 34).

Act V is to a great extent a preparation for *Richard III*.

1 ff.] For the topography, see Sugden, 135.

6. *Daintry*] Daventry.

118

War. Who should that be? Belike, unlook'd for friends.
Som. They are at hand, and you shall quickly know.　　15

　　March. Flourish. Enter EDWARD, RICHARD, *and Soldiers.*

K. Edw. Go, trumpet, to the walls and sound a parle.
Rich. See how the surly Warwick mans the wall.
War. O unbid spite! Is sportful Edward come?
　　Where slept our scouts or how are they seduc'd
　　That we could hear no news of his repair?　　20
K. Edw. Now, Warwick, wilt thou ope the city gates,
　　Speak gentle words, and humbly bend thy knee,
　　Call Edward King, and at his hands beg mercy,
　　And he shall pardon thee these outrages?
War. Nay, rather, wilt thou draw thy forces hence,　　25
　　Confess who set thee up and pluck'd thee down,
　　Call Warwick patron, and be penitent,
　　And thou shalt still remain—the Duke of York?
Rich. I thought at least he would have said the King;
　　Or did he make the jest against his will?　　30
War. Is not a dukedom, sir, a goodly gift?
Rich. Ay, by my faith, for a poor earl to give;
　　I'll do thee service for so good a gift.
War. 'Twas I that gave the kingdom to thy brother.
K. Edw. Why then 'tis mine, if but by Warwick's gift.　　35
War. Thou art no Atlas for so great a weight;
　　And, weakling, Warwick takes his gift again;
　　And Henry is my King, Warwick his subject.

5. S.D.] *F;* Enter *Edward* and his power. *Q.*

16. *trumpet*] trumpeter.

18. *unbid*] uninvited; unwelcome.

spite] vexatious or mortifying circumstance.

sportful] Edward's notorious character—lustful; lascivious.

19. *slept*] metaphorical = were inactive, failed in their duty.

20. *repair*] approach, or return.

21-8.] The two carefully balanced speeches are typical of the formal rhetoric of the play.

26. *set . . . up . . . pluck'd . . . down*] nother reference to Warwick's king-

making activities; cf. II. iii. 37 and III. iii. 157.

27. *patron*] protector; *OED.* 1.

30. *jest*] The only possible jest here lies in a pause after the ambiguous 'remain' in 28.

31, 32. *duke . . . earl*] duke being, of course, higher than earl.

33. *do thee service*] render the service (L. *servitium*) due from a feudal tenant to his lord for the land granted him.

36. *Atlas*] who was credited with supporting the world on his shoulders; cf. Ovid, *Metam.*, ii. 296 ff.

K. Edw. But Warwick's king is Edward's prisoner;
  And, gallant Warwick, do but answer this: 40
  What is the body when the head is off?

Rich. Alas, that Warwick had no more forecast,
  But, whiles he thought to steal the single ten,
  The king was slily finger'd from the deck!
  You left poor Henry at the Bishop's palace,   45
  And ten to one you'll meet him in the Tower.

K. Edw. 'Tis even so: yet you are Warwick still.

Rich. Come, Warwick, take the time; kneel down, kneel
  down.
  Nay, when? Strike now, or else the iron cools.

War. I had rather chop this hand off at a blow   50
  And with the other fling it at thy face,
  Than bear so low a sail to strike to thee.

K. Edw. Sail how thou canst, have wind and tide thy
  friend,
  This hand, fast wound about thy coal-black hair,
  Shall, whiles thy head is warm and new cut off, 55
  Write in the dust this sentence with thy blood:
  'Wind-changing Warwick now can change no more'.

Enter OXFORD, *with drum and colours.*

War. O cheerful colours! See where Oxford comes!

Oxf. Oxford, Oxford, for Lancaster!
          [*He and his forces enter the city.*]

Rich. The gates are open, let us enter too.   60

---

43. whiles] *F; whilst Q.* 57. S.D.] *F; . . .* drum and souldiers & al crie, *Q1,2;*
. . . drum and souldiors. *| Q3.* 59. S.D.] *Capell; Exit. | Q; not in F.*

42. *forecast*] forethought; prudence.
43. *single ten*] the simple ten—the earest card to a court or royal card Hart); cf. *Shr.*, II. i. 397.
44. *finger'd from the deck*] stolen from he pack; cf. *Ham.*, v. ii. 15; 'deck' is still used in this sense in America.
46. *Tower*] dramatic irony; cf. v. vi. 57.
48. *time*] opportunity.
49. *when*] exclamation of impatience; cf. *R 2*, I. i. 162, 'When, Harry, when?'

Strike . . .] Richard, as usual, refers to a proverb, 'Strike while the iron is hot'; cf. Tilley, 194. Warwick's reply plays on the sense of 'yield'.
52. *bear so low a sail*] go so humbly or modestly.
strike] lower, i.e. yield, punning on 'strike' in 49.
53. *wind and tide*] Cf. III. iii. 48, 'This is he that moves both wind and tide'.
57. *Wind-changing*] (*a*) inconstant as the wind, (*b*) able to change the direction of the wind.

K. Edw. So other foes may set upon our backs.
　　　Stand we in good array, for they no doubt
　　　Will issue out again and bid us battle;
　　　If not, the city being but of small defence,
　　　We'll quickly rouse the traitors in the same.　　65
War. O welcome, Oxford, for we want thy help.

Enter MONTAGUE, *with drum and colours.*

Mont. Montague, Montague, for Lancaster!
　　　　　　　[*He and his forces enter the city.*]
Rich. Thou and thy brother both shall buy this treason
　　　Even with the dearest blood your bodies bear.
K. Edw. The harder match'd, the greater victory:　　70
　　　My mind presageth happy gain and conquest.

Enter SOMERSET, *with drum and colours.*

Som. Somerset, Somerset, for Lancaster!
　　　　　　　[*He and his forces enter the city.*]
Rich. Two of thy name, both Dukes of Somerset,
　　　Have sold their lives unto the house of York,
　　　And thou shalt be the third, and this sword hold.　　75

Enter GEORGE, *with drum and colours.*

War. And lo, where George of Clarence sweeps along,
　　　Of force enough to bid his brother battle;
　　　With whom an upright zeal to right prevails
　　　More than the nature of a brother's love.

66, 71, 75. S.D.] *F;* drum and souldiers. *Q.*　　67, 72. S.D.] *Malone; Exit. | Q;*
not in F.　　75. and] *Q1,2;* if *Q3,F.*　　78. whom an] *F2;* whom, in *F1.*

61. *backs*] rear (of an army).
63. *bid*] offer.
64. *of small defence*] feebly fortified.
65. *rouse*] to cause (an animal) to rise from its lair.
68. *buy*] pay the penalty of; atone for. Cf. Q2 'abie', of which 'buy' is an aphetic form: *OED.* 3.
71. *happy*] fortunate.
72. *Somerset*] here substituted for the Exeter of Hall and Holinshed.
73. *Two of thy name*] Edward, second duke, slain at St Albans, 1455, and his

son Henry, third duke, beheaded after the battle of Hexham, 1464. See head-note to IV. i; v. vii. 5; and App. I.
76. *sweeps along*] with a suggestion of the peacock; cf. *1 H 6* (of Talbot and his forces), III. iii. 6, 'And like a peacock sweeps along his tail'.
78. *to*] towards; in favour of.
right] justice.
79. *the nature . . . love*] is due to the natural instinct of brotherly love; brotherly love has in its nature (Vaughan).

Geo. Clarence, Clarence, for Lancaster!   80
K. Edw. Et tu, Brute! wilt thou stab Caesar too?
　　A parley, sirrah, to George of Clarence.
　　　　　　　Sound a parley. Richard and George whisper.
War. Come, Clarence, come; thou wilt if Warwick call.

　　George takes the red rose from his hat and throws it at Warwick.

Geo. Father of Warwick, know you what this means?
　　Look, here I throw my infamy at thee: 85
　　I will not ruinate my father's house,
　　Who gave his blood to lime the stones together,
　　And set up Lancaster. Why, trowest thou, Warwick,
　　That Clarence is so harsh, so blunt, unnatural,
　　To bend the fatal instruments of war   90
　　Against his brother and his lawful King?
　　Perhaps thou wilt object my holy oath:
　　To keep that oath were more impiety
　　Than Jephthah's when he sacrific'd his daughter.
　　I am so sorry for my trespass made,   95
　　That, to deserve well at my brothers' hands,
　　I here proclaim myself thy mortal foe;
　　With resolution, wheresoe'er I meet thee—
　　As I will meet thee if thou stir abroad—
　　To plague thee for thy foul misleading me.   100
　　And so, proud-hearted Warwick, I defy thee,

80-2.] *Q; not in F.*　82. S.D.] *Q (subst.); not in F.*　83. S.D.] *Q (subst., before 82); not in F.*　85. my] *F;* mine *Q.*　94. Jephthah's] *Rowe*[3] *(Jepthah's);* Iephah | *F.*

80–2. S.D.] There can be little doubt that the passage peculiar to Q is authentic, though 82 is metrically defective. No source or other use of the phrase 'Et tu Brute' is known except for *Caes.,* III. i. 77. Shakespeare has already alluded to the events of *Julius Caesar* at III. i. 18, and returns to them at v. v. 53. See note at III. i. 18–20.

83. S.D. hat] 'illustrates the fact that the actors were dressed in Elizabethan costumes, not in mediaeval armour as in modern performances' (Brooke).

84. *Father*] used for 'father-in-law' in the 16th and 17th centuries.

86. *ruinate*] ruin.

87. *lime*] join; bind with mortar.

88. *trowest*] dost thou think or suppose.

89. *blunt*] rough; rude.

90. *To bend*] For the omission of the relative ('as') after 'so', see Abbott, 281.

92. *object*] urge (literally 'throw') against me.

94. *Jephthah's . . . daughter*] a common theme of Shakespeare's, e.g. in *Hamlet;* from *Judges,* xi. 30, and the Homily against swearing and perjury.

99. *abroad*] outside (the walls of Coventry).

And to my brother turn my blushing cheeks.
Pardon me, Edward, I will make amends:
And, Richard, do not frown upon my faults,
For I will henceforth be no more unconstant.　　105

K. Edw.　Now welcome more, and ten times more belov'd,
Than if thou never hadst deserv'd our hate.

Rich.　Welcome, good Clarence; this is brother-like.

War.　O passing traitor, perjur'd and unjust!

K. Edw.　What, Warwick, wilt thou leave the town and fight?
Or shall we beat the stones about thine ears?　　111

War.　Alas, I am not coop'd here for defence!
I will away towards Barnet presently
And bid thee battle, Edward, if thou dar'st.

K. Edw.　Yes, Warwick, Edward dares, and leads the way.　115
Lords, to the field; Saint George and victory!　　*Exeunt.*
March. Warwick and his company follow.

[SCENE II.—*A field of battle near Barnet.*]

*Alarum, and excursions. Enter [*King*] Edward, bringing forth*
Warwick *wounded.*

K. Edw.　So, lie thou there: die thou, and die our fear;
For Warwick was a bug that fear'd us all.

---

02. brother] *F;* brothers *Q.*　　116. S.D.] *F (subst.); Exeunt Omnes. | Q.*

Scene II

SCENE II] *Capell; not in Q,F.　　A . . . Barnet.] Theobald; not in Q,F.　　S.D.] F
Enter Edward . . .*); Alarmes, and then enter *Warwike* wounded. *Q.*　　1–4.] *F;
ot in Q.*

---

102. *brother*] Q 'brothers' may be
orrect here, as referring to 'Edward
. . Richard . . . our' (103–7).

109. *passing*] surpassing; extreme.
The usage is still found in Goldsmith's
passing rich'.

112 ff.] a device to omit events at
Coventry and proceed immediately to
the battle of Barnet; see head-note.

112. *Alas*] forsooth; 'used in mock-
ry' (Hart).

coop'd] enclosed for protection or de-
nce; *OED.* 2.

113. *presently*] immediately—the
normal Elizabethan sense.

Scene II

Source: Hall, 296 (App. I).
Margaret landed at Weymouth the
day of the battle, having been detained
at sea by the weather.

2. *bug*] imaginary object of terror,
as in 'bug-bear'; bogey; cf. *Shr.*, I. ii.
207, 'fear boys with bugs'.

fear'd] terrified.

Now, Montague, sit fast; I seek for thee,
That Warwick's bones may keep thine company.   *Exit.*

War. Ah, who is nigh? Come to me, friend or foe,   5
And tell me who is victor, York or Warwick?
Why ask I that my mangled body shows?—
My blood, my want of strength, my sick heart shows?—
That I must yield my body to the earth,
And, by my fall, the conquest to my foe.   10
Thus yields the cedar to the axe's edge
Whose arms gave shelter to the princely eagle,
Under whose shade the ramping lion slept,
Whose top branch over-peer'd Jove's spreading tree
And kept low shrubs from winter's powerful wind.   15
These eyes, that now are dimm'd with death's black veil,
Have been as piercing as the mid-day sun
To search the secret treasons of the world;
The wrinkles in my brows, now fill'd with blood,
Were liken'd oft to kingly sepulchres;   20
For who liv'd King but I could dig his grave?
And who durst smile when Warwick bent his brow?
Lo now my glory smear'd in dust and blood!
My parks, my walks, my manors that I had,
Even now forsake me; and of all my lands   25
Is nothing left me but my body's length.
Why, what is pomp, rule, reign, but earth and dust?
And live we how we can, yet die we must.

7. that] *This edn, conj. Vaughan;* that? *Q,F+Edd.*   10. foe] *F;* foes *Q.*

3. *sit fast*] Cf. iv. i. 118; see that your
position is secure; look out.

7. *that*] that which; Abbott, 244. The
F mispunctuation is derived from Q.

11 ff. *cedar . . . eagle . . . lion*] Elizabethan types of supremacy, or pri-
mates—the king of evergreen trees, of
birds, and of animals respectively, as
the oak (14) is of deciduous trees: see
e.g. Tillyard, *EWP.*, 27.

13. *ramping lion*] See i. iii. 12 and n.;
rearing on the hind legs and hence
showing fierceness.

14. *over-peer'd*] rose or towered above.
Jove's spreading tree] the oak; cf. Vir-

gil, *Georgics*, iii. 332, 'magna Iouis . .
quercus'.

24. *My parks . . .*] Cf. Horace, *Odes*
ii. iii. 17–18, 'Cedes coemptis saltibu[s]
et domo / Villaque, flavus quam
Tiberis lavit,' and continuing on th[e]
inevitability of death.

walks] tracts of garden, park, o[r]
forest.

25–6.] Cf. Juvenal, *Satires*, x. 172–3
'sarcophago contentus erit. Mors sol[a]
fatetur, / quantula sint hominu[m]
corpuscula'. He is describing Alexan[-]
der, for whom 'non sufficit orbis'
(Baldwin, *Sm. Lat.*, ii. 538.)

Enter OXFORD *and* SOMERSET.

Som. Ah, Warwick, Warwick! wert thou as we are
 We might recover all our loss again.   30
 The Queen from France hath brought a puissant power.
 Even now we heard the news. Ah, couldst thou fly!
War. Why then, I would not fly. Ah, Montague,
 If thou be there, sweet brother, take my hand,
 And with thy lips keep in my soul a while!   35
 Thou lov'st me not; for, brother, if thou didst,
 Thy tears would wash this cold congealed blood
 That glues my lips and will not let me speak.
 Come quickly, Montague, or I am dead.
Som. Ah, Warwick! Montague hath breath'd his last; 40
 And to the latest gasp cried out for Warwick,
 And said, 'Commend me to my valiant brother.'
 And more he would have said; and more he spoke;
 Which sounded like a cannon in a vault
 That mought not be distinguish'd; but at last 45
 I well might hear, deliver'd with a groan,
 'O farewell, Warwick!'
War.   Sweet rest his soul!
 Fly, lords, and save yourselves, for Warwick bids
 You all farewell, to meet in heaven.   *He dies.*
Oxf. Away, away, to meet the Queen's great power! 50
     Here they bear away his body. Exeunt.

28. S.D.] *Q,F.* 44. cannon] *F+some edd.;* clamour *Q+some edd.* 47–9.]
Pope +Steevens; Sweet ... Soule: / Flye ... selues, / For ... Heauen. *F;* Sweet
... selues, / For ... Heauen *Q.* 49. meet] *Q,F;* meet again *Pope.* 49. S.D.]
Q; not in *F.* 50. S.D.] *F;* not in *Q.*

31. *power*] armed force.
35.] Cf. *2 H 6,* III. ii. 396–7.
43, 44.] Cf. II. iii. 17–18.
45. *mought*] might = could; cf.

'might' at 46; and see Franz, 178.
50. S.D. bear away ... body] a physical necessity for clearing the open
Elizabethan stage.

[SCENE III.—*Another part of the field.*]

Flourish. Enter KING EDWARD *in triumph, with* RICHARD, GEORGE, *and the rest.*

K. Edw. Thus far our fortune keeps an upward course,
　　　And we are grac'd with wreaths of victory:
　　　But in the midst of this bright-shining day
　　　I spy a black suspicious threatening cloud
　　　That will encounter with our glorious sun   5
　　　Ere he attain his easeful western bed—
　　　I mean, my lord, those powers that the Queen
　　　Hath rais'd in Gallia have arriv'd our coast,
　　　And, as we hear, march on to fight with us.

Geo. A little gale will soon disperse that cloud   10
　　　And blow it to the source from whence it came;
　　　Thy very beams will dry those vapours up,
　　　For every cloud engenders not a storm.

Rich. The Queen is valu'd thirty thousand strong,
　　　And Somerset, with Oxford, fled to her: 15
　　　If she have time to breathe, be well assur'd
　　　Her faction will be full as strong as ours.

K. Edw. We are advertis'd by our loving friends
　　　That they do hold their course toward Tewkesbury.
　　　We, having now the best at Barnet field,   20
　　　Will thither straight, for willingness rids way;

Scene III

SCENE III] *Capell; not in* Q,F.　　　*Another . . . field.*] *Theobald; not in* Q,F.
S.D.] F; *Enter Edward, Clarence, Gloster, with souldiers.* Q.

For the source, see Hall, 297 ff.

1. *Thus far . . .*] Cf. *1 Tamb.*, II. i. 1, 'Thus far are we towards Theridamas'.

2.] identical with Marlowe, *Massacre at Paris*, 794.

5. *sun*] scil. of York, of which house it was the badge; cf. *R 3*, I. i. 2.

8. *arriv'd*] in the narrower original sense of coming to shore, landing (L. *ad+ripa*).

12. *beams*] of the Yorkist sun.

13.] an Italian proverb: Tilley, C443 (Wilson).

14. *valu'd*] estimated.

thirty thousand] See v. ii. 31. Hart points out Commines's reference (Danett's trans., 89) to the number of 40,000; Hall and Holinshed give none.

18. *advertis'd*] informed; notified.

21. *straight*] immediately.

rids way] annihilates distance; Cotgrave has 'a strong foot and a light head *rid way* apace' (Hart); clears the way by removing obstacles. Cf. 'Vorare viam Catull. To dispatch or *ridde the way*' (Cooper); 'to deuour the way', *2 H 4*, I. i. 47.

And as we march our strength will be augmented
In every county as we go along.
Strike up the drum; cry 'Courage!' and away.   *Exeunt.*

[SCENE IV.—*Plains near Tewkesbury.*]

lourish. March. Enter QUEEN MARGARET, PRINCE EDWARD,
SOMERSET, OXFORD, *and Soldiers.*

. Mar. Great lords, wise men ne'er sit and wail their loss,
But cheerly seek how to redress their harms.
What though the mast be now blown overboard,
The cable broke, the holding anchor lost,
And half our sailors swallow'd in the flood;   5
Yet lives our pilot still: is't meet that he
Should leave the helm and, like a fearful lad,
With tearful eyes add water to the sea
And give more strength to that which hath too much;

. S.D.] F; Ex. Omnes. | Q.

Scene IV

*CENE IV] Capell; not in Q,F.   Plains ... Tewkesbury.] Theobald; not in Q,F.
.D.] F (... the Queene, young Edward ...); Enter the Queene, Prince Edward, Oxford
d Summerset, with drum and souldiers. Q.*

Scene IV

Source: Hall, 298 ff. Shakespeare
nits much of Hall's account of events
:tween Barnet and Tewkesbury, es-
:cially Margaret's despair and me-
ncholy. When she appears again,
e is 'of ... valiant spirit'. Hart points
t that this succinct version is much
ser to that of Commines than to
all or Holinshed.

1–31.] The storm-ship simile has a
ackground in Horace, *Odes*, I. xiv,
uctus ... Nudum remigio latus ... /
ntennaeque gemant ac sine funibus /
ix durare carinae / Possint imperios-
; / Aequor ... ventis ... nitentes...
ycladas' (Baldwin, *Sm. Lat.*). The
rect source here, however, seems to
: Brooke's *Romeus and Iuliet* (*Sh. Lib.*,
134–5), beginning: 'A wise man in
e midst of troubles and distres / Still

standes not wayling present harme,
but seeks his harmes redres.'

Shakespeare uses the same material
in *R 2*, III. ii. 178–85, beginning: 'My
lord, wise men ne'er sit and wail their
woes, / But presently prevent the ways
to wail.' Cf. also *Dido* (McKerrow, II),
III. i. 104–9. Wilson refers to an Italian
proverb, Tilley, M999a. For the full
extract from *Romeus*, see App. I (*b*).

2. *cheerly*] Somerset 'merily required
of them all, to bee of hardy harte and
good chere' (Hall, 298).

4. *holding anchor*] no special term,
such as is implied in the F hyphen,
seems to be known. Possibly 'holding'
is predicative = the anchor, whose
function is to take hold on the sea-
bottom.

7. *fearful*] the Elizabethan sense =
'full of fear'.

Whiles, in his moan, the ship splits on the rock,   1

Which industry and courage might have sav'd?

Ah, what a shame! ah, what a fault were this!

Say Warwick was our anchor; what of that?

And Montague our top-mast; what of him?

Our slaughter'd friends the tackles; what of these?   1

Why, is not Oxford here another anchor?

And Somerset another goodly mast?

The friends of France our shrouds and tacklings?

And, though unskilful, why not Ned and I

For once allow'd the skilful pilot's charge?   2

We will not from the helm to sit and weep,

But keep our course, though the rough wind say no,

From shelves and rocks that threaten us with wrack.

As good to chide the waves as speak them fair.

And what is Edward but a ruthless sea?   2

What Clarence but a quicksand of deceit?

And Richard but a ragged fatal rock?

All these the enemies to our poor bark.

Say you can swim—alas, 'tis but a while!

Tread on the sand—why, there you quickly sink: 3

Bestride the rock—the tide will wash you off,

Or else you famish; that's a threefold death.

This speak I, lords, to let you understand,

If case some one of you would fly from us,

That there's no hop'd-for mercy with the brothers   3

More than with ruthless waves, with sands, and rocks.

Why, courage then! what cannot be avoided

'Twere childish weakness to lament or fear.

---

23. wrack] *F*; wreck *Theobald+most edd.*   27. ragged] *Rowe*; raged *F*.

11. *industry*] hard work.
sav'd] prevented.

15. *tackles*] the ropes, rigging, or cables of a ship.

16. *Oxford*] not present at Tewkesbury. He fled after Barnet, but was captured in Cornwall, and sent to Hames Castle (v. v. 2) in Picardy (French, 183).

18. *of France*] from France; French.
shrouds] sail-ropes.

tacklings] Cf. 2 *Tamb.*, 2550, 'ma and tacklings'.

20. *the . . . pilot's charge*] Cf. the stor metaphor in *Mirror*, 409, 'My Cabl crakte. . . The *Pilotes* charge, who si teth at the stearne'.

23. *shelves*] shoals; sandbanks.

27. *ragged*] rugged; uneven; c 'ragged staff'.

34. *If case*] if it should chance (*casus*).

Prince. Methinks a woman of this valiant spirit
  Should, if a coward heard her speak these words,   40
  Infuse his breast with magnanimity
  And make him, naked, foil a man at arms.
  I speak not this as doubting any here;
  For did I but suspect a fearful man,
  He should have leave to go away betimes,   45
  Lest in our need he might infect another
  And make him of like spirit to himself.
  If any such be here—as God forbid!—
  Let him depart before we need his help.
Oxf. Women and children of so high a courage,   50
  And warriors faint! why, 'twere perpetual shame.
  O brave young Prince! thy famous grandfather
  Doth live again in thee: long may'st thou live
  To bear his image and renew his glories!
Som. And he that will not fight for such a hope   55
  Go home to bed and, like the owl by day,
  If he arise, be mock'd and wonder'd at.
Q. Mar. Thanks, gentle Somerset; sweet Oxford, thanks.
Prince. And take his thanks that yet hath nothing else.

      Enter a Messenger.

Mess. Prepare you, lords, for Edward is at hand   60
  Ready to fight; therefore be resolute.
Oxf. I thought no less: it is his policy
  To haste thus fast, to find us unprovided.
Som. But he's deceiv'd; we are in readiness.

59. S.D.] *Q,F.*

41. *magnanimity*] the Renascence
ideal of the noble mind.

42. *naked*] unarmed.

foil] overthrow; defeat; cf. *AYL.*, ii.
ii. 14, 'the Wrastler / That did but
lately foile the synowie Charles'.

44–9.] Cf. Henry V's address before
Agincourt (iv. iii. 35–7). Both plays
seem indebted to Edward's proclamation at Towton (Hall, 255), 'that al
men, whiche were afrayde to fighte,
shoulde incontinent departe'. Both
this passage and the source at Hall,

300, promise rewards to the troops.

51. *faint*] faint-hearted.

54. *image*] likeness.

glories] The achievements of Henry
V run like a continuous theme through
these historical plays.

56. *the owl by day*] Ovid, *Metam.*, ii.
742–52; xi. 25–6.

59. *his thanks*] the thanks of him—
L. construction.

62. *policy*] cunning; craft.

63. *unprovided*] unprepared; not
having foreseen eventualities.

Q. Mar. This cheers my heart, to see your forwardness.   65
Oxf. Here pitch our battle; hence we will not budge.

Flourish, and march. Enter [KING] EDWARD, RICHARD, GEORGE,
and Soldiers.

K. Edw. Brave followers, yonder stands the thorny wood
Which by the heavens' assistance and your strength
Must by the roots be hewn up yet ere night.
I need not add more fuel to your fire,   70
For well I wot ye blaze to burn them out.
Give signal to the fight, and to it, lords!

Q. Mar. Lords, knights, and gentlemen, what I should say
My tears gainsay; for every word I speak
Ye see I drink the water of my eye.   75
Therefore no more but this: Henry, your sovereign,
Is prisoner to the foe, his state usurp'd,
His realm a slaughter-house, his subjects slain,
His statutes cancell'd, and his treasure spent;
And yonder stands the wolf that makes this spoil.   80
You fight in justice: then, in God's name, lords,
Be valiant, and give signal to the fight.

                         Alarum. Retreat. Excursions. Exeunt.

66. S.D. *Flourish, and march.*] F; *not in* Q.   Enter . . . Soldiers.] F (*Enter Edward,* . . .); Enter king *Edward, Cla. Glo. Hast.* and Souldiers. Q.   75. my eye]
F; mine eyes Q, *Capell.*   80. stands] Q; is F.   82.] F; togither cry saint
George. | *All.* Saint *George* for *Lancaster.* | Q.   82. S.D.] F; Alarmes to the battell,
Yorke flies, then the chambers be / discharged. Then enter the king, *Cla.* & *Glo.*
& the rest, / & make a great shout, and crie, for *Yorke*, for *Yorke*, and / then the
Queene is taken, & the prince, & *Oxf.* & *Sum.* | Q.

65. *forwardness*] eagerness; ardour.

66. *pitch . . . battle*] set . . . a body of
troops in battle array.

69. *yet*] adversative, with 'hewn up',
to 'stands'.

74. *gainsay*] say the contrary; forbid.

77. *state*] sovereignty.

80. *stands*] F sophisticates to 'is'; cf.
II. ii. 55.

wolf] ironical, coming from the 'she-
wolf of France'.

spoil] havoc; destruction.

[SCENE V.—*Another part of the field.*]

Flourish. Enter [KING] EDWARD, RICHARD, GEORGE,
[*and Soldiers*]; *with* QUEEN [MARGARET], OXFORD,
[*and*] SOMERSET[, *prisoners*].

K. Edw. Now here a period of tumultuous broils.
        Away with Oxford to Hames Castle straight:
        For Somerset, off with his guilty head.
        Go, bear them hence; I will not hear them speak.

Oxf. For my part, I'll not trouble thee with words.   5

Som. Nor I; but stoop with patience to my fortune.
                Exeunt Oxford and Somerset[, *guarded*].

Q. Mar. So part we sadly in this troublous world,
        To meet with joy in sweet Jerusalem.

K. Edw. Is proclamation made that who finds Edward
        Shall have a high reward, and he his life?   10

Rich. It is: and lo where youthful Edward comes.

        Enter [*Soldiers, with*] PRINCE [EDWARD].

K. Edw. Bring forth the gallant: let us hear him speak.
        What, can so young a thorn begin to prick?
        Edward, what satisfaction canst thou make
        For bearing arms, for stirring up my subjects,   15

Scene v

SCENE V] *Capell; not in Q,F.   Another . . . field.*] *Edd., after Capell; not in Q,F.*
.D.] *Capell; Flourish. Enter Edward, Richard, Queene, Clarence, Oxford, Somerset.* | *F;*
nd then sound and enter all againe. Q.   6. S.D.] *Capell; Exeunt.* | *F; Exit*
Oxford. (after 5) | *Exit Sum.* | *Q.*   11. S.D.] *Capell; Enter the Prince.* | *F.*

Source: Hall, 300-4, 343.

1. *period*] end; full stop.

2. *Hames Castle*] See n. to IV. 16
bove.
    straight] immediately.

3. *For*] as for.
    guilty] transferred epithet = the
ead of him who is guilty.

6. *fortune*] here = ill fortune; the
nse has since narrowed; cf. 'success'.

7-8.] The sentiment seems out of
haracter for Margaret. The wording
s from Rev., xxi. 2, and the refer-

ence to the New Jerusalem, or heaven.

9. *who*] he who; the L. construction;
Abbott, 251.

10. *he his life*] Cf. 38-40 for the
breach of this promise.

11. *youthful Edward*] to distinguish
him from the king, the 'lascivious
Edward', of 34.

13. *so young a thorn*] proverbial; cf.
'Young doth it prick, that will be a
thorn', *Jacob and Esau* (Dodsley, ii. 196,
234).

14. *satisfaction*] amends; atonement.

And all the trouble thou hast turn'd me to?

Prince. Speak like a subject, proud ambitious York.
Suppose that I am now my father's mouth;
Resign thy chair, and where I stand kneel thou,
Whilst I propose the self-same words to thee   2
Which, traitor, thou would'st have me answer to.

Q. Mar. Ah, that thy father had been so resolv'd!

Rich. That you might still have worn the petticoat
And ne'er have stol'n the breech from Lancaster.

Prince. Let Aesop fable in a winter's night;   2
His currish riddles sorts not with this place.

Rich. By heaven, brat, I'll plague ye for that word.

Q. Mar. Ay, thou wast born to be a plague to men.

Rich. For God's sake, take away this captive scold.

Prince. Nay, take away this scolding crookback rather.   3

K. Edw. Peace, wilful boy, or I will charm your tongue.

Geo. Untutor'd lad, thou art too malapert.

Prince. I know my duty; you are all undutiful:
Lascivious Edward, and thou perjur'd George,
And thou misshapen Dick, I tell ye all   3
I am your better, traitors as ye are,
And thou usurp'st my father's right and mine.

K. Edw. Take that, the likeness of this railer here.   *Stabs hin*

26. sorts] *Q,F; sort Rowe+most edd.*   33. are all] *Q,F; are Pope, conj. this ed*
36. are] *F; be Q.*   38. the] *Q1,2,F; thou Q3.*   S.D.] *F; not in Q.*

18. *mouth*] mouthpiece.

19. *chair*] throne.

23–4. *petticoat . . . breech*] Cf. *2 H 6*,
I. iii. 145, where this metaphor is also
applied to Margaret. The implication
here is that if Henry had been 'resolv'd', Margaret would not have been
able to assume his powers, and things
would have turned out otherwise.

24. *breech*] plural = breeches; see
Franz, 193.

25–6. *Aesop . . . currish*] Aesop the
author was often confused with Aesop
the actor, a hunchback (Cicero, *Pro
Roscio Comoedio*) (J. A. K. Thomson).
This, and Richard's gnomic style,
make two palpable hits, to which is
added a third—'currish', which is associated with one of Aesop's animals,

but also with the Cynic philosophe
(κύων = a dog), so called from the
attitude to life and ordinary value
Richard's reply shows that the sho
have gone home.

26. *sorts*] For the concord, s
Abbott, 333.

27. *brat*] child. The sense was st
general, and not, as now, pejorativ
cf. I. iii. 4.

31. *charm*] silence (as by magic).

32. *Untutor'd*] untaught.
malapert] impudent; saucy.

37. *right*] just claim.

38. *the likeness*] Cf. 'Farewell ti
latter spring', *1 H 4*, I. ii. 177, and
in the New Arden edn.

38–40.] Note the breach of the pr
mise given at 10.

Rich. Sprawl'st thou? Take that to end thy agony. *Stabs him.*
Geo. And there's for twitting me with perjury. *Stabs him.* 40
Q. Mar. O, kill me too!
Rich.   Marry, and shall. *Offers to kill her.*
K. Edw. Hold, Richard, hold; for we have done too much.
Rich. Why should she live to fill the world with words?
K. Edw. What, doth she swoon? Use means for her recovery.
Rich. Clarence, excuse me to the King my brother: 45
    I'll hence to London on a serious matter:
    Ere ye come there, be sure to hear some news.
Geo. What? what?
Rich.   The Tower! the Tower! I'll root them out.
                                Exit.
Q. Mar. O Ned, sweet Ned, speak to thy mother, boy!
    Canst thou not speak? O traitors! murderers! 50
    They that stabb'd Caesar shed no blood at all,
    Did not offend, nor were not worthy blame,
    If this foul deed were by to equal it.
    He was a man; this, in respect, a child;
    And men ne'er spend their fury on a child. 55
    What's worse than murderer, that I may name it?
    No, no, my heart will burst and if I speak;

39. thy] *F; not in Q;* thine *conj. this edn.*   S.D.] *F* (*Rich. stabs him.*)*; not in Q.*
40. S.D.] *F* (*Clar. stabs him.*)*; not in Q.*   41. S.D.] *F; not in Q.*   48. The . . .
out.] *Q* (. . . Tower man, the . . .)*;* Tower, the Tower. *F.*   S.D.] *F; Exit
Gloster. | Q.*   56. name it?] *F; name. Q.*

39.] Richard comes one step nearer the throne.

Sprawl'st thou?] Do you writhe (in death agony)?

41.] The line is metrically defective. It was taken over unaltered from Q.

Marry, and shall] Indeed I will.

43. *fill the world with words*] prophetic of her future rôle (Wilson).

47. *be sure to*] you may expect to; be sure you will.

48. *The Tower*] Hall, 303, 343. The special hurried journey to London is invented; the murder of King Henry came after Edward and his forces had returned to London. Shakespeare took Edward's ignorance and Richard's intention to 'root them out' (not in

Holinshed) from Hall, 343, 'now is there no heire male of Kynge Edwarde the thirde, but wee of the house of Yorke'.

50 ff.] Ironically Margaret is now placed like York in I. iv, and delivers the sort of speeches he then made to her.

51. *Caesar*] Cf. the references at III. i. 18, and v. i. 81.

53. *to equal it*] either 'to compare with their deed'; or, more probably, 'to make it (Caesar's murder) just or fair by comparison', as Vaughan suggests.

54. *in respect*] in comparison; or 'if regarded with due consideration' (Vaughan).

And I will speak, that so my heart may burst.
Butchers and villains! bloody cannibals!
How sweet a plant have you untimely cropp'd!   60
You have no children, butchers; if you had,
The thought of them would have stirr'd up remorse:
But if you ever chance to have a child,
Look in his youth to have him so cut off
As, deathsmen, you have rid this sweet young prince!   65

K. Edw. Away with her; go bear her hence perforce.

Q. Mar. Nay, never bear me hence; dispatch me here:
Here sheath thy sword; I'll pardon thee my death.
What, wilt thou not? Then, Clarence, do it thou.

Geo. By heaven, I will not do thee so much ease.   70

Q. Mar. Good Clarence, do; sweet Clarence, do thou do it.

Geo. Didst thou not hear me swear I would not do it?

Q. Mar. Ay, but thou usest to forswear thyself.
'Twas sin before, but now 'tis charity.
What! wilt thou not? Where is that devil's butcher?   75
Richard, hard-favour'd Richard, where art thou,
Thou art not here: murder is thy alms-deed;
Petitioners for blood thou ne'er put'st back.

75-6. devil's butcher, / Richard, ... Richard,] *This edn;* diuels butcher *Richard?* /
Hard fauor'd *Richard? Richard,* / *F;* Diuels butcher, hardfauored *Richard,* / Richard *Q;* Devil's butcher, / Richard? hard-favour'd Richard, *Pope;* Devil-butcher,/
Richard? hard-favour'd Richard, *Theobald.*   76. thou,] *This edn;* thou? *Q,F.*
77. thy] *Q,F;* thine *conj. this edn.*

60. *How sweet a plant . . .*] Cf. Kyd,
Sp. Tr., II. v. 47, 'Sweet lovely Rose,
ill pluckt before thy time'; and *1 H 4,*
I. iii. 175, 'To put down Richard, that
sweet lovely rose'.

untimely] prematurely; before his
time.

61. *no children*] Cf. *Mac.,* IV. iii. 216.
This is not, of course, true historically,
since Edward had several children,
and Clarence had a son (Brooke).

62. *remorse*] pity; *OED.* 3.

63-5, 80.] prophecies, or curses, to
be amply fulfilled in *R 3.*

65. *deathsmen*] executioners; cf. *2 H 6,*
III. ii. 217.

rid] destroyed; made away; cf. *2 H 6,*
III. i. 233.

70. *do . . . ease*] give . . . comfort; cf.
Ham., I. i. 131.

73. *usest*] art in the habit of.

forswear] perjure; cf. 34, 40; V. i. 105,
109; and *R 3,* I. iv. 50, 55.

75-6.] What seems to have happened is that 'Richard' was transferred, in
the Q copy, to follow 'butcher', but
was also printed where it stood; and
the indication for the line-ending was
not made clear.

76. *hard-favour'd*] hard-featured; cf.
Hall, 342, 'eiuill featured'; and
Pharaoh's 'ill-favoured kine'.

77. *Thou art*] i.e. that thou art.

alms-deed] act of charity.

78. *put'st back*] repulsed; reject-
ed.

K. *Edw.* Away, I say; I charge ye bear her hence.

Q. *Mar.* So come to you and yours as to this prince!   80

curse   *Exit[, led out forcibly].*

*but
and she has
as begun.
(way)*

K. *Edw.* Where's Richard gone?

Geo. To London all in post, and, as I guess,
To make a bloody supper in the Tower.

K. *Edw.* He's sudden if a thing come in his head.
Now march we hence: discharge the common sort   85
With pay and thanks, and let's away to London
And see our gentle Queen how well she fares:
By this, I hope, she hath a son for me.   *Exeunt.*

[SCENE VI.—*London. The Tower.*]

Enter KING HENRY *and* RICHARD, *with the Lieutenant, on the walls.*

Rich. Good day, my lord. What, at your book so hard?

K. *Hen.* Ay, my good lord—my lord, I should say rather.
'Tis sin to flatter; 'good' was little better:
'Good Gloucester' and 'good devil' were alike,
And both preposterous; therefore not 'good lord'.   5

80. S.D.] *Capell; Exit Queene. | F; Ex. | Q1; Exit. | Q2,3.*   84. come] *Q; comes
+Edd.*   88. S.D.] *Rowe; Exit. | F; Exeunt Omnes. | Q.*

Scene VI

SCENE VI] *Capell; not in Q,F.*   *London. The Tower.*] *after Pope; not in
Q,F.*   S.D.] *F (Enter Henry the sixt, and . . .); Enter Gloster to king Henry in
the Tower. Q.*

80. *come to*] happen to; befall.

84.] Edward's remark is meant to emphasize his fatuous disregard of his royal responsibilities.

sudden] prompt; impulsive.

85. *common sort*] common class or kind; ordinary soldiers.

Scene VI

The scene is an elaboration of suggestions from Hall, 303 and 342-3. It carries forward the 'bookish' character of Henry, whose 'rule' had pulled all England down. In the main it serves to develop the character and designs of Richard, both from his own long speeches, and from Henry's 'prophecy'. The dying Henry thus takes his place in the chain with the dying Gaunt in *Richard II* and Margaret in *Richard III*.

1. *book*] probably, as Hart suggests, *the* book, the Bible.

3. '*Tis sin to flatter*] Cf. Daniel, xi. 32, 'to sinne by flatterie' (Carter).

better] scil. than flattery.

5. *preposterous*] the original L. sense (*prae* = before; *post* = after) of something that inverts the natural order; putting the cart before the horse.

Rich. Sirrah, leave us to ourselves; we must confer.

            [*Exit Lieutenant.*

K. Hen. So flies the reckless shepherd from the wolf;
 So first the harmless sheep doth yield his fleece,
 And next his throat unto the butcher's knife.
 What scene of death hath Roscius now to act?   1

Rich. Suspicion always haunts the guilty mind;
 The thief doth fear each bush an officer.

K. Hen. The bird that hath been limed in a bush
 With trembling wings misdoubteth every bush;
 And I, the hapless male to one sweet bird,   1
 Have now the fatal object in my eye
 Where my poor young was lim'd, was caught, and kill'd

Rich. Why, what a peevish fool was that of Crete,
 That taught his son the office of a fowl!
 And yet, for all his wings, the fool was drown'd.   2

K. Hen. I, Daedalus; my poor boy, Icarus;

---

6. S.D.] *Rowe; not in Q,F.* 7. reckless] *Hanmer;* wreaklesse *F.* 10. Rosciu
Q (Rosius); F (Rossius); Pope. 16. my] *F;* mine *Q.*

---

6. *Sirrah*] form of address to an inferior.

 confer] talk together; converse (L. *confero*).

7 ff. *wolf . . . sheep . . . butcher's . . . bird . . . lim'd*] a return to the imagery of *2 H 6*, and of the early scenes of *3 H6*.

7. *reckless*] careless; thoughtless; having no care for.

10. *Roscius*] the great Roman actor (d. 62 B.C.). The Elizabethans often referred to Richard Burbage, of Shakespeare's Company, by this name, usually in tragic rôles, though in fact Roscius was best known for comedy. Cf. *Ham.*, II. ii. 387.

11. *Suspicion . . .*] proverbial; see Tilley, F117; typical of Richard's speech and irony.

 Suspicion] apprehension of something ill (Schmidt).

12. *The thief . . .*] proverbial; Tilley, T112; cf. *MND.*, v. i. 20–1.

13, 17. *limed*] caught with bird-lime; Tilley, B394.

14. *misdoubteth*] suspects; mistrusts.

15. *male*] father; parent; begette
cf. II. i. 42; *2 H 4*, III. ii. 141.

 bird] offspring; cf. II. i. 91.

16. *fatal*] death-dealing; ill-omene

 object] here = anything regarde
with love or with dislike, inspirin
sympathy or antipathy (Schmidt
Henry seems to be saying that, bein
innocent, he does not fear as the thi
does; nor does he fear every bus
since he has 'the fatal object' befo
him. Cf. *MND.*, v. i. 21–2, and Juve
nal, *Sat.*, x. 21, 'motae ad lunam trep
dabis harundinis umbram'.

18. *peevish*] foolish; childish; *OE*
1. obs.

18–20. *fool . . . fowl . . . fool*] Note t
pun on the two words, then pr
nounced alike. See *Sh. Qu.*, II (1951
212 ff.

19. *office*] function.

21. *Daedalus . . . Icarus*] from Ovi
Ars Amatoria, ii. 21–100, rather th:
Metam., viii. 183–235 (J. A. K. Thor
son). Escaping with his father, Da
dalus, from Minos, King of Crete, wi

Thy father, Minos, that denied our course;
The sun that sear'd the wings of my sweet boy,
Thy brother Edward; and thyself, the sea
Whose envious gulf did swallow up his life.   25
Ah, kill me with thy weapon, not with words!
My breast can better brook thy dagger's point
Than can my ears that tragic history.
But wherefore dost thou come? Is't for my life?

Rich. Think'st thou I am an executioner?   30

K. Hen. A persecutor I am sure thou art:
If murdering innocents be executing,
Why then thou art an executioner.

Rich. Thy son I kill'd for his presumption.

K. Hen. Hadst thou been kill'd when first thou didst
        presume,   35
Thou hadst not liv'd to kill a son of mine.
And thus I prophesy: that many a thousand
Which now mistrust no parcel of my fear,
And many an old man's sigh, and many a widow's,
And many an orphan's water-standing eye—   40
Men for their sons', wives for their husbands',
Orphans for their parents' timeless death—
Shall rue the hour that ever thou wast born.
The owl shriek'd at thy birth—an evil sign;

---

23. boy] F (Boy.).   28. my] F; mine Q.

---

the help of wings fastened with wax,
Icarus flew too near the sun, which
melted the wax, and he fell into the
sea. Cf. Talbot and his son in *1 H 6*,
IV. vi. 55; IV. vii. 16.

22. *denied*] forbad.

23. *sun*] referring to Edward's
badge; cf. II. vi. 9.

25. *envious*] malicious; spiteful.

gulf] whirlpool; sucking eddy, like
a gullet.

27. *brook*] endure.

dagger] in Hall, 303.

28. *history*] story.

37. *I prophesy*] Cf. Gaunt, in *R 2*; a
common device of Shakespeare's to
impose unity on the series of histories;
see Intro., lvi.

38. *mistrust*] apprehend.

parcel] part; portion.

40. *water-standing*] flooded with
tears; cf. water-flowing, IV. viii. 43.

41 ff.] possibly suggested by Hall, 73
(1415, after Agincourt), 'the ladies
souned for the deathes of their huse-
bandes, the Orphalines wept and rent
their heares for the losse of their
parentes, the faire damoselles defied
that day in the whiche they had lost
their paramors, the seruauntes waxed
mad for destruccion of their masters,
and finally, euery frend for his frend,
euery cosyn for his alye, euery neighbor for his neighbor, was sorry, dis-
pleased & greued'.

42. *timeless*] untimely; premature.

The night-crow cried, aboding luckless time;   45
Dogs howl'd, and hideous tempests shook down trees;
The raven rook'd her on the chimney's top,
And chattering pies in dismal discords sung;
Thy mother felt more than a mother's pain,
And yet brought forth less than a mother's hope,   50
To wit, an indigest deformed lump,
Not like the fruit of such a goodly tree.
Teeth hadst thou in thy head when thou wast born,
To signify thou cam'st to bite the world;
And if the rest be true which I have heard,   55
Thou cam'st—

Rich. I'll hear no more: die, prophet, in thy speech. *Stabs him.*
For this, amongst the rest, was I ordain'd.

K. Hen. Ay, and for much more slaughter after this.

O God, forgive my sins and pardon thee!   *Dies.* 60

Rich. What, will the aspiring blood of Lancaster
Sink in the ground? I thought it would have mounted.
See how my sword weeps for the poor King's death.
O, may such purple tears be alway shed
From those that wish the downfall of our house!   65
If any spark of life be yet remaining,

46. tempests] *Q;* Tempest *F.*   51. indigest deformed] *Malone;* indigested and
deformed *F;* vndigest created *Q.*   55. which] *F;* that *Q.*   56. Thou cam'st—]
F; Thou camst into the world *Q.*   57. S.D.] *F;* He stabs him. *Q (after 56).*
60. S.D.] *F;* He dies. *Q.*

45. *night-crow*] a bird of supersti-
tion incapable of exact identification (Hart); the night-raven in Spenser,
F.Q., II. vii. 23; Tilley, R33.

aboding] foreboding; cf. abodement,
IV. vii. 13.

46. *tempests*] The Q plural is supported by the full measure of the F line,
the F tendency to omit final *s*, and the
accumulation of sibilants to echo the
sense.

47. *rook'd her*] crouched; cowered;
OED. rook, and ruck, v¹.

48. *pies*] magpies.
dismal] ill-boding; sinister.

51. *indigest . . . lump*] Ovid's 'rudis
indigestaque moles', *Metam.,* I. 7. Cf.
2 H 6, v. i. 157, 'indigested lump'; *R 3,*

I. ii. 57, 'lump of foul deformity' =
shapeless mass. F has sophisticated
and added 'and' for the metre.

58. *ordain'd*] Richard adopts the fate
of which he is the instrument and the
victim. Cf. II. ii. 137 and v. vii. 23.

59.] Henry continues his prophecy.

60.] 'A plain echo of the dying
words of Christ' (Goddard, *The Meaning of Shakespeare,* 32).

61–2. *aspiring . . . mounted*] Cf. Marlowe, *Ed. 2,* 93; and 1999–2000, 'highly scorning that the lowly earth /
Should drinke his bloud, mounts vp
into the ayre:' and *1 H 6,* v. iv. 99.

64. *purple*] blood-red.

66.] Cf. Kyd, *Sp. Tr.,* II. v. 17, 'O
speak if any spark of life remaine'.

Down, down to hell; and say I sent thee thither—

Stabs him again.

I that have neither pity, love, nor fear.
Indeed 'tis true that Henry told me of:
For I have often heard my mother say   70
I came into the world with my legs forward.
Had I not reason, think ye, to make haste
And seek their ruin that usurp'd our right?
The midwife wonder'd, and the women cried
'O Jesu bless us, he is born with teeth!'   75
And so I was, which plainly signified
That I should snarl, and bite, and play the dog.
Then, since the heavens have shap'd my body so,
Let hell make crook'd my mind to answer it.
I have no brother, I am like no brother;   80
And this word 'love', which greybeards call divine,
Be resident in men like one another,
And not in me: I am myself alone.
Clarence, beware; thou keep'st me from the light,
But I will sort a pitchy day for thee;   85
For I will buzz abroad such prophecies
As Edward shall be fearful of his life;
And then, to purge his fear, I'll be thy death.

7. thither—] *Wilson;* thither. *Q1,2,F;* thither *Q3.*   S.D.] *F; Q* (Stab . . .)
after 56).   75. Jesu] *This edn;* Iesus *Q,F.*   80. brother . . . brother] *F;*
brothers . . . brothers *Q1,3;* brother . . . brothers *Q2.*   86. prophecies]
Q1,2,F; Prophesies, / Vnder pretence of outward seeming ill, *Q3.*   87. As] *Q;*
That *F.*

68 ff.] a typical Machiavellian
speech, that sums up Richard, and
3 *H 3,* and links the two plays closely.
69.] See 56.
75. *Jesu*] In F, the form 'Iesus' occurs only here and in *2 H 6,* I. ii. 70;
both instances derive from bad quartos. All other eighteen examples, including two where Q had 'Iesus'—
1 H 4, II. ii. 79, and *2 H 6,* v. i. 215—
read 'Iesu', which may therefore be
taken as Shakespeare's usage.
79. *answer*] correspond to; *OED.*
8.

81. '*love*' . . . *divine*] Cf. 1 John, iv. 7,
'Beloved, let us love one another, for
love cometh of God'.
85. *sort* . . . *day*] arrange a black
future; *OED.* 'sort', 1; Tilley, D88.
86. *buzz abroad*] spread around (false
rumours).
87. *As*] For the F sophistication to
'That', cf. I. iv. 151; *R 3,* III. vii. 161;
III. iv. 40; *Ham.,* II. i. 95; *Lear,* I. i. 232;
Oth., III. iii. 227; etc.
of] for.
88. *purge*] expel as 'humours' are ex-
pelled from the bowels.

King Henry and the Prince his son are gone;
Clarence, thy turn is next, and then the rest,   90
Counting myself but bad till I be best.
I'll throw thy body in another room,
And triumph, Henry, in thy day of doom.

Exit[, with the body].

[SCENE VII.—*The same. The palace.*]

Flourish. Enter KING [EDWARD], QUEEN [ELIZABETH], GEORGE
RICHARD, HASTINGS, [*a*] *Nurse* [*with the young Prince*], *and
Attendants.*

K. Edw. Once more we sit in England's royal throne,
Repurchas'd with the blood of enemies.

89–90.] *F*; Henry and his sonne are gone, thou *Clarence* next, / And one by on
I will dispatch the rest, *Q1*; King *Henry* and the Prince his sonne are gone, / An
Clarence thou art next must follow them, / So one by one dispatching all the res
Q3.   94. S.D. *with the body*] *Capell; not in Q,F.*

Scene VII

SCENE VII] *Capell; not in Q,F.   The same. The palace.*] *Edd., after Theobald*
not in Q,F.   S.D.] F (. . . Hastings, Nurse, and . . .); Enter . . *Elizabeth*
and a Nurse / with the young prince, and *Clarence*, / and *Hastings*, and others
Q.

89–90.] *Q3* and F vary from *Q1*
and from each other. With only a
single exemplar of *Q1* extant, it is impossible to decide the authority, at this
point, of *Q3*, which was printed from it
and may incorporate a *Q1* variation.
It seems best to adopt F.

91. *bad . . . best*] proverbial 'bad is
the best'; *ODP.*, 58.

93. *triumph*] exult.
   day of doom] last day of life; death-
day.

Scene VII

The scene, which is purely fictitious,
draws many threads together, and sets
the stage for *Richard III*, all with con-
summate irony. York has triumphed.
Edward first calls the roll of his formid-
able enemies now dead, and goes on to
rejoice in the birth of an heir. Wars are

at an end, and he is now surrounded
as he thinks, by his 'brothers' loves
Margaret, for whom the wheel ha
come full circle since she came in tr
umph to England as Henry's bride,
now ruined by her own ambitions, an
is to be sent back to France. To com
plete the ironical conclusion to *3 Hen
VI*, she is to be ransomed by th
pawning of kingdoms which the
sounded so grand among her father
titles.

   Finally, Richard's Judas kiss throw
into relief the dramatic irony of Ed
ward's self-satisfaction, and prepare
the way for the tragedy to come.

   1. *Once more*] referring to his coron
tion (II. vi. 109–10 and II. i), captu
(IV. iii), escape (IV. v), return (IV. viii
and victory (V. ii and iii).

   2. *Repurchas'd*] acquired or obtaine

What valiant foemen, like to autumn's corn,
Have we mow'd down in tops of all their pride!
Three Dukes of Somerset, threefold renown'd   5
For hardy and undoubted champions;
Two Cliffords, as the father and the son;
And two Northumberlands—two braver men
Ne'er spurr'd their coursers at the trumpet's sound;
With them, the two brave bears, Warwick and
    Montague,   10
That in their chains fetter'd the kingly lion
And made the forest tremble when they roar'd.
Thus have we swept suspicion from our seat
And made our footstool of security.
Come hither, Bess, and let me kiss my boy.   15
Young Ned, for thee thine uncles and myself
Have in our armours watch'd the winter's night,
Went all afoot in summer's scalding heat,
That thou might'st repossess the crown in peace;
And of our labours thou shalt reap the gain.   20

---

4. tops] *Q,F*; top *Pope.*   5. renown'd] *Q ;* Renowne *F.*   6. undoubted] *Q,F;*
redoubted *Hudson, conj. Capell.*

---

again; a legal term for acquisition
otherwise than by inheritance or descent, and here of more general application than now.

4. *in tops of*] at the height of.

5. *Three Dukes of Somerset*] Edmund,
second duke, killed at St Albans, 1455
(I. i. 16); and his sons, Henry, third
duke, beheaded at Hexham, 1464
(v. i. 73–5), and Edmund, fourth
duke, beheaded at Tewkesbury, 1471
(v. v)—see IV. i. head-note, and v. i.
73 n.

6. *For*] As; Franz, 482.
undoubted] fearless (Schmidt); free
from doubt or fear.
champion] man of valour; *OED.* 1.

7. *Cliffords*] See *2 H 6*, v. ii, and *3 H 6*,
I. vi.
as] namely.

8. *Northumberlands*] See I. i. 54, and
App. II.

10. *bears*] an allusion, of course,
to the badge of Warwick, the bear
and ragged staff; cf. *2 H 6*, v. i. 144–
60.

11. *chains*] a continuation of the
'bear' metaphor; the bears were led in
chains.

13. *suspicion*] apprehension; anxiety.

14.] The same line (with 'on' for
'of') is in Marlowe's *Massacre at Paris*,
744.

17–18.] derived, like *2 H 6*, I. i. 78–9,
from Hall, 112 (reign of Henry V),
'No colde made him slouthfull, nor
heat caused him to loyter'.

17. *watch'd*] kept watch; stayed
awake.

20–1. *reap . . . harvest*] Cf. John, iv.
37–8, 'one soweth and another reap-
eth; . . . other men laboured and yee
are entered into their labours' (Carter).

Rich. [*Aside.*] I'll blast his harvest, and your head were laid;
  For yet I am not look'd on in the world.
  This shoulder was ordain'd so thick to heave,
  And heave it shall some weight, or break my back:
  Work thou the way, and that shall execute. 25

K. Edw. Clarence and Gloucester, love my lovely Queen;
  And kiss your princely nephew, brothers both.

Geo. The duty that I owe unto your Majesty
  I seal upon the lips of this sweet babe.

Q. Eliz. Thanks, noble Clarence; worthy brother, thanks. 30

Rich. And, that I love the tree from whence thou sprang'st,
  Witness the loving kiss I give the fruit.
  [*Aside*] To say the truth, so Judas kiss'd his master
  And cried 'All hail!' when as he meant all harm.

K. Edw. Now am I seated as my soul delights, 35
  Having my country's peace and brothers' loves.

Geo. What will your Grace have done with Margaret?
  Reignier, her father, to the King of France
  Hath pawn'd the Sicils and Jerusalem,
  And hither have they sent it for her ransom. 40

K. Edw. Away with her and waft her hence to France.

21, 33. *Aside*] *Rowe; not in* Q,F. 21. and] *Q1,2; if Q3,F.* 25. that shall]
Brooke, conj. Vaughan; thou shalt *Q;* that shalt *F.* 30. *Q. Eliz.*] *Q (Queen.);*
Cla. | F. Thanks] *Q;* Thanke *F.* 38. Reignier] *Rowe;* Ranard | *Q1,2;*
Reynard | *Q3,F.*

21. *blast*] blight; wither.

and] if; possibly a sign of Q3 copy,
but alternatively an independent sophistication in F.

head] a double reference to Edward's
head and the head of the corn, both of
which could be laid—one in the grave,
the other flat on the ground ('blasted').
Richard could easily deal with the
young prince once his father was out
of the way.

22. *look'd on*] regarded.

25. *that*] his shoulder; 'thou' must
be Richard himself. In the Q copy
for F, 'shalt' remained uncorrected.

30.] typical formal chiasmus.

31. *I love the tree*] i.e. his own stock.
For the irony, cf. III. ii. 126; and *R 3,*
v. iii. 187, 'I love myself'.

32. *kiss*] Tilley, K312, 'Many kiss
the child for the nurse's sake'.

33. *Judas*] The allusion was probably suggested by Hall, 343, 'not lettynge to kisse whom he thought to
kill'. But Shakespeare has many allusions to Judas when he wishes to brand
ingratitude, e.g. *R 2,* IV. i. 169–70.

34. *when as*] adversative = though
on the contrary: Franz, 554.

35. *my soul delights*] Cf. Isaiah, xlvi.
3; xlii. 1.

39. *pawn'd*] Hall says 'sold'. Reignier's many kingdoms were listed as
a sign of his importance in *2 H 6.*

the Sicils] The Kingdom of the two
Sicilies—Naples and Sicily; Hall, 301,
263.

40. *it*] the money raised.

41. *waft*] convey by sea.

And now what rests but that we spend the time
With stately triumphs, mirthful comic shows,
Such as befits the pleasure of the court?
Sound drums and trumpets! Farewell, sour annoy!   45
For here, I hope, begins our lasting joy.   *Exeunt.*

. pleasure] *F;* pleasures *Q.*   46. S.D.] *Q,F* (Exeunt omnes.).

43. *triumphs*] public rejoicings; 'pub-
ue processions', Hall, 301.
44. *befits*] for this use of the third
person plural in -*s* see Abbott, 333
45. *sour*] bitter; harsh.
annoy] vexation, trouble; *OED.* 1.

Appendix I

(a) From Edward Hall's *The Union of the Two Noble and Illustre Famelies of Lancastre and Yorke*, 1548

References are to (i) the 1548 edition, (ii) the reprint of 1809. Readers may be further referred to:
(a) Geoffrey Bullough, *Narrative and Dramatic Sources of Shakespeare*, iii (1960).
(b) W. G. Boswell-Stone, *Shakespeare's Holinshed*, 1896.

THE TROUBLEOUS SEASON OF KYNG HENRY THE SIXT

3H6

xviij 233   The xxxiii yere [1454–5]. . . there died . . . Edmond duke of Somerset . . . and beside hym, lay Henry the second erle of Northumberlande, and Humfrey erle of Stafforde, sonne to the duke of Buckyngham, Ihon lorde Clifford, and viij. M. men and more. Humfrey duke of Buckyngham, beyng wounded, & Iames Butler erle of Wilshire & Ormond, seyng fortunes loweryng chaunce, left the kyng poste a lone & with a great numbre fled away. This was thend of the first bataill

xviij^v   at S. / Albons. . .

I. i

     After this victory obteined, by the Duke of Yorke . . ., he usyng all lenitie, mercy, and bounteousness, would not once touche or apprehend the body of kyng Henry. . . But . . . conveyed hym to London, & so to Westminster, to whiche place was somoned and appoynted, a great assemble of the thre estates, commonly called a Parliament. . . In whiche Parliament also, the duke of Yorke was made protector of the Realme, and therle of Salisbury, was appoynted to be Chauncellor, and had the greate seale to hym delivered: and the erle of Warwicke, was elected to the office of the capitain of Calice. . .

it was agreed, that king Henry should reigne, in name and dignitie, but neither in deed nor in aucthoritie: not myndyng either to depose or destroy thesaid kyng, least they might sodainly provoke and stirre the fury and ire of the common people against theim: which for his holines of life, and abundant clemencie, was of the simple sort, muche favored, and highly estemed.

Clxxvij

The xxxviij yere. [1459–60] Duryng this troble, was a Parliament somoned to begyn at Westmynster, in ye moneth of October next folowyng. Before which tyme, Richarde duke of Yorke, beyng in Ireland . . . was advertised of

245

the great victorie, gayned by hys parte, at the feld of Northampton, and also knew that the kynge was now in case to be kepte, & ordered at his pleasure and wil: wherfor losyng no tyme, nor sluggyng one houre, he . . . came to the citie of London, . . . and toke his lodgynge in the kynges awne palayce, wherupon the common people babbeled, that he should be Kyng, & that kyng Henry should no longer reigne. Durynge the tyme of this Parliamente, the duke of Yorke, with a bolde contenaunce, entered into the chamber of the peres, and sat downe in the trone royall, under the cloth of estate (which is the kynges peculiar seate) & in the presence aswel of the nobilitie, as of ye spiritualtie (after a pause made) saide these wordes in effect. /

Clxxvijv

". . . here I sit, as in the place to me by very justice lawfully belongyng, & here I rest, as he to whome this chayre of righte apperteineth. . . /

246

For all you know . . . that the high and mightie prince kynge Richard the. ii. was the trew and indubitate heyre, to . . . Edwarde the iij. . . . Which kyng Richard . . . Henry of Derby . . . by force & violence, contrary both to the duetie of his allegiaunce, and also to his homage, to him both done and sworne, raysed warre and battayle . . . agaynst the sayd kyng Richard

Clxxviij

. . . / After whose piteous death, and execrable murder . . . the right & title of the croune . . .

was lawfully reverted and returned to Rogier
Mortimer, erle of Marche . . . to which Rogiers
doughter called Anne, my most derest and wel-
beloved mother, I am the very trew and lyneall
heyre . . . Likewise my most derest lord & father,
so farre set furth that right and title, that he loste

viij^v 247 his life . . . / Henry the v. obteyned notable victories, and immortall prayses, for his noble
actes, done in the realme of Fraunce: . . . Is not
Normandy . . . regayned, and conquered agayn
. . . ? Is not the whole duchye of Aquitayn . . .
gotten out of ower handes and seignorie? What
should I speake of Angeow and mayne or the
losse, of the Isle of Fraunce, with the riche citie

xj 248 of Parys. . ." / When the duke has thus ended
his oracion, the lordes sat still like Images graven
in the wall, or domme Gods, neither whisperyng
nor spekyng, as though their mouths had been
sowed vp. . .

xij 249   The xxxix. yere. [1460–1] After long argu-
mentes made, & deliberate consultation had
emong the peeres, prelates, and commons of the
realme: upon the vigile of all sainctes, it was
condescended and agreed, by the three estates,
for so muche as kyng Henry had been taken as
kyng, by the space of. xxxviij. yeres and more,
that he should inioye the name and title of
Kyng, and haue possession of the realme, duryng his life naturall: And if he either died or
resigned, or forfeted thesame, for infringing any
poynt of this concorde, then the saied Croune
and aucthoritie royal, should immediately bee
divoluted to the Duke of Yorke, if he then lived,
or els to the next heire of his line or linage, and
that the duke from thensefurth, should be Protector and Regent of the lande. Provided all-
waie, that if the kyng did closely or apertly,
studie or go aboute to breake or alter this agrement, or to compesse or imagine the death or
destruccion, of the saiede Duke or his bloud,
then he to forfet the croun, and the duke of
Yorke to take it. These articles with many other,

were not onely written, sealed, and sworne to by
the twoo parties; but also wer enacted, in the
high court of Parliament. . .

The Duke of Yorke well knowyng, that the
Quene would spurne and impugne the conclusions agreed and taken in this parliament, caused
her and her sonne, to be sent for by the kyng:
but she beyng a manly woman, usyng to rule
and not to be ruled, & therto counsailed by the
dukes of Excester and Somerset, not onely denied to come, but also as- / sembled together a
great army, intending to take the kyng by fine
force, out of the lordes handes, and to set them
to a new skoole. The Protector liyng in London,
havyng perfite knowledge of all these doynges:
assigned the Duke of Norffolke and the Erle of
Warwicke, his trustie frendes, to be about the
kyng, and he with therles of Salisbury, and Rut-
lande: with a convenient company, departed
out of London, the second daie of Decembre
Northward, and sent to the Erle of March his
eldest sonne to folowye hym with all his power.
The Duke by small iorneis, came to his Castle of
Sandall, beside Wakefelde, on Christmas eve,
and there began to assemble his tenauntes and
frendes. The quene beyng thereof asserteined,
determined to couple with hym while his power
was small and his ayde not come: And so havyng
in her company, the Prince her sonne, the
Dukes of Excester and Somerset, the Erle of
Devonshire, the Lorde Clifford, the Lorde
Rosse, and in effect all the Lordes of the Northe
parte, with eightene thousande men, or as some
write, twentie and twoo thousande, marched
from Yorke to Wakefelde, and bad base to the
Duke, even before his Castle he havyng with
hym not fully five thousande persones, determined incontinent to issue out, and to fight with
his enemies, and all though sir Dauy Halle, his
old servaunt and chief counsailer, avised hym to
kepe his Castle, and to defende thesame with his
smal numbre, till his sonne the Erle of Marche
wer come with his power of Marchemen and

250

Welshe souldiours, yet he would not be counsailed, but in a great fury saied, a Davy, Davy,
has thou loved me so long, and now wouldest
haue me dishonored? Thou never sawest me
kepe fortres when I was Regent in Normandy,
when the Dolphyn hymself, with his puissaunce
came to besiege me, but like a man, and not like
a bird included in a cage, I issued and fought
with myne enemies, to their losse ever (I thanke
God) and to my honor: If I have not kepte my
self within walles, for feare of a great and strong
prince, nor hid my face from any man livyng,
wouldest thou that I for dread of a scoldyng
woman. . . / . . . Their great numbre shall not
appall my spirites, but incorage theim. . .

xxxiij

. . . in the plain ground betwene his Castle and
the toune of Wakefelde, he was environed on
every side, like a fish in a net, or a deere in a
buckestall: so that he manfully fightyng, was
within halfe an houre slain and ded, and his
whole army discomfited, & with hym died of his
trusty frendes, his two bastard uncles, sir Ihon,
& sir Hugh Mortimers. . .

I. iv
II. i

I. ii

. . . While this battaill was in fightyng, a /
prieste called sir Robert Aspall, chappelain and
schole master to the yong erle of Rutland ii.
sonne to the above named duke of Yorke,
sca[r]ce of ye age of. xii. yeres, a faire gentleman,
and a maydenlike person, perceivyng y^t flight
was more savegard, then tariyng, bothe for him
and his master, secretly conveyed therle out of y^e
felde, by the lord Cliffordes bande, toward the
towne, but or he coulde enter into a house, he
was by the sayd lord Clifford espied, folowed,
and taken, and by reson of his apparell, demaunded what he was. The yong gentelman
dismaied, had not a word to speake, but kneled
on his knees imploryng mercy, and desiryng
grace, both with holding up his handes, and
making dolorous countinance, for his speache
was gone for feare. Save him sayde his Chappe-
lein, for he is a princes sonne, and peradventure
may do you good hereafter. With that word,

I. iii

the lord Clifford marked him and sayde: by
Gods blode, thy father slew myne, and so wil I
do the and all thy kyn, and with that woord,
stacke the erle to ye hart / with his dagger, and
bad his Chappeleyn bere the erles mother &
brother worde what he had done, and sayde.
In this acte the lord Clyfford was accompted a
tyraunt, and no gentelman, for the propertie of
the Lyon, which is a furious and an unreasonable beaste, is to be cruell to them that with-
stande hym, and gentle to such as prostrate or
humiliate them selfes before him. Yet this cruell
Clifforde, & deadly bloudsupper not content
with this homicyde, or chyldkillyng, came to y^e
place wher the dead corps of the duke of Yorke
lay, and caused his head to be stryken of, and
set on it a croune of paper, & so fixed it on a pole,
& presented it to the Quene, not lyeng farre from
the felde, in great despite, and much derision,
saiyng: Madame, your warre is done, here is
your kinges raunsome, at which present, was
much ioy, and great reioysing, but many laugh-
ed then, that sore lamented after, as the Quene
her self, and her sonne: And many were glad
then of other mens deaths, not knowing that
their awne were nere at hande, as the lord Clifford, and other. But surely, mans nature is so
frayle, that thinges passed be sone forgotten,
and mischiefes to come, be not forsene. After this
victory by ye Quene and her parte obteyned,
she caused the erle of Salisbury, with all the
other prisoners, to bee sente to Pomfret, and
there to bee behedded, and sent all their heddes,
and the dukes head of Yorke, to be set upon
poles, over the gate of the citie of Yorke, in despite of them, and their lignage: whose chyldren
shortly revenged their fathers querell, both to
the Quenes extreme perdicion, and the utter
undoynge of her husband and sonne. This ende
had the valeant lord, Rychard Plantagenet,
duke of Yorke, & this fyne ensued of his to much
hardines. The erle of Marche, so commonly
called, but after the death of his father, in dede

and in right very duke of Yorke, lyeng at Glocester, heryng of the death of his noble father,
and lovyng brother, and trusty frendes was
wonderfully amased, but after comfort given to
him, by his faithful lovers and assured alyes, he
removed to Shrewsbury, and other townes upon
the ryver of Severne. . . The duke of Yorke,
called erle of Marche, . . . mett with his enemies
in a faire playne, nere to Mortimers crosse, not
farre from Herford east, on Candelmas day in
the mornyng, at whiche / tyme the sunne (as
some write) appered to the erle of March, like.
iii. sunnes, and sodainly ioined al together in
one, and that upon the sight thereof, he toke
suche courage, y^t he fiercely set on his enemies,
them shortly discomfited: for which cause, men
imagined, that he gave the sunne in his full
brightnes for his cognisaunce or badge.

xxiiij

II. i. 25

. . . During this season, ye quene was greatly en-
couraged with the victory, obteined late at
Wakefeld, . . . wherfore with a great multitude
of Northren people, she marched toward London, . . . entendynge to subverte and defaict all
conclusions and agrementes, enacted and assented to, in the last Parliament. And so after
her long iorney, she came to the town of sainct
Albons: wherof ye duke of Northfolke, ye erle of
Warwycke, and other, whom ye duke of Yorke
had lefte to governe the kyng in his absence,
beyng advertised, by the assent of ye kyng, gathered together a great hoste, and set forward towarde sainct Albons, havyng the kyng in their
company, as the head and chefetayn of the
warre, and so not myndyng to differre the time
any farther, upon shrovetuesday early in the
morning, set upon their enemies. Fortune y^t day
so favored the Quene, that her parte prevayled,
and the duke and the erle were discomfited, and
fled: leaving the king accompanied with the
lord Bonvile, and syr Thomas Kyriell of Kent,
whiche upon assurance of his promise, taried
still and fled not, but their trust, them deceived.

II. i. 95 ff.

For after the victorie obteyned, and the kynge
broughte to the Quene, they two were deteyned
as prisoners, and so continued till the kynges
departyng from that towne. In this battayl were
slayn. xxiii C men, and not above, of whom no
noble man is remembred, save syr Ihon Gray,   I
which thesame day was made knight, with. xii.
other, at ye village of Colney. Happy was the   II. ii. 7
quene in her two battayls, but unfortunate was   II. v. 17
the kyng in all his enterprises, for where his person was presente, ther victory fled ever from him
to the other parte, & he commonly was subdued
& vanqueshed. When quene Margaret had thus   II ii
wel sped, first she caused the kyng, to dubbe
prince Edward his sonne, knyght, with. xxx.
other persons, which in the morning fought on
Clxxxiiij^v   the quenes side, against / his parte. . .

253   . . . trew report was brought, not onely to the
citie but also to the quene, that / the erle of
Marche had vanquesed the erles of Penbroke
and Wilshyre, and that the erle of Warwycke,
in whome rested the chefe trust of that faction,
after the last conflict, had at saincte Albons, had
mete with the sayd erle of Marche at Chippyng
Norton, by Cottesold, and that they with both
their powers were cominge toward London.
These trew tales turned the quenes purpose, and
altered all her long devised ententes, in so
muche that she litle trustinge Essex, and lesse
Kent, but London least of all, with her husband
and sonne, departed from sainct Albons, into
the Northcountrey, where the roote, & foundacion of her ayde and refuge, onely consisted. . .

The duches of Yorke, seyng her husband and
sonne slayne, and not knowyng what should   II. i.
succede of her eldest sonnes chaunce, sent her.
ii. yonger sonnes, George & Richard, over the
sea, to the citie of / Utrechte in Almayn: where
they were of Philippe, duke of Bourgoyne, wel
receyved and fested, and so there thei remayned, till their brother Edwarde had obteyned the
Clxxxv   Realme, and gotten the regiment. . . / . . . The
erles of Marche and Warwycke, havyng perfite

knowledge, that the kyng and quene with their
adherentes, were departed from sainct Albons,
determined first to ryde to London, as the chefe
key, and common spectacle to the whole
Realme, thinking there to assure them selfs of
the East and West parte of the kingdome, as
king Henry and his faction nesteled and strengthened him and his alyes in the North regions.
. . . And so these two great lordes . . . entered the
citie of London . . . this lusty prince and flower
of chivalry . . . called a great counsaill both of
lordes spirituall and temporall, & to them re-
peted the title, and right that he had to the
Realme, & dignitie royall: . . . After the lordes
had considered, & weyghed his title and de-
claracion, thei determined . . . for as much as
kyng Henry, contrary to his othe, honor and
agrement, had violated and infringed, the order
taken and enacted in the last Parliament . . . he
was therfore . . . deprived & deiected of all kyngly honor, and regall sovereigntie. And incontinent, Edward erle of Marche . . . was named,
elected, & admitted, for kyng and governour of
the realme: on which day, the people of the erles
parte, beyng in their muster in sainct Ihons felde
. . . sodaynly the lord Fawconbridge, which toke
the musters, wisely declared to the multitude,
the offences and breaches of the late agremente
done and perpetrated by kyng Henry the. vi.
and demaunded of the people, whether thei
would haue the sayd kyng Henry to rule and
reigne any lenger over them: To whome they,
with a whole voyce, aunswered nay, nay. Then
he asked them, if thei would serve, love and
obey the erle of March as their earthly prince

xxxv^v
4
and sovereign lord. To which question / they
aunswered, yea, yea, crieng, king Ed- / ward,
with many great showtes and clappyng of   ii. i. 192 ff.
handes. . . Dayly makyng provision to go North-   ii. ii. 66 ff.
warde against his adverse faccion and open
xxxvj
enemies. . . / . . . When his army was redy, and
al thinges prepared, he departed out of London
the. xii. day of Marche, & by easy iourneys

came to the castell of Pomfret, where he rested,
appoyntyng the lorde Fitzwater, to kepe ye passage at Ferybridge. . . / the lord Clifforde determined with his light horsemen, to make an assaye to suche as kepte the passage of Ferybridge, . . . and early or his enemies were ware, gat the bridge, and slew the kepers of thesame, and al suche as woulde withstand him. The lord Fitzwater hearyng the noyse, sodainly rose out of his bed, and unarmed, with a pollax in his hande, thinking y^t it had byn a fray emongst his men, came doune to appeace thesame, but or he either began his tale, or knew what the matter meant, he was slayne, and with hym the bastard of Salisbury, brother to the erle of Warwycke, a valeaunt yong gentelman, and of great audacitie. When the erle of Warwycke was enformed of this feate, he like a man desperate, mounted on his Hackeney, and came blowyng to kyng Edward saiyng: syr I praye God have mercy of their soules, which in the beginnyng of your enterprise, hath lost their lifes, and because I se no succors of the world, I remit the vengeaunce and punishment to God our creator and redemer, and with that lighted doune, and slewe his horse with his swourde, saiyng: let him flie that wil, for surely I wil tary with him that wil tary with me, and kissed the crosse of his swourde.

The lusty kyng Edward, perceiving the courage of his trusty frend the erle of Warwycke, made proclamacion that all men, whiche were afrayde to fighte, shoulde incontinent departe, and to all men that tar/ried the battell, he promised great rewardes with this addicion, that if any souldiour, which voluntariely would abide, and in, or before the conflict flye, or turne his backe, that then he that could kil him should haue a great remuneracion and double wages. . .
. . . the lord Clifforde, either for heat or payne, putting of his gorget, sodainly w^t an arrowe (as some say) without an hedde, was striken into the throte, and incontinent rendered hys spirite,

and the erle of Westmerlandes brother, and all
his company almost were there slayn, at a place
. . . not farr from Towton. This ende had he,
which slew the yong erle of Rutland, kneling on
his knees: . . . When this conflict was ended at
Ferebridge, the lord Fawconbridge . . . came to
Saxton, where he might apparantly perceyve
the hoste of his adversaries, which were accompted. lx. M. men, and therof advertised
kyng Edward, whose whole army, thei that
knew it, and payed the wages, affirme to. xlviii.
M. vi. C. &. lx. persons, . . /

. . . This deadly battayle and bloudy conflicte,   II. v. 1–13
continued. x. houres in doubtfull victorie. The
one parte some time flowyng, and sometime
ebbyng, . . . The dukes of Somerset and Excester
fled from the felde and saved themselfes. This   II. v
conflict was in manner unnaturall, for in it the
sonne fought against the father, the brother
against the brother, the nephew against the
uncle, and the tenaunt against his lorde, . . .

After this great victorie, kyng Edward rode to
Yorke, . . . / . . . and first he caused the heddes of
his father, the erle of Salisbury, and other of his
frendes to be taken from the gates, and to be   II. vi. 52 ff.,
buried with their bodies. And there he caused   85–6
the erle of Devonshyre and. iii. other to be behedded, and set their heddes in the same place.
After that he sent out men on light horses, to
espye in what parte kyng Henry lurked, which
hearinge of the irrecuperable losse of his frendes,
departed incontinent with his wife and sonne,
to the towne of Barwycke, and . . . came to the   II. v. 128
kynges courte of Scotland, requiring of him and
his counsaill, ayde succor, relief & comfort . . . /
. . . Henry . . . sent his wyfe and hys sonne into   III. i. 28
Fraunce, to kynge Rene her father.

THE PROSPEROUS REIGNE OF KYNG EDWARD THE
FOURTH

The first yere [1461–2]. . . this yong Prince   II. vi
. . . after the fashion and maner of a triumphant

conqueror, and victorious champion, with great
pompe returned to London. Where (according
to the old custome of the realme) he called a
great assemble of persons of all degrees: and the.
xxix. daie of Iune, was at Westminster with all
solempnitie crouned and anoynted kyng. . .

258

. . . In the whiche Parliament, the erle of Oxford
farre striken in age and the Lord Awbrey Vere,
his sonne and heire, whether it were for malice
of their enemies, or thei were suspected, or had
offended the Kyng, they both and diverse of
their counsailors, were attainted and put to exe- III. iii. 10
cution, which caused Ihon erle of Oxford, ever
after to rebell. And afterward he created his
twoo younger brethern Dukes, that is to saie:
Lorde George, Duke of Clarence, lorde Richard, Duke of Gloucester, . . .

Cxci^v 261

[1463–4]. . . kyng Henry, . . . whether he wer
past all feare, or was not well stablished in his
perfite mynde, or could not long kepe hymself
secrete, in a disguysed apparell, boldely entered
into Englande. He was no soner entered, but he
was knowen and taken of one Cantlowe, and
brought towarde the kyng, whom the erle of
Warwicke met on the waie, by the kynges com-
maundement, and brought hym through London, to the toure, and there he was laied in sure
holde. Quene Margarete his wife, hearyng of
the captivitie of her husbande, mistrustyng the
chaunce of her sonne, all desolate and comfort-
les, departed out of Scotlande, and sailed into
Fraunce, where she remained with Duke Reyner her father, till she toke her infortunate iorney into Englande again: where she lost bothe
husband and sonne, and also all her wealth,
honor, and worldly felicitie. . .

II. vi. 8

Cxciij 263

. . . the erle of Warwicke . . . cam to kyng Lewes
the. xi. then beyng Frenche kyng, liyng at
Tours, and with greate honor was there received, and honorably interteined: of whom, for
kyng Edward his master, he demaunded to haue

III. i.

in mariage the lady Bona, doughter to Lewes
duke of Sauoy, and suster to the lady Carlot,
then French Quene, beyng then in the Frenche
court. This mariage semeth pollitiquely devised, and of an high imaginacion to be invented,
if you will well consider, the state and condicion
of kyng Edwardes affaires, which at this time,
had kyng Henry ... in safe custody, in the strong
toure of London, and the moste parte of his adherentes, he had as he thought, either profli-
gated or extinct, Quene Margaret onely except,
and Prince Edward her sonne, which wer then
soiornyng at Angiers, with old Duke Reiner of
Aniow her father, writyng hymself kyng of
Naples, Scicile, and Ierusalem, having as
muche profites of the letters of his glorious stile,
as rentes and revenues out of thesaid large and
riche realmes and dominions, (because the kyng
of Arragon toke the profites of thesame, and
would make no accompt therof to duke Reiner)
ij^v 264   ... / ... the matrimony ... was clerely assented
to. .. After these thinges thus concluded, the
erle of Warwycke was dismissed and highly re-
warded, & for the great & noble corage that
was in him, he obteyned such favor of the kynge,
the quene and the nobles of Fraunce, that when
he fled out of England, he was there honorably
received, frendly maynteined, and lovingly suc-
cored. ..

BUT now consider the old Proverbe to be   III. ii
true y^t saieth: that mariage is destinie.[1]

[1464–5]. AND in the next yere after, she [Lady
Grey] was with great solempnitie crouned   III. iii
quene at Westmynster. Her father also was   IV. i. 46–59
created erle Ryvers, and made high Constable
of Englande: her brother lorde Anthony, was
maried to ye sole heyre of Thomas lord Scales,
& by her he was lord Scales. Syr Thomas Grey,
sonne to syr Ihon Grey, the quenes fyrst husband, was created Marques Dorset, and maried

There follows an account of Edward's wooing of Lady Grey, repeated more fully at
(365).

to Cicilie, heyre to the lord Bonvile. Albeit this
mariage, at the first apparaunce was very pleas-
aunt to the king, but more ioyous to the quene
& profitable to her bloud, which were so highly
exalted, yea, & so sodainly promoted, that all
the nobilitie more marvayled then allowed this
sodayne risyng and swift elevacion: Yet who so
wil marke the sequele of this story, shall manifestly perceyve, what murther, what miserie, &
what troble ensued by reason of this mariage:
for it can not be / denied, but for this mariage
kyng Edward was expulsed the Realm, & durst
not abide, And for this mariage was therle of
Warwicke & his brother miserable slain. By this
mariage were kyng Edwardes. ii. sonnes declared bastardes, & in conclusion prived of their
lifes. And finally by this mariage, the quenes
bloud was confounded, and utterly in maner
destroyed. So y^t men did afterward divyne, that
either God was not contented, nor yet pleased
with this matrimony, or els that he punished
kyng Edward in his posteritie, for the diepe dis-
simulynge and covert clokynge, with hys faith-
full frende the erle of Warwycke. But such con-
iectures for ye most part, be rather more of mens
phantasies, then of divine reuelacion. When this
mariage was once blowen abrode, forren kynges
and prynces marvayled and musyd at it: noble
men detested and disdained it: the common
people grudged and murmured at it, and al with
one voyce sayde, that hys vnadvised wowyng,
hasty lovyng, and to spedy mariage, were neither
meete for him beyng a kyng, nor consonant to
the honor of so high an estate. The French kyng
and his quene were not a littell discontent (as I
can not blame them) to have their syster, first
demaunded and then graunted, and in conclusion reiected, and apparantly mocked, without
any cause reasonable. . . But when the erle of
Warwycke had perfit knowledge by the letters of
his trusty frendes, that kyng Edward had gotten him a new wyfe, & that all that he had done
with kyng Lewes in his ambassade for the con-

265

ιᵛ ioynyng of this new affinitie, was both frustrate
& vayn, he was earne / stly moved and sore
chafed with the chaunce, and thought it neces-
sarye that king Edward should be deposed from
his croune and royal dignitie, as an inconstant
prince, not worthy of such a kyngly office. All
men for the moste parte agre, that this mariage
was the only cause, why the erle of Warwycke
bare grudge, and made warre on kynge Edwarde... yet he thought it best to dissimule the
matter, tyll such a time were come, as he might
fynd the king without strength, and then to im-
brayd him with the pleasure that he had done
for him. And farther it erreth not from yᵉ treuth   III. iii. 188
that kynge Edward did attempt a thyng once in
the erles house which was much agaynste the
erles honestie (whether he woulde haue de-
flowred hys doughter or his nece, yᵉ certayntie
was not for both their honors openly knowen)
for surely such a thyng was attempted by king
Edward, which loved well both to loke and to
fele fayre dammosels. But whether the iniury
that the erle thought he had taken at king Edwardes handes, or the disdayne of aucthoritie
that the erle had under the king, was the cause
of dissolucion of their amitie and league, trueth
it is that the privie intencions in their hartes
brake into so many smal peces, that England,
Fraunce, and Flaunders, could never ioyne
them agayn, duryng their naturall lyfes.

xᵛ 271   [1467–8]. . . The erle of Warwicke beeynge a   IV. i
man of a greate wit, farre castyng, and many
thynges vigilantly foreseyng, either perceived
by other, or had perfect knowledge of hymself,
that the duke of Clarence, bare not the best will
to kyng Edward his brother (as he did not in
dede) thought firste to prove hym a farr of, as it
wer in a probleme, and after to open to him (if
he sawe hym flexible to his purpose) the secrete
imaginacions of his stomacke: thynkyng that if
he might by pollicie or promise, allure the duke
to his partie, that kyng Edward should be desti-

tute, of one of his best Hawkes, when he had
moste nede to make a flight. So at tyme and
place convenient, the erle began to complain to
the duke, of the ingratitude and doublenes of
kyng Edward, saiyng: that he had neither
handled hym like a frende, nor kepte promise
with hym, accordyng as the estate of a Prince required. The erle had not halfe tolde his tale, but
the duke in a greate fury answered, why my lorde,
thynke you to have hym kynde to you, that is
unkynd, yea, and unnatural to me beyng his awne
brother, thynke you that frendship will make
hym kepe promise, where neither nature nor
kynred, in any wise can provoke or move hym,
to favor his awne bloud? Thynke you that he
will exalte and promote his cosin or alie, whiche
litle careth for the fall or confusion, of his awne
line and lignage: This you know well enough,
that the heire of the Lord Scales he hath maried
to his wifes brother, the heire also of the lorde
Bonvile and Haryngton, he hath geven to his
wifes sonne, and theire of the lorde Hungerford,
he hath graunted to the lorde Hastynges: thre
mariages more meter for his twoo brethren and
kynne, then for suche newe foundlynges, as he
hath bestowed theim on: But by swete saincte
George I sweare, if my brother of Gloucester
would ioyne with me, we would make hym
knowe, that wee were all three one mannes
sonnes, of one mother and one lignage discended, whiche should be more preferred and promoted, then straungers of his wifes bloud. . . /
. . . And the rather to wynne the dukes hart the
erle beside diverse and many faire promises
made to the duke, offered hym his eldest daughter (beeyng of ripe age and elegant stature) in
mariage. . . thei first determined to saile to
Caleis, of the which toune the erle was chief capitain, where his wife and twoo doughters then
soiorned. . . But the erle continually remem-
bryng the purpose that he was set on, thought
to begin and kindle the fire, of his ungracious
coniuracion . . . before his departure, wherefore

CC

he appoynted his brethren the Archebishop and
the Marques, that thei should by some meane
in his absence, stirre vp newe commocion or rebellion, in the Countie of Yorke and other places
adiacente: so that / this civill warre should seme
to all men, to haue been begon without his assent or knowledge (he beyng in the partes of beyond the sea).

[1469–70]. When all these thynges wer thus determined, and in grave counsaill allowed, the
erle and the duke sailed directly to Caleis:
where thei were solempnely received, and ioy-
ously interteined of the Countesse and her twoo
daughters. And after that the duke had sworne
on the Sacrament to kepe his promise and pacte
inviolate made and concluded with the erle of
Warwicke, he maried the lady Isabell, eldest
daughter to thesaied erle, in our Lady Churche
at Caleis, . . . After whiche . . . the duke and
therle consulted sadly together, by what meanes
thei should continue the warre (whiche as it was
by theim appoynted) was recently and within
few daies begonne in Yorkeshire, not without
great rumore and disturbaunce, . . . /
. . . But the lorde Marques Montacute, governor
and presedent of that countrey for the kyng, . . .
encountered the rebelles, before the gates of
Yorke: where after long conflicte, he toke . . .
their capitain, and before theim commaunded
his hed there to bee striken of. . .

Here is to be marveiled, why the Marques
thus put to death the capitain and ruler of the
people, stirred and reised vp by hym, and the
felowes of his coniuracion and conspiracie:
Some saie he did it to the intent, that he would
seme fautles and innocent, of all his brothers
doynges, and privie imaginacions: But other
affirme and saie, that he for all his promise /
made to his brother, was then deliberatly determined to take parte with kyng Edward, with
whom (as it shall after appere) he in small space
entered into greate grace and high favor. . . /

CCi   When kyng Edwarde . . . was by diverse letters sent to hym, certified that the great armie
of the Northren men, wer with all spede com-
myng toward London . . . in greate hast he sent
to Wyllyam lorde Herbert, whom, within twoo
yeres before he had created erle of Penbroke,
that he should without delaye encountre with
the Northren men. . .

And to assiste and furnishe hym with archers,
was appoynted Humffray lorde Stafford. . . /
CClᵛ   . . . The Yorke shire men . . . toke their waie
toward Warwicke, lokyng for aide of therle,
whiche was lately come from Caleis, with the
Duke of Clarence his sonne in lawe, and was
gatheryng and reisyng of men, to succor his
CCijᵛ 275 frendes and kynsfolke. . . / . . . The erle of Warwycke had by his espialles perfyt, knowlege how
the kyng with his armye was bent toward hym,
& sent in all hast possible to the duke of Clarence (which was not far from him with a great
power). . . When all thynges were redy prepared
to fight: by the meanes of frendes, a meane was
founde how to common of peace, . . . the kynge
conceyvinge a certayne hope of peace in hys
awne imaginacion, toke bothe lesse hede to him
selfe, and also lesse fered the outward attemptes
of hys ennemyes, thinkyng and trustynge truely
that all thynges were at a good poynt and should
be well pacified. All the kynges doynges were by
espials declared to the erle of Warwycke, which
lyke a wyse and politique Capitayne entendyng
not to lese so great an avauntage to hym geven,
but trustyng to brynge all his purposes to a
fynall ende and determinacion, by onely ob-
teynyng this enterprise: in the dead of the nyght,   ɪv. ii. i
with an elect company of men of warre, as
secretly as was possible set on the kynges felde,
kylling them that kept the watche, and or the
kynge were ware (for he thought of nothynge
lesse then of that chaunce that happened) at a
place called Wolney. iiii. myle from Warwycke,
he was taken prysoner, and brought to the
Castell of Warwicke. And to the entent that the

kynges frendes myghte not know where he was, nor what was chaunced of hym, he caused hym by secret iorneys in the nyght to be conveyed to Myddelham Castell in Yorkeshyre, & there to be kept under the custody of the Archebishop of Yorke his brother, and other hys trusty frendes, which entertayned the kyng, like his estate, and served hym lyke a prynce. But there was no place so farre of but that the taking of the kyng was shortly knowen there with ye wynde which newes made many men to feare, and greatly to dread, and many to wonder and lament the chaunce. Kyng Edward beyng thus in capti-/ vitie, spake ever fayre to the Archebishop and to the other kepers, (but whether he corrupted them with money or fayre promises) he had libertie divers dayes to go on huntynge, and one day on a playne there met with hym syr William Stanley, syr Thomas of Borogh, and dyvers other of hys frendes, with suche a great bend of men, that neither his kepers woulde, nor once durst move him to retorne to prison agayn.

IV. V

^v 281 [1470–1]. . . When Quene Margarete, whiche soiorned with Duke Reyner her father, called kyng of Scicile, &c. Harde tell that the erle of Warwicke and the duke of Clarence, had abandoned Englande, and wer come to the Frenche Courte: hopyng of newe confort, with all diligence came to Amboyse, with her onely son Prince Edward. And with her came Iasper erle of Penbroke, and Ihon erle of Oxenford, . . . thei determined by meane of the Frenche kyng, to conclude a league and a treatie betwene them: And first to begin with all, for the more sure foundacion of the newe amitie, Edward Prince of Wales, wedded Anne second daughter to therle of Warwicke, . . . / . . . This mariage semed very straunge to wise men, consideryng that the erle of Warwicke, had first disherited the father, and then to cause his sonne, to mary with one of his daughters, whose suster the duke of Clarence before had maried, whiche was ever ex-

III. iii

treme enemie to the house of Lancastre: whereupon thei divined that the mariage of the
Prince, should ever be a blot in the Dukes iye,
or the mariage of the Duke, a mote in the iye of
the Prince, . . .

While these Lordes wer thus in the Frenche
Courte, there landed at Caleis a damosell, belongyng to the Duches of Clarence (as she saied)
whiche . . . perswaded the Duke of Clarence,
that it was neither naturall, not honorable to
hym, either to condiscende or take parte, against
the house of Yorke (of whiche he was lineally
discended). . . Farthermore she declared, that
the mariage with therles daughter with Prince
Edward, was for none other cause, but to make
the Prince kyng, and clerely to extingishe all the
house of Yorke, of whom the duke hymself was
one, and next heire to the croune, after his eldest
brother and his children. These reasons, and the
mariage of the Prince to the Erles daughter, so
sancke in the Dukes stomacke, that he promised
at his returne, not to be so an extreme enemie
to his brother, as he was taken for, whiche promise afterwarde, he did not forget. With this
answere the damosell departed into Englande,
therle of Warwicke therof beyng clerely ignor-
aunt.

v. i. 8

When the league was concluded (as you before have harde) the Frenche kyng lent them
shippes, money, and men. . . / . . . Kyng Reyner
also did help his daughter, to his smal power,
with menne, and municions of warre. When
this armie (whiche was not small) was con-
scribed and come together to Harflete, at the
mouthe of the river of Seyne, expectyng wind /
and wether. The Erle of Warwicke received
letters out of Englande, that men so muche
daily and hourely, desired and wished so sore
his arrival and returne, that almoste all men
were in harnesse, lokyng for his landyng: . . . he
was farther assured, that assone as he had once
taken lande, there should mete hym many thou-
sandes (as after it proved in deede) to doo hym

CCvii^v

282

what service or pleasure, thei could or might:
all this was the offer of the common people...

ij^v 283 Kyng Edward beyng...in diffidence of reysyng
any army, with such trusty frendes as he had
departed into Lyncolnshyre, consulting what
was best to be done, but sodainly or he was
fully determined on any certayn purpose, newes
were brought to hym, that all the Townes and
all the countrey adiacent was in a great rore,
and made fiers and sang songes, cryeng kynge
Henry, kyng Henry, a Warwycke a Warwycke.   iv. iii. 27
King Edward was much abashed with these
new tidynges, and more and more his especials
and explorators declared and accompted to
hym, that all the Realme was up, ... wherfore
hys nere frendes advised and admonished hym   iv. vi. 77
to flye over the sea to the duke of Burgoyne, hys   iv. v
brother in lawe, there to tary tyll God and fortune should sende him better luck and chaunce,
he ... with all hast possible ... came to the
towne of Lynne, where he founde an English
shyp &. ii. Hulkes of Holland redy (as fortune
wolde) to make sayle ... whereupon he ... with
his brother the duke of Glocester, the lord
Scales, & divers other his trusty frendes entered
into the ship.

285   When the fame was spred of kynge Edwardes
flyenge, innumerable people resorted to the erle
of Warwycke to take his parte, but all kyng Edwardes trusty frendes went to divers sentuaries,
dayly loking, & howerly harkening, to hear of
his health, & prosperous retorne... / ...
Emongst other, Quene Elizabeth hys wyfe, all   iv. iv. 31 ff.
moste desperate of all comfort, toke sentuarie at
Westmynster, & their in great penurie forsaken
of all her frendes, was delivered of a fayre sonne
called Edwarde, which was with small pompe
lyke a pore mans chyld Christened & Bap-
tised, ...
Vpon the. xij. daye of October he [Warwick]
rode to the towre of London, whiche was to him   iv. vi
without resistence delivered, & there toke kyng
Henry the vi. out of the warde, where he before

was kept, & was brought to the kynges lodgyng & there served, according to his degre. And the. xxv. daye of the sayd moneth, the duke of Clarence accompanied with the erles of Warwycke, Shrewsbury, & the Lord Stanley, & other lordes & Gentelmen, some for feare, & some for love, and some onely to gase at the waveryng world, resorted with a greate company to the towre of London, & from thence with great pompe broughte kynge Henry the. vi. appareled in a longe gowne of blew velvet, through the high streates of London, too the cathedrall church of sainct Paule, the people on the right hand and on the left hand, reioysing & cryeng God save the Kynge, as though all thyng had succeded as they would have it, and when he had offered as kynges use to do, he was conveyed to the palleys of the bishop of London, and there kept hys housholde lyke a kynge.

King Henry the. vi. thus readepted . . . hys croune & dignitie Royall, . . . newly, after so many overthrowes beginnynge to reygne, lykely within short space to fall agayn, & to taste more of his accustomed captivitie & usuall misery. This yll chaunce & misfortune, by many mens opinions happened to him, because he was a man of no great wit, such as men comonly call an Innocent man, neither a foole, neither very wyse, whose study always was more to excell, other in Godly liuynge & vertuous example, then in wordly regiment, or temporall dominion, in so much, that in comparison to the study & delectacion that he had to vertue / and godlines, he littel regarded, but in manner despised al worldly power & temporal authoritie, which syldome folow or seke after such persons, as from them flye or disdayne to take them. But hys enemies ascri / bed all this to hys coward stommack, . . . Other there be that ascribe his infortunitie, onely to the stroke & punishment of God, afferming that the kyngdome, whiche Henry the. iiij. hys grandfather wrongfully gat, and uniustly possessed agaynst kyng Richard

CCxᵛ

the. ii. & his heyres could not by very divyne
iustice, longe contynew in that iniurious stocke:
And that therfore God by his divine providence,
punished the offence of the grandfather, in the
sonnes sonne.

When kyng Henry had thus obteined agayn,
the possession & dominion of the Realme, he
called his hygh court of Parliament . . . in the
whyche kyng Edwarde was declared a traytor to
hys countrey, & usurpor of ye Realme, because
he had uniustly taken on hym, the Croune &
Scepter, & all hys goodes were confiscate. . . The
Crounes of the realmes of England & Fraunce,
was by ye authoritie of thesame Parliament entayled to kyng Henry the. vi. and the heyres
males of hys body lawfully begotten, & for default of suche heyre male . . . then ye sayd
Crounes & dignities were entayled to George
duke of Clarence, . . . Beside this, the erle of
Warwycke as one to whome the common welthe
was much beholden, was made Ruler, Governor
of the Realme, with whom as felow and com-
paignion was associated, George duke of Clarence his sonne in law. So that by these meanes
the whole estate, both / of the realme, and the
publique wealth of thesame, wer newly altred
and chaunged, yea, and in maner clerely trans-
figured and transmuted. To this Parliament
came the lorde Marques Montacute, excusyng
hymself that onely for feare of death, he declined
to kyng Edwardes parte, whiche excuse was so
accepted that he obteined his pardon, whiche,
after was the destruccion, of hym and his brother: For if he had manfully and appartly taken
kyng Edwardes parte, surely he beyng an open
enemie, had much lesse hurted, then beyng a
fained, false and a coloured frende: . . .

Quene Margaret, after that the erle of Warwicke was sailed into England, . . . with Prince
Edwarde her sonne, and her trayne, entered
their shippes, to take their voyage into Englande: but the Wynter was so sore, the wether
so / stormie, and the wynde so contrariant, that

she was fain to take land again, and defer her iorney till another season. . .

In this season Iasper erle of Penbroke, went into Wales, to visite his Countie of Penbroke, wher he found lorde Henry, sonne to his brother Edmond Erle of Richmond, hauyng not fully ten yeres of his age complete, whiche was kept in maner like a captive: but well and honorably educated, and in all kynde of Civilitie brought CCxiᵛ   vp, by the Lady Harbert, . . . / . . . Penbroke toke this child beyng his nephew, out of the custodie of the Lady Harbert, and at his returne, he brought the childe to London, to kyng Henry the sixte, whom, when the kyng had a good space by hymself, secretly beholden and mark-ed, bothe his wit and his likely towardnes, he saied to suche princes, as were then with hym: Lo, surely this is he, to whom both wee and our adversaries levyng the possession of all thynges, shall hereafter geve rome and place. So this holy man shewed before, the chaunce that should happen, that this erle Henry so ordeined by God, should in tyme to come (as he did in deede) have and enioye the kyngdome, and the whole rule of the realme.

CCxiiiᵛ 290   [1471–2]. Kyng Edwarde . . . sailed into Eng-land, and came on the cost of Yorke shire, to a place called Ravenspurr . . . no doubte, but that the Duke of Clarence and he, were secretly agreed before, and that the Marques Monta-cute, had secretly procured his favor. . . all the tounes rounde aboute, wer permanent and stiffe on the parte of kyng Henry, and could not bee CCxiiii¹   removed: . . . / . . . Which . . . when kynge Ed-warde had perfitly digested, of very necessitie he chaunged hys purpose: for where before his clayme was to be restored to the croune and / 291   kyngdome of England, nowe he caused it to be published that he only claymed the Duchie of Yorke, to yᵉ entent that in requyryng nothyng, but that which was bothe trew and honest, he

1. CCxv in Hall.

might obtayne the more favor of the common
people. It was almost incredible to se what effect
this new imaginacion (all though it were but
fayned) sorted and toke immediatly. . . . All men
moved with mercye and compassion, began out
of hande either to favor hym or els not to resist
him, . . . he determined to take hys iorney toward Yorke, . . . The erle of Warwycke which
then lay in Warwykeshyre, beyng enformed
that king Edward was landed, and goyng toward Yorke, with all hast wrote to the Marques
Montacute hys brother . . . commaunding him
to set on kyng Edward with all expedicion, &
byd hym battayle, or els to kepe the passage,
. . . tyll he hym self had gathered a greater host,
which with all diligence, he was assemblynge to
come and ioyne with hys brother the Marques.
And . . . he wrote to . . . the citie also, com-
maundyng all men on the kynges behalfe to be
redy in harnes, and to shutte their gates against
the kynges enemyes. Kyng Edward . . . came
peaceably nere to Yorke, of whose commynge,
when the citezens were certefied, without delay
they armed them selfe, and came to defende the
gates, sendyng to hym two of the chiefest Aldermen of the citie, . . . / . . . The citezens heryng . . .
that he entended nothynge preiudiciall to kynge
Henry . . . began to commen with hym from
their walles . . . / . . . fell to this pact & conven-
cion, that if kyng Edward woulde swere . . . to
be obedient, and faythfull to all kyng Henryes
commaundementes and preceptes, that then
they woulde receyve hym into their citie. . . /

iiii^v

v

When kyng Edward had appesed the citie-
zens, and that their fury was past, he entred in
to the citie, & clerely forgettinge his othe, he
first set a garrison of souldiers in the towne, to
the entent y^t nothyng should be moved agaynst
hym by the citezens, & after he gathered a great
host, by reason of his money. . . he thought it
necessarie . . . to make hast toward London: . . .
and came savely to the towne of Nottingham,
where came to him . . . syr Thomas Montgom-

IV. viii. 4

erie, and divers other of hys assured frendes with
their aydes, which caused hym at the fyrst com-
ming to make Proclamacion in hys owne name,
kyng Edward the. iiii. boldely sayng to hym,
that they would serve no man but a kynge...

293

... the erle of Warwycke ... marched forward
toward Coventry, ... In the meane season, kyng
Edward came to Warwycke, where he founde
all the people departed, and from thence with
al diligence avaunced his power toward Cov-
entre, & in a playne by the citie he pytched his
felde. And the next day after that he cam
thither, hys men were set forwarde, and mar-
shalled in array, & he valiantly bad the erle
battayle: which mistrustyng that he should be
deceaved by the duke of Clarence (as he was in
dede) kepte hym selfe close within the Walles.
... When eche host was in sight of other, Rychard duke of Glocester, brother to them both, as
though he had bene made arbitrer betwene
them, fyrst rode to the duke, and with hym
commoned very secretly: from him he came to
kyng Edward, and with lyke secretnes so used
hym, that in conclusion no unnaturall warre,
but a fraternall amitie was concluded... It was
no mervayll that the duke of Clarence... turned
from the erle of Warwyckes parte, ... /

CCxvi

294
CCxviᵛ

From thence kyng Edward thus beyng fur-
nished of a strong host, went without any
maner / of diffidence or mistrust toward London: ... / ... the communaltie ... ranne in
hepes out of the citie, to mete him, and saluted
hym as their kyng and sovereygne lord. When
the duke of Somerset and other of kynge Henryes
frendes, saw the world thus sodaynly chaunged,
euery man fledde, and in hast shyfted for hym
selfe, levyng kyng Henry alone, as an host that
should be sacrificed, in the Bishops palace of
London, adioyning to Poules churche, not
knowing of whom nor what counsayll to aske,
as he which with troble and adversitie was clerely dulled and appalled, in which place he was

IV.

by kynge Edward taken; and agayne committed to prison and captivitie. . .

    Therle of Warwicke ponderyng, that the gain   v.i
of the whole battaill stode in makyng haste, with

xvii   all diligence, followed his enemies, . . . / . . . he
was enformed that kyng Edward, peaceably
was entered into London, . . . he rested with his
army, at the toune of sainct Albons, . . . In the
erles armie wer Ihon Duke of Excester, Edmond
Erle of Somerset, Ihon Erle of Oxenford, and
Ihon Marques Montacute, whom the erle his
brother well knewe, not to bee well mynded
(but sore against his stomacke) to take part with
these Lordes, . . . And from sainct Albones, he
removed to a village in the meane waie, betwene London and sainct Albones called Barnet, . . . /

xviij 296   But when his souldiers beyng sore wounded,
weried with so long a conflict, did geve litle regarde to his wordes, he beyng a manne of a
mynde invincible, rushed into the middest of
his enemies, where as he (aventured so farre
from his awne compaignie, to kil and sley his
adversaries, that he could not be rescued) was
in the middes of his enemies, striken doune and
slain. The marques Montacute, thinkyng to
succor his brother, whiche he sawe was in greate
ieoperdy, and yet in hope to obtein the victory,
was likewise over throwen and slain. After the
erle was ded, his parte fled and many were
taken, but not one man of name, nor of nobilitie. . .

viij^v 297   In the meane season, quene Margaret . . .
gathered together no small compaignie, of
hardy and valiaunt souldiours, determined with   v. iii–iv
all hast and diligence, with Prince Edwarde her
soonne, to saile into Englande, but yet once
again (suche was her destinie) beyng letted for
lacke of prosperous wynd, and encombered with
to muche rigorous tempeste, a daie after the
faire, as the common proverbe saieth, landed at

ix 298   the Port of Weymouth, in Dorset shire. . . / . . .
When it was knowen that she was landed, Ed-

mond Duke of Somerset . . . with Iasper Erle of
Penbroke . . . presented theimselfes to the
Quene: . . . /

CCxxi 300   . . . When all these battayles were thus ordered and placyd, the Quene and her sonne prince
Edward rode about the felde, encouragyng
theyr souldiers . . . after no long conflict, the
Quenes part went almost all to wrecke, for the
most part were slayne. The Quene was founde
in her Chariot almost dead for sorow, ye prince
was apprehended and kepte close. . . /

301   After the felde ended, kyng Edward made a
Proclamacion, that who so ever could bring
prince Edward to hym alyve or dead, shoulde
haue an annuitie of an. C. l. duryng his lyfe, and
the Princes life to be saved. Syr Richard Croftes,
. . . nothing mistrusting the kynges former pro-
myse, brought furth his prisoner prince Edward,
beynge a goodly femenine & a well feautered
CCxxi^v   yonge gentelman, whome / when kynge Edward
had well advised, he demaunded of him, how
he durst so presumptuously enter in to his
Realme with banner displayed. The prince,
beyng bold of stomacke & of a good courage,
answered sayinge, to recover my fathers kyngdome & enheritage, from his father & grandfather to hym, and from him, after him, to me
lyneally divoluted. At which wordes kyng Edward sayd nothyng, but with his hand thrust
hym from hym (or as some say, stroke him with
his gauntlet) whom incontinent, they that stode
about, whiche were George duke of Clarence,
Rychard duke of Gloucester . . . sodaynly murthered. . . And on the Monday next ensuyng was
Edmond duke of Somerset . . . behedded in the
market place at Tewkesbury. / . . .

302   Quene Margaret lyke a prisoner was brought to   v. vii. 3
London, where she remayned tyll kyng Reiner
her father raunsomed her with money, whiche
summe . . . he borowed of kyng Lewes. . . to re-
paye so greate a dutie, he solde to the French
kynge & his heyres, the kyngdomes of Naples,
and both the Siciles, with the countye of Pro-

uynce. . . After the raunsom payd, she was conveyed in to Fraunce with small honor. . . / . . .

Poore kyng Henry the sixte, a litle before deprived of his realme, and Imperiall Croune, was
now in the Tower of London, spoyled of his life,
and all worldly felicitie, by Richard duke of
Gloucester . . . whiche . . . murthered thesaid
kyng with a dagger. . .

Kyng Henry was of stature goodly, of body
slender, to which proporcion, al other members
wer correspondent: his face beautifull, in the
which continually was resident, the bountie of
mynde, with whiche, he was inwardly endued.
He did abhorre of his awne nature, all the vices,
as well of the body as of the soule, and from his
verie infancie, he was of honest conversacion
and pure integritie, no knower of evill, and a
keper of all goodnes: a dispiser of all thynges,
whiche bee wonte to cause, the myndes of mor-
tall menne to slide, fall, or appaire. Beside this,
pacience was so radicate in his harte, that of all
the iniuries to him committed, (whiche were no
small nombre) he never asked vengeaunce nor
punishement, but for that, rendered to al-
mightie God, his creator, hartie thankes, thinking that by this trouble, and adversitie, his
synnes were to him forgotten and forgeven.
What / shall I saie, that this good, this gentle,
this meke, this sober and wisman, did declare
and affirme, that those mischefes and miseries,
partly, came to hym for his awne offence, and
partly, for the hepyng of synne upon sinne,
wretchedly by his aunceters and forfathers:
wherefore, he litle or nothing estemed, or in
anywise did turment or macerate hymself, what
so ever dignitie, what honor, what state of life,
what child, what frend he had lost, or missed,
but if it did but sound an offence toward God,
he loked on that, and not without repentaunce,
both mourned and sorowed for it: these and
other like offices of holynes, caused God to
worke miracles for him in his life tyme.

The. xi. yere [1472–3]. Ihon Erle of Oxenford, whiche after Barnet feld, bothe manfully
gat, and valiantly kept, sainct Mighels Mount
in Cornewal: either for lacke of aide, or perswaded by his frendes, gaue vp the Mount, and
yelded himself to kyng Edward, (his life only
saved) whiche to hym was graunted: but to be
out of all doubtfull imaginacions, kyng Edward
sent hym over the sea, to the Castle of Hammes,
. . .

Edward the V. [1483–4]. Richard duke of Gloucester . . . was in witte and courage egall with the
other [Edward and George], but in beautee and
liniamentes of nature far underneth bothe, for
he was litle of stature, eivill featured of limnes,

croke backed, the left shulder / muche higher
than the righte, harde favoured of visage, such
as in estates is called a warlike visage, and
emonge commen persones a crabbed face. He
was malicious, wrothfull and envious, and as it
is reported, his mother the duches had muche
a dooe in her travaill, that she could not bee
delivered of hym uncut, and that he came into
the worlde with the fete forwarde, . . . and as the
same ran, not untothed: . . . He was close and
secrete, a depe dissimuler, lowlye of counten-
aunce, arrogante of herte, outwardely familier
where he inwardely hated, not lettynge to kisse
whom he thought to kill, despiteous and cruell,
not alwaie for eivill will, but ofter for ambicion
and too serve his purpose, frende and fooe were
all indifferent, where his avauntage grew, he
spared no mannes deathe whose life withstode
his purpose. He slewe in the towre kynge Henry
the sixte, saiynge: now is there no heire male of
kynge Edwarde the thirde, but wee of the house
of Yorke: . . . Some wise menne also wene, that

his drifte lacked not in helpynge / furth his
owne brother of Clarence to his death, which
thyng in all apparaunce he resisted, although
he inwardly mynded it. /

After kyng Edwarde the fourthe had deposed kyng Henry the sixte and was in peaceable possession of the realme, determinyng him selfe to mary (as was requisite) bothe for hym selfe and for the realme, he sente therle of Warwike & diverse other noble men in ambassade to the Frenche kyng to entreate a mariage betwene the kyng and Bona sister to the Frenche quene, then beyng in Fraunce. In which thyng therle of Warwike founde the parties so towarde and willyng, that he spedely without any difficultie accordyng to his instruccions brought the matter to a good conclusion. Nowe happeneth it in the meane season, there came to make a sute to the kyng by peticion dame Elizabeth Grey (whiche after was his quene) then a widdowe, borne of noble bloude, specially by her mother, whiche was Duchesse of Bedforde, and she was maried to sir Richarde Woodvile lorde Rivers, her father.

Howbeit, this Elizabeth beyng in service with quene Margaret wife to kyng Henry the sixte, was maried to one Ihon Grey Esquire whom kyng Henry made knight at the laste battaill of sainct Albones, but litle while he enioyed his knighthod, for at that same feld he was slain.

After, when that kyng Edward was kyng and the Erle of Warwike beyng on his ambassad, this poore lady made sute to the kyng to be restored to suche smal landes as her husbande had geven her in ioyntoure, whom when the kyng behelde and harde her speake, as she / was bothe faire and of good favoure, moderate of stature, well made and very wyse, he not alonely pitied her, but also wexed enamored on her, and takyng her secretly a syde began to enter into talkyng more familierly, whose appetite when she perceyved, she verteously denied hym, but that she dyd so wysely and that with so good maner and woordes so wel set, that she rather kyndeled his desyre then quenched it. And finally, after / many a metyng and much wow-

ii^v

yng and many great promises she well espied
the kyng his affeccion towarde her so greately
encreased that she durst somewhat the more
boldely saye her mynde, as to hym whose hert
she perceyved more fervently set then to fall of
for a worde. And in conclusion she shewed him
plain, that as she wist her self to simple to be his
wife, so thought she her self to good to be his
concubine. The kyng much marveilyng of her
constancy, as he that had not been wonte els
where so stiefly sayed nay, so muche estemed
her continency and chastitee, that he sette her
vertue in steade of possession and richesse: And
this takyng counsaill of his owne desyre determined in haste to mary her. And after that he
was thus apoincted and had betwene them
twayn ensured her, then asked he counsaill of
his secrete frendes, and that in suche maner that
they might easly perceyve that it boted not
to saye nay. Notwithstanding, the duches of
Yorke his mother, was so sore moved therewith
that she disswaded that mariage as muche as she
possible might: allegyng that it was his honor,
profyte & surety, to mary in some noble progeny
out of hys realme, where upon depended greate
strengthe to hys estate by that affinite, and great
possibilite of encrease of his dominions... The

xxij 367   kyng... saied... / That she is a widdowe and
hath alredy children: By God his blessed lady,
I am a bachelor and have some to, & so eche of
us hath a proofe, that neither of us is like to be
barren.

(b) Arthur Brooke, *Romeus and Juliet*, 1359–77 (see v. iv. 1–33).

A wise man in the midst of troubles and distres
Still standes not wayling present harme, but seeks his harmes
  redres.
As when the winter flawes, with dredfull noyse arise,
And heave the fomy swelling waves up to the starry skies,
So that the broosed barke in cruell seas betost,
Dispayreth of the happy haven in daunger to be lost.
The pylate bold at helme, cryes, mates strike now your sayle,

And tornes her stemme into the waves that strongly her assayle;
Then driven hard upon the bare and wrackfull shore,
In greater daunger to be wract, then he had been before,
He seeth his ship full right against the rocke to ronne,
But yet he dooth what lyeth in him the perilous rocke to shonne;
Sometimes the beaten boate, by cunning government,
The ancors lost, the cables broke, and all the tackle spent,
The roder smitten of, and over boord the mast,
Doth win the long desyred porte, the stormy daunger past.
But if the master dread, and overprest with woe,
Begin to wring his handes, and lets the gyding rodder goe,
The ship rents on the rocke, or sinketh in the deepe ...

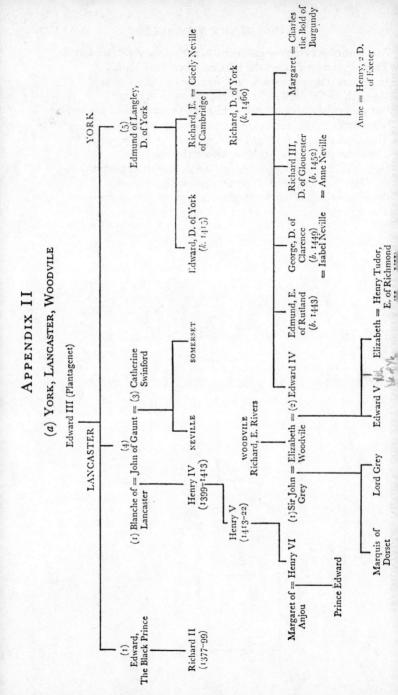

APPENDIX II

(a) YORK, LANCASTER, WOODVILE

Edward III (Plantagenet)

LANCASTER

YORK

(1) Edward, The Black Prince

Richard II (1377–99)

(1) Blanche of = John of Gaunt = (3) Catherine Lancaster (4) Swinford

NEVILLE

SOMERSET

Henry IV (1399–1413)

Henry V (1413–22)

Margaret of = Henry VI Anjou

Prince Edward

(5) Edmund of Langley, D. of York

Richard, E. = Cicely Neville of Cambridge

Edward, D. of York (k. 1415)

Richard, D. of York (k. 1460)

WOODVILE Richard, E. Rivers

(1) Sir John = Elizabeth = (2) Edward IV Grey Woodvile

Edmund, E. of Rutland (b. 1443)

George, D. of Clarence (b. 1449) = Isabel Neville

Richard III, D. of Gloucester (b. 1452) = Anne Neville

Margaret = Charles the Bold of Burgundy

Marquis of Dorset

Lord Grey

Edward V

Elizabeth = Henry Tudor, E. of Richmond

Anne = Henry, 2 D. of Exeter

178

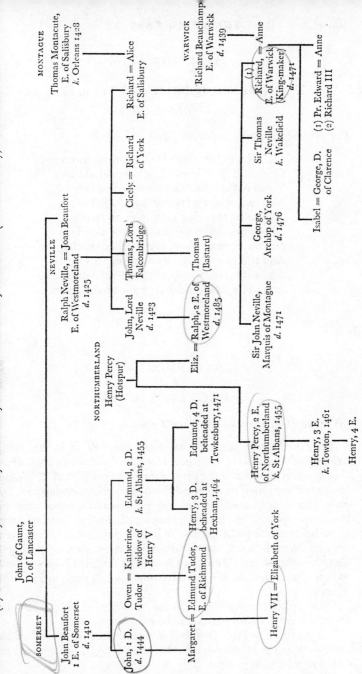

(*b*) MONTAGUE, NEVILLE, SOMERSET, NORTHUMBERLAND, WARWICK (BEAUCHAMP), FALCONBRIDGE

179

Appendix III

ALTERNATIVE Q PASSAGE TO II. iii. 15–22
(*Tr. Tr.*, 599)

For discussion, see Introduction, xxii.

> *Rich.* . . . Thy noble father in the thickest thronges,
> Cride still for *Warwike* his thrise valiant son,
> Vntill with thousand swords he was beset,
> And manie wounds made in his aged brest,
> And as he tottering sate vpon his steede,
> He waft his hand to me and cride aloud:
> *Richard*, commend me to my valiant sonne,
> And still he cride *Warwike* reuenge my death,
> And with those words he tumbled off his horse,
> And so the noble Salsbury gaue vp the ghost.

Appendix IV

RECOLLECTIONS

(*a*) From other plays in *The True Tragedy*

The True Tragedy (the bad quarto of *3 Henry VI*) is, in the main, a defective version as reconstructed by a group of actors from what they could remember of the play as they had performed it. Where their memory failed or deceived them, they often introduced, by association of ideas, similar words and phrases from other plays in their repertoire. The clearest examples of the 'recollections' are given below, arranged according to the plays from which they were derived. In each case the phrase from the external source is quoted first; then the passage, if any, in *3 Henry VI*, which the actors wished to reproduce; and last, the defective result as it appears in *The True Tragedy*.

Other recollections are given in the Introduction; but, even with these, the list does not pretend to be exhaustive.

The text of *The True Tragedy* is most conveniently consulted in volume IX of the Cambridge Shakespeare (1893). References are to the *pages* of that volume.

Many of the following recollections have been previously identified.

Titus Andronicus

    pardon what is past *Tit.*, I. i. 431
    let former grudges passe *3 H 6*, III. iii. 195
    pardon what is past *Tr. Tr.*, 614

    To see the generall Hunting in this Forrest *Tit.*, II. iii. 59
    Comes hunting this way *3 H 6*, IV. v. 8
    Should come a hunting in this forest heere *Tr. Tr.*, 620

    thy Rosed (=roseate) lips *Tit.*, II. iv. 24
    the lips *3 H 6*, v. vii. 29
    the rosiate lips *Tr. Tr.*, 636

    dangerous warres *Tit.*, III. i. 3
    —   *3 H 6*, II. i
    dangerous warres *Tr. Tr.*, 600

    reuerse the doome of death *Tit.*, III. i. 24
    Reuoke that doome of mercy *3 H 6*, II. vi. 46
    Reuerse that doome of mercie *Tr. Tr.*, 604 (cf. *Cont.*, 545)

2 Henry VI

                     Lord Marques kneel down,
    We heere create thee the first Duke of Suffolke,
    And girt thee with the Sword. *2 H 6*, I. i. 58 ff.
    Richard, I will create thee Duke of Gloucester,
    And *George* of Clarence; *3 H 6*, II. vi. 103–4
    Wee heere create thee Duke of *Clarence*, and girt thee with the
        sword. *Tr. Tr.*, 605

    my lord, away, take horse *2 H 6*, IV. iv. 54
    Mount you my Lord *3 H 6*, II. v. 128
    Take horse *Tr. Tr.*, 602

    with all contempt *2 H 6*, v. i. 209
    (in all despight) *3 H 6*, II. vi. 80
    in all contempt *Tr. Tr.*, 605

Richard III

    Why lookes your Grace so heauily *R 3*, ɪ. iv. 1

    But what art thou, whose heauie Lookes fore-tell
                                3 H 6, ɪɪ. i. 43

    But what art thou? that lookest so heauilie? *Tr. Tr.*, 590

    I must talke a word with you *R 3*, ɪv. iv. 198

    While I vse further conference with Warwicke
                                  3 H 6, ɪɪɪ. iii. 111

    Till I doe talke a word with *Warwike* *Tr. Tr.*, 612

    A bloudy Tyrant, and a Homicide: *R 3*, v. iii. 246

    O Traitors, Murtherers!... bloudy Caniballes,
                                  3 H 6, v. v. 52, 61

    Traytors, Tyrants, bloudie Homicides, *Tr. Tr.*, 632

The Spanish Tragedy

    let Fortune doe her worst *Sp. Tr.*, ɪ. iii. 19

    Though Fortunes mallice ouerthrow my State *3 H 6*, ɪv. iii. 46

    let fortune doe her worst *Tr. Tr.*, 619

    O speak if any sparke of life remaine *Sp. Tr.*, ɪɪ. v. 17

    If any sparke of Life be yet remaining *3 H 6*, v. vi. 66

    If anie sparke of life remaine in thee *Tr. Tr.*, 634

    But liue t'effect thy resolution *Sp. Tr.*, ɪɪɪ. ii. 47

    But sound the Trumpets, and about our Taske. *3 H 6*, ɪɪ. i. 200

    But forward to effect these resolutions *Tr. Tr.*, 594

Soliman and Perseda

    Ah, stay, no more, for I can hear no more *S. P.*, ɪɪ. ii. 28

    Oh speake no more, for I haue heard too much *3 H 6*, ɪɪ. i. 48

    O speake no more, for I can heare no more *Tr. Tr.*, 590

    Their horse, I deeme them fiftie thousand strong;
                                  S. P., ɪɪɪ. i. 48

    Their power (I thinke) is thirty thousand strong:
                                  3 H 6, ɪɪ. i. 177

Their power I gesse them fifty thousand strong *Tr. Tr.*, 593

A glorious death or famous victorie *S. P.*, III. iii. 8

And cry'de, A Crowne, or else a glorious Tombe,

3 H 6, I. iv. 17

And cried courage Father: Victorie or death *Tr. Tr.*, 585

I saist thou so? why then it shall be so. *S. P.*, IV. i. 242

Richard, enough; *3 H 6*, I. ii. 35

I, saist thou so boie? why then it shall be so.

Tr. Tr., 582 (cf. 622)

(*b*) Common to *The True Tragedy* (*3 Henry VI*, Q) and either *The Contention* (*2 Henry VI*, Q) or the bad quarto of *Richard III*.

(i) And he that throwes not vp his cap for joy,
Shall for the Fault make forfeit of his head. *3 H 6*, II. i. 196–7

And he that breakes a sticke of Glosters groue,
Shall loose his head for his presumption. *2 H 6*, I. ii. 33–4

That he that breakes a sticke of *Glosters* groue,
Shall for th'offence, make forfeit of his head. *Cont.*, 514

And he that casts not vp his cap for ioie,
Shall for the offence make forfeit of his head. *Tr. Tr.*, 594

(ii) A ... Mother to a many Sonnes *R 3*, III. VII. 184

the Father vnto many Sonnes: *3 H 6*, III. ii. 105

the Father of manie children *Tr. Tr.*, 609

A ... mother of a many children *R 3* (Q)

(iii) Come Grey, come Vaughan, let vs here embrace.
Farewell, vntill we meet againe in Heauen. *R 3*, III. iii. 24–5

Now Lords, take leaue, vntill we meete againe
Where ere it be, in heauen, or in earth...
Giue me thy hand, ...
Let me imbrace thee ... farwell. *3 H 6*, II. iii. 42 ff.

Brothers, giue me your hands, and let vs part
And take our leaues vntill we meet againe,
Where ere it be in heauen or in earth ... farewel. *Tr. Tr.*, 600

Come Gray, come Vaughan, let vs all imbrace
And take our leaue vntill we meete in heauen. *R 3* (Q)

See also Introduction, xvii.

APPENDIX V

PARALLELS, SOURCES, AND DERIVATIVES

These suggest Shakespeare's debt to (a) *The Spanish Tragedy*, and to (b) *The Faerie Queene* and the metrical Psalms of Sternhold and Hopkins; and (c) borrowings from *3 Henry VI* in *The Troublesome Raigne of King Iohn* (1591).

(a) *The Spanish Tragedy*

III. xiii

80   my murdred Sonne, ...

83   Heere take my *handkercher*,
    and *wipe* thine *eies*,
    ... a *bloudie Napkin*.

86 O no, not this; Horatio,
  this was thine;
  And when I dyde it in thy
  deerest *blood*,

IV. iv. 122–4

And heere *beholde* this *bloudie
hand-kercher*,

Which at Horatio's death I
weeping dipt

Within the riuer of his bleeding
wounds:

3 Henry VI

I. iv. 79 ff.

Looke Yorke, I stayn'd this *Napkin* with the *blood* ...

And if thine *eyes* can water for
his death,

I give thee this to drie thy
Cheekes withall.

157 ff.

This Cloth thou *dipd'st* in *blood*
of my sweet Boy,

And I with teares doe wash the
blood away.

Keepe thou the *Napkin*, ...

II. i. 61–3

... gaue him, to dry his Cheekes,

A *Napkin*, steeped in the harm-
lesse *blood*

Of sweet young Rutland, ...

Richard III

IV. iv. 275–8

... steept in Rutlands *blood*,

A *hand-kercheefe*, ...

And bid her *wipe* her *weeping eyes*
withall.

(b) 3 Henry VI, II. i. 9 ff.

Richard. I cannot *ioy*, vntill I be resolu'd
      Where our right *valiant* Father is become . . .   15
      . . . as a Beare *encompass'd* round with Dogges: 20
      Me thinkes 'tis *prize* enough to be his *Sonne.*
      See how the Morning *opes* her *golden Gates,*
      And takes her farwell of the *glorious Sunne.*
      How well resembles it the prime of Youth,
      Trimm'd like a Yonker prauncing to his Loue?
Ed. Dazle mine eyes, or doe I see three *Sunnes*?
Rich. Three *glorious Sunnes*, each one a perfect *Sunne,*
      Not seperated with the racking Clouds,
      But seuer'd in a pale *cleare-shining Skye.*
      See, see, they ioyne, *embrace*, and seeme to kisse,
      As if they vow'd some league inuiolable.
      Now are they but one *Lampe*, one *Light*, one *Sunne.*
      In this the *Heauen* figures some euent.
Edward. 'Tis *wondrous* strange,
      The like yet neuer heard of.
      I thinke it cites vs (Brother) to the field,
      That wee, the *Sonnes* of braue Plantagenet,
      Each one alreadie blazing by our meedes,
      Should notwithstanding ioyne our *Lights together*,
      And ouer-*shine* the *Earth*, as this the World.
      What ere it bodes, hence-forward I will beare
      Vpon my Targuet three *faire shining Sunnes.*
          . . . Ile venge thy death,   88
      Or dye *renowned* by attempting it.
Ed. His name that *valiant* Duke hath left with thee:

The Faerie Queene, Book I, Canto v

  2. At last the *golden* Orientall *gate*
      Of greatest *heauen* gan to *open faire,*
      And Phoebus fresh, *as bridegroom to his mate,*
      Came *prauncing* forth, shaking his deawie haire:

19. So wept Duessa vntill euentide,
      That *shining lampes* in Ioues high house were *light*:

21. Who when she saw Duessa *Sunny* bright,
      Adornd with *gold* and iewels *shining cleare,*

Psalm xix (Sternhold and Hopkins)

1. *The heauens* and the firmament / do *wondrously* declare
   The *glory* of God omnipotent, / his works, and what they are.
3. In all the *earth* and coasts thereof / . . .
4. In them the Lord made for the *Sun* / a place of great *renown*:
   Who *like a bride-groome* ready *trim'd*, / doth from his chamber
   come.
5. And as a *valiant* champion, / who for to get a *prize*,
   With *joy* doth hast to take in hand, / some noble enterprise.
6. And all the *skie* from end to end / he *compasseth* about:
9. . . . and righteous *altogether*.
10. And more to be *imbrac'd* alway, / then fined *gold* I say:

Psalm xxiv

7. Ye Princes *ope* your *gates*, stand *ope* / the euerlasting *gate*:
   For there shall enter in thereby / the King of *glorious* state.

(*c*) *3 Henry VI*, i. iv

3   And all my followers, to *the eager foe*
     Turne back, and flye, like Ships *before* the Winde,
     Or *Lambes* pursu'd by hunger-starued *Wolues*.

ii. i
50   Enuironed he was with many foes,
     And stood against them, *as the* hope *of Troy*
     Against the Greekes, that would haue entred Troy.
105 And now to adde more *measure* to your woes,
     I come *to tell* . . .
119 *Short tale to make*, we at S. Albons met, . . .
122 But whether 'twas the coldnesse of the King, . . .
126 Or more then common *feare* of Cliffords Rigour,
     Who thunders to his *Captiues*, Blood and Death,
     I cannot iudge: . . .
133 I *cheer'd* them vp . . .
135 But all in vaine, they had *no heart* to fight, . . .
137 So that we *fled*; *the King* vnto the Queene, . . .
140 . . . in the Marches heere we heard you were,
     Making another *head* to fight againe.
148 'Twas oddes belike, when valiant Warwick *fled*;
     Oft haue I heard his praises in Pursuite,
     But ne're till now, his *Scandall of Retire*.
204 Then strike vp Drums, God and *S. George* for vs

v. vi

24   ... and thy Selfe, the Sea
      Whose enuious Gulfe did *swallow vp* his life:
28   ... *that Tragicke History.*
58   For this (*among'st the rest*) was I ordain'd

2 *Troublesome Raigne*, vi

26   Another moan, to make the *measure* full ...
30   ... *the King* had left the field.
33   ... ignominious *scandal by retire.*
      I *cheer'd* the troops, *as* did *the* prince *of Troy.* ...
36   Crying aloud, '*Saint George*, the day is ours!'
      But *fear* had *captivated* courage quite;
      And, like the *lamb before* the greedy *wolf,*
      So *heartless fled* our warmen from the field.
      Short tale to make,—myself, *amongst the rest,*
      Was fain to fly before *the eager foe.*
46   When in the morning our troops did gather *head,* ...
48   The impartial tide ...
50   ... *swallow'd vp* the most of all our men.
52   I so escap'd, *to tell this tragic tale.*

(Cf. also *tragic tale, Tit.,* iv. i. 47)